Functions of several variables

Functions of several variables

B.D. CRAVEN

Reader in Mathematics,
University of Melbourne

LONDON AND NEW YORK
CHAPMAN AND HALL

First published 1981
by Chapman and Hall Ltd
11 New Fetter Lane, London EC4P 4EE
Published in the USA by
Chapman and Hall
in association with Methuen, Inc.
733 Third Avenue, New York NY 10017

ISBN 0 412 23330 4 (cased)
ISBN 0 412 23340 1 (paperback)

Printed and bound in the
United States of America

British Library Cataloguing in Publication Data

Craven, B.D.
Functions of several variables.
1. Functions of several real variables
I. Title
515.8′4 QA331.5 80-42132

ISBN 0–412–23330–4
ISBN 0–412–23340–1 Pbk

Contents

Preface

This book is aimed at mathematics students, typically in the second year of a university course. The first chapter, however, is suitable for first-year students. Differentiable functions are treated initially from the standpoint of approximating a curved surface locally by a flat surface. This enables both geometric intuition, and some elementary matrix algebra, to be put to effective use. In Chapter 2, the required theorems – chain rule, inverse and implicit function theorems, etc. – are stated, and proved (for n variables), concisely and rigorously. Chapter 3 deals with maxima and minima, including problems with equality and inequality constraints. The chapter includes criteria for discriminating between maxima, minima and saddlepoints for constrained problems; this material is relevant for applications, but most textbooks omit it. In Chapter 4, integration over areas, volumes, curves and surfaces is developed, and both the change-of-variable formula, and the Gauss–Green–Stokes set of theorems are obtained. The integrals are defined with approximative sums (expressed concisely by using step-functions); this preserves some geometrical (and physical) concept of what is happening. Consequent on this, the main ideas of the 'differential form' approach are presented, in a simple form which avoids much of the usual length and complexity. Many examples and exercises are included.

The background assumed is elementary calculus of functions of one real variable, and some matrix algebra. In modern syllabuses, this material is taught in schools, or at the beginning of a university course, and so the students will already know it. However, the essential material is summarized in an appendix, for those who need it.

Why is another textbook written? Existing textbooks on 'functions of several variables' are often too advanced for a student beginning this topic. Any 'advanced calculus' textbook has a 'chapter *n*' on functions of several variables; but this is only accessible to students who have worked through the preceding many chapters, and thus only if the same book has been prescribed for various earlier courses. To fill this gap, a concise, and inexpensive, text is offered, specifically on functions of several variables.

1. Differentiable functions

1.1 INTRODUCTION

Let f be a real function of two real variables, x and y say. This means that, to each pair x, y in some region in the plane, there corresponds a real number $f(x, y)$. This number may, but need not, be given by a formula, e.g.

$$f(x, y) = x^2 - 3xy - y^3 \text{ or } f(x, y) = \cos(2x + 3y).$$

If x, y, z are Cartesian coordinates in three-dimensional space, then the equation $z = f(x, y)$ represents, geometrically, a surface. Some examples are as follows.

The *unit sphere*, namely the sphere with centre (0, 0, 0) and radius 1, has equation $x^2 + y^2 + z^2 = 1$. Solving this equation for z gives two values: $z = \pm(1 - x^2 - y^2)^{1/2}$. If we pick out the positive square root, the equation

$$z = +(1 - x^2 - y^2)^{1/2},$$

of which the right side is a function of x and y, represents the hemisphere which lies above the x, y coordinate plane. The region in the x, y plane for which this function is defined is the disc $\{(x, y) : x^2 + y^2 \leq 1\}$. (Note that here a *circle* means a curve, the plane region inside it is a *disc*. Similarly a *sphere* means the surface; the 'solid sphere' is called a *ball*.)

Consider the parabola in the z, x plane, given by the equation $z = x^2$. If this parabola is rotated about the z-axis, it traces out a surface, called a *paraboloid of revolution*. The equation of this paraboloid is obtained by replacing x^2, which is the squared distance from the z-axis of a point in the z, x plane, by x^2+y^2, which is the squared distance from the z-axis of a point (x, y, z) in three-dimensional space. So the paraboloid has the equation

$$z = x^2+y^2.$$

The function of x and y occurring here is defined for all values of x and y. The paraboloid is a bowl-shaped surface (see Fig. 1.1).

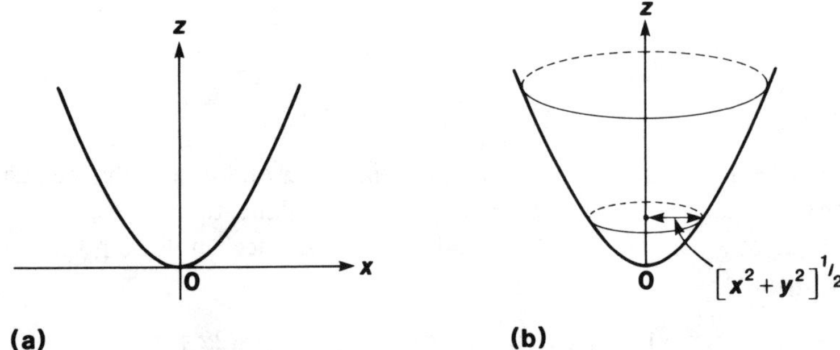

Figure 1.1 Parabola and paraboloid

Consider the sphere $x^2+y^2+z^2 = 1$, and stretch it in the direction of the x-axis by the ratio a, in the direction of the y-axis by the ratio b, and in the direction of the z-axis by the ratio c; thus the point (x, y, z) moves to (ax, by, cz). The sphere is thus stretched to a surface whose equation is

$$\left(\frac{x}{a}\right)^2+\left(\frac{y}{b}\right)^2+\left(\frac{z}{c}\right)^2 = 1.$$

This surface is called an *ellipsoid* with semiaxes a, b, c (see Fig. 1.2). If this equation is solved for z, and the positive square root taken, this gives

$$z = +c\left[1-\left(\frac{x}{a}\right)^2-\left(\frac{y}{b}\right)^2\right]^{1/2}$$

The right side of this equation defines a function of x and y, for the region in the x, y plane inside the ellipse $(x/a)^2+(y/b)^2 = 1$.

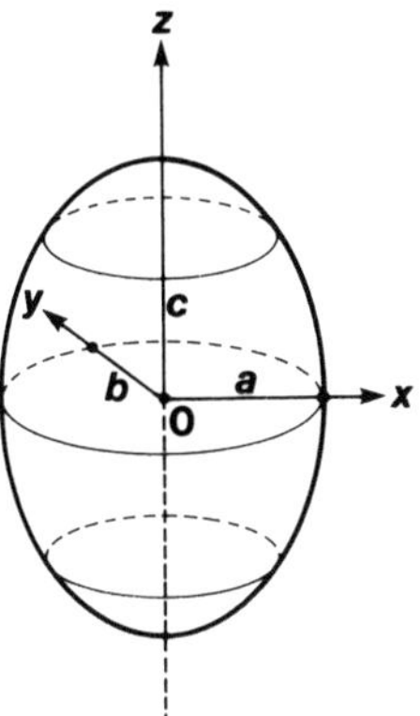

Figure 1.2 Ellipsoid

These examples have some properties in common. An equation $z = f(x, y)$ usually describes only part of the geometrical surface, such as a sphere or ellipsoid. The surface consists of one untorn piece; this means that the points $(x, y, f(x, y))$ and $(x_0, y_0, f(x_0, y_0))$ on the surface are close together if the points (x, y) and (x_0, y_0) are close together in the plane; this expresses the concept that f is a *continuous* function of its variables x, y. Any small part of the surface (near one point) is in some sense 'nearly flat', even though the surface is actually curved. Thus a man standing on the (spherical) earth sees his local neighbourhood as roughly flat.

These ideas must now be made precise. We start with the concept of 'nearly flat'.

1.2 LINEAR PART OF A FUNCTION

Consider the function f, where

$$f(x, y) = x^2-3xy-y^3;$$

and try to approximate $f(x, y)$ near the point $(x, y) = (2, -1)$ by a simpler function. To do this, set $x = 2+\xi$ and $y = -1+\eta$. Then

$$\begin{aligned} f(x, y) = f(2+\xi, -1+\eta) &= (4+4\xi+\xi^2)-3(-2-\xi+2\eta+\xi\eta) \\ &\quad -(-1+3\eta-3\eta^2+\eta^3) \\ &= 11+(7\xi-9\eta)+(\xi^2-3\xi\eta+3\eta^2+\eta^3). \end{aligned} \tag{1.2.1}$$

Here $11 = f(2, -1)$; $7\xi - 9\eta$ is a *linear* function of the variables ξ and η; and $v = \xi^2 - 3\xi\eta + 3\eta^2 + \eta^3$ is small, compared to the linear function $7\xi - 9\eta$, if ξ and η are both small enough. This means that, if ξ and η are both small enough, then

$$f(x, y) \approx 11 + (7\xi - 9\eta) \tag{1.2.2}$$

is a good approximation, the terms omitted being small in comparison to the terms retained.

To make the idea of 'small enough' precise, denote by d the distance from $(2, -1)$ to $(2+\xi, -1+\eta)$; then

$$d = [\xi^2 + \eta^2]^{1/2}.$$

Then $|\xi| \leq d$ and $|\eta| \leq d$, so that, as $d \to 0$,

$$|\xi^2|/d \leq d^2/d = d \to 0; \qquad |-3\xi\eta|/d \leq 3d^2/d = 3d \to 0;$$

and similarly for the remaining terms in v. This motivates the following definition.

Definition

The function f of the two real variables x, y is *differentiable* at the point (a, b) if

$$f(x, y) = f(a, b) + p(x-a) + q(y-b) + \theta(x, y), \tag{1.2.3}$$

where p and q are constants, and

$$|\theta|/d \to 0 \text{ as } d = [(x-a)^2 + (y-b)^2]^{1/2} \to 0. \tag{1.2.4}$$

The linear function $p(x-a) + q(y-b)$ will be called the *linear part* of f at (a, b). (Some books call it the *differential*.)

The numbers p and q can be directly calculated. If y is fixed at the value b, then $d = |x-a|$, and

$$\frac{f(x, b) - f(a, b)}{x-a} = p + 0 + \frac{\theta(x, b)}{x-a} \to p + 0$$

as $d = |x-a| \to 0$, thus as $x \to a$. Thus p equals the *partial derivative* of f with respect to x at a, holding y fixed at b. This will be written

$$p = \frac{\partial f}{\partial x}(a, b) = f_x(a, b) = \mathrm{D}_x f(a, b), \text{ or as } \frac{\partial f}{\partial x} \text{ or } f_x \text{ or } \mathrm{D}_x f$$

for short. Similarly q equals $\dfrac{\partial f}{\partial y}(a, b) = f_y(a, b)$, the partial derivative of f with respect to y at b, holding x fixed at a.

Thus, in the above example, $f_x = 2x-3y-0$ (differentiating with respect to x, holding y constant), and so, at $(x, y) = (2, -1)$, $f_x = 2(2)-3(-1) = 7 = p$. Similarly, $f_y = 0-3x-3y^2 = -9 = q$ (at $(2, -1)$).

Exercise 1.2.1 Calculate the linear part of f at $(\pi/4, 0)$, where $f(x, y) = \cos(2x+3y)$. (*Note:* it is not yet shown that this function f is *differentiable*; it certainly has partial derivatives f_x and f_y, but *differentiable* implies more than this.)

Exercise 1.2.2 Calculate the linear part of g at $(0, \frac{1}{2}\pi)$, where $g(x, y) = \sin(x^2+y^2)$.

Exercise 1.2.3 Calculate the partial derivatives f_x and f_y when: (i) $f(x, y) = g(x)h(y)$; (ii) $f(x, y) = g(x)^{h(y)}$; (iii) $f(x, y) = g(x)$; where g and h are suitable differentiable functions of one variable.

1.3 VECTOR VIEWPOINT

It will be convenient to regard f as a function of a *vector variable* $\mathbf{w}$, whose components are x and y. Denote $\mathbf{w} = \begin{bmatrix} x \\ y \end{bmatrix}$, as a column vector, in matrix language; denote also $\mathbf{c} = \begin{bmatrix} a \\ b \end{bmatrix}$. Define also the row vector

$$f'(\mathbf{c}) = [p, q] = [f_x(a, b), f_y(a, b)].$$

(The notation $f'(\mathbf{c})$ suggests a derivative; we have here a sort of vector derivative.) Then, since f is differentiable,

$$f(\mathbf{w}) = f(\mathbf{c})+f'(\mathbf{c})(\mathbf{w}-\mathbf{c})+\theta(\mathbf{w}),$$

where the product

$$f'(\mathbf{c})(\mathbf{w}-\mathbf{c}) = [p, q]\begin{bmatrix} x-a \\ y-b \end{bmatrix} = p(x-a)+q(y-b)$$

is the usual matrix product. Now let $\|\mathbf{w}-\mathbf{c}\|$ denote the length of the vector $\mathbf{w}-\mathbf{c}$; then the previous $d = \|\mathbf{w}-\mathbf{c}\|$, and so $\theta(\mathbf{w})/\|\mathbf{w}-\mathbf{c}\| \to 0$ as $\|\mathbf{w}-\mathbf{c}\| \to 0$.

Example

For $f(x, y) = x^2-3xy-y^3$, $a = 2$, $b = -1$, set $\mathbf{c} = \begin{bmatrix} 2 \\ -1 \end{bmatrix}$; then $f'(\mathbf{c}) = [7, -9]$.

Exercise 1.3.1 Discuss Exercise 1.2.1 in terms of vectors.

1.4 DIRECTIONAL DERIVATIVE

Suppose that the point (x, y) moves along a straight line through the point (a, b); thus $x = a+\ell\beta$, $y = b+m\beta$, where β is the distance from (a, b) to (x, y), and ℓ and m are constants specifying the direction of the line (with $\ell^2+m^2 = 1$). Note, in Fig. 1.3, that $\ell = \cos\gamma$ and $m = \sin\gamma$. In vector language, let $\mathbf{w} = \begin{bmatrix} x \\ y \end{bmatrix}$, $\mathbf{c} = \begin{bmatrix} a \\ b \end{bmatrix}$, $\mathbf{t} = \begin{bmatrix} \ell \\ m \end{bmatrix}$; then $\beta = \|\mathbf{w}-\mathbf{c}\|$; and the line has equation $\mathbf{w} = \mathbf{c}+\beta\mathbf{t}$.

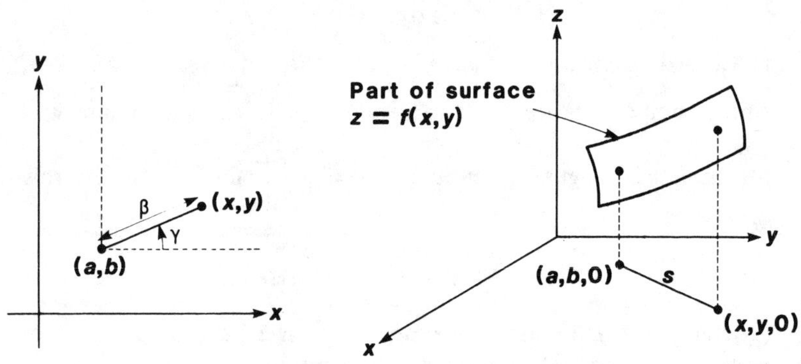

Figure 1.3 Directional derivative

The rate of increase of $f(\mathbf{w})$, measured at $\mathbf{w} = \mathbf{c}$, as $\mathbf{w}$ moves along the line $\mathbf{w} = \mathbf{c}+\beta\mathbf{t}$, is called the *directional derivative of f at* $\mathbf{c}$ *in the direction* $\mathbf{t}$. This may be calculated, assuming f differentiable, as follows:

$$\frac{f(\mathbf{c}+\beta\mathbf{t})-f(\mathbf{c})}{\beta} = \frac{f'(\mathbf{c})(\beta\mathbf{t})+\theta}{\beta} = f'(\mathbf{c})\mathbf{t}+\theta/\beta.$$

The required directional derivative is the limit of this ratio as $\beta \to 0$, namely $f'(\mathbf{c})\mathbf{t} = [p, q]\begin{bmatrix} \ell \\ m \end{bmatrix} = p\ell + qm$ (since $|\theta|/\beta \to 0$ as $\beta \to 0$). Note that $\mathbf{t}$ is here a unit vector.

Example

Let $f(x, y) = x^2 - 3xy - y^3$. The directional derivative of f at $\begin{bmatrix} 2 \\ -1 \end{bmatrix}$ in the direction $\begin{bmatrix} \cos\gamma \\ \sin\gamma \end{bmatrix}$ is $[7, -9]\begin{bmatrix} \cos\gamma \\ \sin\gamma \end{bmatrix} = 7\cos\gamma - 9\sin\gamma$.

Exercise 1.4.1 Let $f(x, y) = \cos(2x + 3y)$. Calculate the directional derivative of f at $(\pi/4, 0)$ in the direction $\begin{bmatrix} \ell \\ m \end{bmatrix}$.

Exercise 1.4.2 Calculate the directional derivative of g at $(0, \frac{1}{2}\pi)$ in the direction $\begin{bmatrix} \cos\gamma \\ \sin\gamma \end{bmatrix}$, where $g(x, y) = \sin(x^2 + y^2)$.

1.5 TANGENT PLANE TO A SURFACE

Let $z = f(x, y)$ be the equation of a surface, and let f be a differentiable function. Let $(a, b, f(a, b))$ be a point on the surface. The *tangent plane* to the surface at this point is the plane whose equation is

$$z - f(a, b) = p(x-a) + q(y-b),$$

or, in vector terms, $z - f(\mathbf{c}) = f'(\mathbf{c})(\mathbf{w} - \mathbf{c})$; here $f'(\mathbf{c}) = [p, q]$, $\mathbf{w} = \begin{bmatrix} x \\ y \end{bmatrix}$, and $\mathbf{c} = \begin{bmatrix} a \\ b \end{bmatrix}$. Since f is differentiable, this plane clearly approximates the surface, and does so arbitrarily closely for points near enough to $\mathbf{c}$. Consider the line whose equations are $x = a + \beta\ell$, $y = b + \beta m$, $z = f(a, b) + \beta n$, where $n = p\ell + qm$ is the directional derivative calculated in Section 1.4. For these values of x and y, the surface is described by the equation $z = f(a, b) + \beta n + \theta$, where $|\theta|/\beta \to 0$ as $\beta \to 0$; so the line may be regarded as a *tangent line* to the surface. Substitution shows that this tangent line lies in the tangent plane; thus the tangent plane contains all lines tangent to the surface at $(a, b, f(a, b))$.

Example
The tangent plane to the paraboloid $z = x^2+y^2$ at the point (a, b, a^2+b^2) has equation $z-(a^2+b^2) = 2a(x-a)+2b(y-b)$.

Example
The tangent plane to the half-ellipsoid $z = c[1-(x/a)^2-(y/b)^2]^{1/2}$ at the point (α, β, γ) (on the half-ellipsoid) is obtained as follows. Calculate

$$z_x = \frac{-cx/a^2}{[\quad]^{1/2}} = \frac{-c\alpha/a^2}{\gamma/c} \qquad \text{at } (\alpha, \beta, \gamma).$$

A similar expression holds for z_y. So the tangent plane has equation

$$z-\gamma = -\frac{c^2\alpha}{\gamma a^2}(x-\alpha)-\frac{c^2\beta}{\gamma b^2}(y-\beta),$$

which reduces to

$$\frac{x\alpha}{a^2}+\frac{y\beta}{b^2}+\frac{z\gamma}{c^2} = 1,$$

using $(\alpha/a)^2+(\beta/b)^2+(\gamma/c)^2 = 1$.

Exercise 1.5.1 Fill in the details of this calculation.

Exercise 1.5.2 Calculate similarly the equation of the tangent plane to the hyperboloid

$$\frac{x^2}{a^2}+\frac{y^2}{b^2}-\frac{z^2}{c^2} = 1$$

at a point (α, β, γ) on the hyperboloid.

1.6 VECTOR FUNCTIONS

Let φ and ψ each be differentiable real functions of the two real variables x and y. The pair of equations

$$u = \varphi(x, y)$$
$$v = \psi(x, y)$$

define a mapping from the point (x, y) to the point (u, v). If, instead of considering points, we consider a vector **w**, with components x, y, and a vector **s**, with components u, v, then the two equations define a mapping from the vector **w** to the vector **s**. This mapping is then specified by the *vector function* $\mathbf{f} = \begin{bmatrix} \varphi \\ \psi \end{bmatrix}$.

Example
Let $\varphi(x, y) = x^2+y^2$ and $\psi(x, y) = 2xy$. These functions are differentiable at (1, 2), and calculation shows that

$$\begin{aligned} u &= 5+2(x-1)+4(y-2)+((x-1)^2+4(y-2)^2); \\ v &= 4+4(x-1)+2(y-2)+(2(x-1)(y-2)). \end{aligned}$$

This pair of equations combine into a single matrix equation:

$$\begin{bmatrix} u \\ v \end{bmatrix} = \begin{bmatrix} 5 \\ 4 \end{bmatrix} + \begin{bmatrix} 2 & 4 \\ 4 & 2 \end{bmatrix}\begin{bmatrix} x-1 \\ y-2 \end{bmatrix} + \begin{bmatrix} (x-1)^2+4(y-2)^2 \\ 2(x-1)(y-2) \end{bmatrix}.$$

In vector notation, this may be written as

$$\mathbf{f}(\mathbf{w}) = \mathbf{f}(\mathbf{c})+\mathbf{f}'(\mathbf{c})(\mathbf{w}-\mathbf{c})+\boldsymbol{\theta}(\mathbf{w}), \tag{1.6.1}$$

where now $\mathbf{f}'(\mathbf{c})$ is a 2×2 matrix. Since the components θ_1, θ_2 of $\boldsymbol{\theta}$ satisfy $|\theta_1(\mathbf{w})|/\|\mathbf{w}-\mathbf{c}\| \to 0$ and $|\theta_2(\mathbf{w})|/\|\mathbf{w}-\mathbf{c}\| \to 0$ as $\|\mathbf{w}-\mathbf{c}\| \to 0$, it follows that $\|\boldsymbol{\theta}(\mathbf{w})\|/\|\mathbf{w}-\mathbf{c}\| \to 0$ as $\|\mathbf{w}-\mathbf{c}\| \to 0$. So this vector function **f** may be regarded as *differentiable*, by the following definition.

Definition
The vector function **f** is *differentiable* at **c** if there is a matrix $\mathbf{f}'(\mathbf{c})$ such that Equation (1.6.1) holds, with

$$\frac{\|\boldsymbol{\theta}(\mathbf{w})\|}{\|\mathbf{w}-\mathbf{c}\|} \to 0 \text{ as } \|\mathbf{w}-\mathbf{c}\| \to 0. \tag{1.6.2}$$

The term $\mathbf{f}'(\mathbf{c})(\mathbf{w}-\mathbf{c})$ is called the *linear part* of **f** at **c**.

Example
For the function discussed above, the linear part at $\begin{bmatrix} 1 \\ 2 \end{bmatrix}$ is

$$\begin{bmatrix} 2 & 4 \\ 4 & 2 \end{bmatrix}\begin{bmatrix} x-1 \\ y-2 \end{bmatrix}.$$

Exercise 1.6.1 Let $f\left(\begin{bmatrix} x \\ y \end{bmatrix}\right) = \begin{bmatrix} x^2-y^2 \\ xy^2 \end{bmatrix}$. Calculate $\mathbf{f}'\left(\begin{bmatrix} 1 \\ 2 \end{bmatrix}\right)$, both from the definition, and also by using partial derivatives.

1.7 FUNCTIONS OF FUNCTIONS

Let the differentiable function $\mathbf{f}$ map the vector $\mathbf{w}$ to the vector $\mathbf{s}$; let the differentiable function $\mathbf{g}$ map the vector $\mathbf{s}$ to the vector $\mathbf{t}$. Diagrammatically,

$$\mathbf{w} \xrightarrow{\mathbf{f}} \mathbf{s} \xrightarrow{\mathbf{g}} \mathbf{t}.$$

Then the composition $\mathbf{h} = \mathbf{g} \circ \mathbf{f}$ of the functions $\mathbf{g}$ and $\mathbf{f}$ maps $\mathbf{w}$ to $\mathbf{t}$. Since $\mathbf{f}$ and $\mathbf{g}$ are differentiable,

$$\begin{aligned} \mathbf{f}(\mathbf{w})-\mathbf{f}(\mathbf{c}) &= A(\mathbf{w}-\mathbf{c})+\boldsymbol{\theta}; \\ \mathbf{g}(\mathbf{f}(\mathbf{w}))-\mathbf{g}(\mathbf{f}(\mathbf{c})) &= B(\mathbf{f}(\mathbf{w})-\mathbf{f}(\mathbf{c}))+\boldsymbol{\rho}; \end{aligned}$$

where A and B are suitable matrices, and $\boldsymbol{\theta}$ and $\boldsymbol{\rho}$ are 'small' terms. If, when $\|\mathbf{w}-\mathbf{c}\|$ is small enough, $\boldsymbol{\theta}$ and $\boldsymbol{\rho}$ can be neglected, then approximately

$$\mathbf{g}(\mathbf{f}(\mathbf{w}))-\mathbf{g}(\mathbf{f}(\mathbf{c})) \approx BA(\mathbf{w}-\mathbf{c}). \tag{1.7.1}$$

It will be proved in Section 2.3 that, if $\mathbf{f}$ and $\mathbf{g}$ are differentiable, then so is $\mathbf{h} = \mathbf{g} \circ \mathbf{f}$, and the linear part of $\mathbf{h}$ is, in fact, $BA(\mathbf{w}-\mathbf{c})$. Thus

$$\mathbf{h}'(\mathbf{c}) = \mathbf{g}'(\mathbf{f}(\mathbf{c}))\mathbf{f}'(\mathbf{c}). \tag{1.7.2}$$

This equation is called the *chain rule*. (The expression on the right of (1.7.2) is given by a product of two matrices.)

Example

Let $\mathbf{f}$ and $\mathbf{c}$ be as in the example of Section 1.6, and let g be the real-valued function given by $g(u, v) = 3u-v^2$. The chain rule then gives

$$h'\left(\begin{bmatrix}1\\2\end{bmatrix}\right) = [3 \quad -8]\begin{bmatrix}2 & 4\\4 & 2\end{bmatrix} = [-26 \quad -4].$$

Here $h(x, y) = g(u, v) = 3(x^2+y^2)-(2xy)^2$, so, at $(x, y) = (1, 2)$, the partial derivatives of h are $h_x = 6x-8xy^2 = -26$ and $h_y = 6y-8x^2y = -4$. If $t = h(x, y)$, then

$$\frac{\partial t}{\partial x} = \frac{\partial g}{\partial u}\frac{\partial \varphi}{\partial x}+\frac{\partial g}{\partial v}\frac{\partial \psi}{\partial x}; \tag{1.7.3}$$

other components of the matrix product can be similarly expressed. Formulas of this type are also often called 'chain rules'.

Note that the notations $h(1, 2)$ and $h\left(\begin{bmatrix}1\\2\end{bmatrix}\right)$ mean the same function evaluation. (Symbols along a line are easier to print!)

Example

$z = 2-x^2-y^2$, $x = \cos t$, $y = \sin t$. Here

$$f(t) = \begin{bmatrix}\cos t\\ \sin t\end{bmatrix}, \; g\left(\begin{bmatrix}x\\y\end{bmatrix}\right) = 2-x^2-y^2.$$

Taking partial derivatives,

$$f'(t) = \begin{bmatrix}-\sin t\\ \cos t\end{bmatrix}; \; g'\left(\begin{bmatrix}x\\y\end{bmatrix}\right) = [-2x \quad -2y].$$

Hence

$$\frac{dz}{dt} = [-2x \quad -2y]\begin{bmatrix}-\sin t\\ \\ \cos t\end{bmatrix} = [-2\cos t \quad -2\sin t]\begin{bmatrix}-\sin t\\ \\ \cos t\end{bmatrix} = 0$$

as it should.

Example

On the surface $z = A-A^{-1}(x^2+y^2)$, where A is a positive constant, a curve is specified by $x = A\cos^3\varphi$, $y = A\sin^3\varphi$. Find the slope of the curve (i.e. the rate of increase of height z per horizontal distance travelled). By the chain rule,

$$\frac{\mathrm{d}z}{\mathrm{d}\varphi} = [-2A^{-1}x \quad -2A^{-1}y]\begin{bmatrix}-3A\cos^2\varphi\sin\varphi\\ \\ 3A\sin^2\varphi\cos\varphi\end{bmatrix}.$$

By the formula for arc-lengths of a plane curve,

$$\frac{\mathrm{d}s}{\mathrm{d}\varphi} \quad \left[\left(\frac{\mathrm{d}x}{\mathrm{d}\varphi}\right)^2+\left(\frac{\mathrm{d}y}{\mathrm{d}\varphi}\right)^2\right]^{1/2} = 3A\sin\varphi\cos\varphi,$$

and

$$\frac{\mathrm{d}z}{\mathrm{d}s} = \frac{\mathrm{d}z}{\mathrm{d}\varphi}\Big/\frac{\mathrm{d}s}{\mathrm{d}\varphi} = 2\cos 2\varphi,$$

after simplification.

Further applications of the chain rule are given later, in connection with implicit functions.

Exercise 1.7.1 Let $f\left(\begin{bmatrix} x \\ y \end{bmatrix}\right) = \begin{bmatrix} x^2 - y^2 \\ 2xy \end{bmatrix}$; let $\varphi(t) = \begin{bmatrix} \cosh t \\ \sinh t \end{bmatrix}$. Calculate $(f \circ \varphi)'(t)$ first using the chain rule, and second, by calculating $f(\varphi(t))$.

Exercise 1.7.2 Use the chain rule to calculate $f'\left(\begin{bmatrix} x \\ y \end{bmatrix}\right)$, where $f\left(\begin{bmatrix} x \\ y \end{bmatrix}\right) = \sin(x^2+y^2)$, also $g'\left(\begin{bmatrix} x \\ y \end{bmatrix}\right)$ where $g\left(\begin{bmatrix} x \\ y \end{bmatrix}\right) = \arctan(x^2+xy+y^2)$.

Exercise 1.7.3 Define $u(x, y) = f(x+ky)+g(x-ky)$, where f and g are real twice-differentiable functions of real variables, and k is constant. By using the chain rule, show that $\dfrac{\partial^2 u}{\partial y^2} = k^2 \dfrac{\partial^2 u}{\partial x^2}$.

Exercise 1.7.4 By considering the function $\mathbf{w} \to f(\mathbf{w})+g(\mathbf{w})$ as the composition of the two functions $\mathbf{w} \to \begin{bmatrix} f(\mathbf{w}) \\ g(\mathbf{w}) \end{bmatrix}$ and $\begin{bmatrix} u \\ v \end{bmatrix} \to u+v$, show that, if f and g are differentiable, then so is $f+g$, with $(f+g)'(\mathbf{w}) = f'(\mathbf{w})+g'(\mathbf{w})$.

Exercise 1.7.5 Let $f(\mathbf{w}) = 1/g(\mathbf{w})$ where $\mathbf{w}$ is a vector variable, and g is a real differentiable function, with $g(\mathbf{w}) \neq 0$. Use the chain rule to show that $f'(\mathbf{w}) = -[g(\mathbf{w})]^{-2}g'(\mathbf{w})$.

2. Chain rule and inverse function theorem

2.1 NORMS

In this chapter, precise definitions are given, and theorems proved, concerning the ideas introduced informally in Chapter 1. The reader is assumed to be familiar with matrix multiplication and matrix inverse. Some preliminary discussion of vectors and norms is first required.

Let $\mathbb{R}^n$ denote the Euclidean vector space of n dimensions. A typical element of $\mathbb{R}^n$ will be represented (in matrix language) as a column vector with n components; each component is a real number. Addition of two vectors in $\mathbb{R}^n$, and multiplication of a vector by a constant, follow the rules for matrices. In Chapter 1, the length of a vector was calculated using Pythagoras' theorem; the n-dimensional version of this defines the length, or *norm*, of the vector $\mathbf{w} \in \mathbb{R}^n$ (with components $w_1, w_2, \ldots, w_n$) as the number

$$\|\mathbf{w}\|_2 = [w_1^2 + w_2^2 + \ldots + w_n^2]^{1/2}. \tag{2.1.1}$$

Another kind of norm is defined by

$$\|\mathbf{w}\|_1 = |w_1| + |w_2| + \ldots + |w_n|. \tag{2.1.2}$$

Various other norms may also be defined, but they are not needed here.

Any definition of *norm* (denoted $\|\cdot\|$) is required to satisfy the following properties:

(N1) For each vector $\mathbf{w}$, $\|\mathbf{w}\| \geq 0$; and $\mathbf{w} = \mathbf{0} \Leftrightarrow \|\mathbf{w}\| = 0$.
(N2) If α is a constant number, and $\mathbf{w}$ is a vector, then

$$\|\alpha\mathbf{w}\| = |\alpha|\,\|\mathbf{w}\|.$$

(N3) For each two vectors $\mathbf{w}$ and $\mathbf{s}$, $\|\mathbf{w}+\mathbf{s}\| \leq \|\mathbf{w}\|+\|\mathbf{s}\|$.

The *triangle inequality* (N3) means, geometrically, that the length of one side of a triangle is not greater than the sum of the lengths of the other two sides. Properties (N1) and (N2) are obvious for the norms $\|\cdot\|_1$ and $\|\cdot\|_2$; so is (N3) for $\|\cdot\|_1$; (N3) for $\|\cdot\|_2$ is proved below from Equation (2.1.4).

For any two vectors $\mathbf{w}$ and $\mathbf{s}$ in $\mathbb{R}^n$, and each number α,

$$0 \leq \|\mathbf{w}+\alpha\mathbf{s}\|_2^2 = \sum_{j=1}^{n}(w_j+\alpha s_j)^2 = \sum_1^n w_j{}^2+2\alpha\sum_1^n w_j s_j{}^2+\alpha^2\sum_1^n s_j. \tag{2.1.3}$$

This quadratic in α is nonnegative for all α, hence it can have no real zeros (unless they coincide); therefore $|\Sigma w_j s_j|^2 \leq \Sigma w_j^2 \cdot \Sigma z_j^2$. This proves *Schwarz's inequality* (for $\mathbb{R}^n$), namely

$$|\sum_{j=1}^{n} w_j s_j| \leq \|\mathbf{w}\|_2 \cdot \|\mathbf{s}\|_2. \tag{2.1.4}$$

The *inner product* $\sum_{j=1}^{n} w_j s_j$ is sometimes denoted $\langle\mathbf{w}, \mathbf{s}\rangle$. From Equation (2.1.3) with $\alpha = 1$, and Equation (2.1.4),

$$\begin{aligned}\|\mathbf{w}+\mathbf{s}\|_2^2 &= \|\mathbf{w}\|_2^2+\|\mathbf{s}\|_2^2+2\langle\mathbf{w}, \mathbf{s}\rangle \\ &\leq \|\mathbf{w}\|_2^2+\|\mathbf{s}\|_2^2+2\|\mathbf{w}\|_2 \cdot \|\mathbf{s}\|_2 \\ &= (\|\mathbf{w}\|_2+\|\mathbf{s}\|_2)^2,\end{aligned}$$

which proves (N3) for $\|\cdot\|_2$. Note that Equation (2.1.4) does *not* hold for every norm.

From the inequalities $|w_j| \leq \|\mathbf{w}\|_2$ and

$$\left[\sum |w_j|\right]^2 = \sum |w_j|^2+2\sum_{j>k} |w_j w_k| \geq \sum w_j^2$$

it follows that, for all $w \in \mathbb{R}^n$,

$$\|\mathbf{w}\|_2 \leq \|\mathbf{w}\|_1 \leq n\|\mathbf{w}\|_2. \tag{2.1.5}$$

Consequently, if $\mathbf{w}$ is 'small' in terms one of these norms, then $\mathbf{w}$ is also 'small' in terms of the other norms. (This is actually true for every pair of norms on $\mathbb{R}^n$, although we shall not prove it.) Consequently, we can use either $\|\cdot\|_1$ or $\|\cdot\|_2$ to define differentiability, and the result will be the same. We shall often write the norm as $\|\cdot\|$, without needing to specify which norm.

Any linear map $A : \mathbb{R}^n \to \mathbb{R}^m$ can be represented by a matrix with m rows and n columns; denote by $\mathbb{R}^{m\times n}$ the set of all such matrices, with real elements. To show this, let $\mathbf{e}_1, \mathbf{e}_2, \ldots, \mathbf{e}_n$ be a set of basis vectors for $\mathbb{R}^n$, and similarly $\mathbf{e}_1', \mathbf{e}_2', \ldots, \mathbf{e}_m'$ for $\mathbb{R}^m$. Then $A(\mathbf{e}_j) = \sum_{i=1}^{m} a_{ij}\mathbf{e}_i'$ for some coefficients a_{ij}. Let $\mathbf{x} \in \mathbb{R}^n$; then $\mathbf{x} = \sum_{j=1}^{n} x_j\mathbf{e}_j$, with some coefficients x_j. Since A is a linear map, $A\mathbf{x} = \sum_{j=1}^{n} x_jA(\mathbf{e}_j) = \sum_{i=1}^{m}\left[\sum_{j=1}^{n} a_{ij}x_j\right]\mathbf{e}_i'$. Thus A is represented by the $m \times n$ matrix with elements a_{ij}. We shall usually assume the standard basis vectors:

$$\mathbf{e}_1 = \begin{bmatrix}1\\0\\0\\\vdots\\0\end{bmatrix}, \mathbf{e}_2 = \begin{bmatrix}0\\1\\0\\\vdots\\0\end{bmatrix}, \mathbf{e}_3 = \begin{bmatrix}0\\0\\1\\\vdots\\0\end{bmatrix}, \text{etc.},$$

and then ignore the distinction between the linear map A and the matrix representing it, and thus refer only to matrices.

By fixing some order for the matrix elements, matrices in $\mathbb{R}^{m\times n}$ may also be considered as vectors in $\mathbb{R}^{mn}$, and then the addition of these vectors gives the same rule as matrix addition. Let $A \in \mathbb{R}^{m\times n}$ have elements a_{ij}. Then the norm $\|\cdot\|_2$ on $\mathbb{R}^{mn}$ defines a norm on $\mathbb{R}^{m\times n}$, as

$$\|A\|_2 = \left[\sum_{i=1}^{n}\sum_{j=1}^{n} a_{ij}{}^2\right]^{1/2}. \tag{2.1.6}$$

Moreover, from Equation (2.1.4), for each $\mathbf{w} \in \mathbb{R}^n$,

$$\|A\mathbf{w}\|_2^2 = \sum_i \left[\sum_j a_{ij} w_j\right]^2 \leq \left[\sum_i \sum_j a_{ij}{}^2\right]\left[\sum_k w_k{}^2\right] = \|A\|_2^2 \cdot \|\mathbf{w}\|_2^2.$$

Hence, for these $\|\cdot\|_2$ norms,

$$\|A\mathbf{w}\| \leq \|A\| \cdot \|\mathbf{w}\|. \tag{2.1.7}$$

Note also that

$$|a_{ij}| \leq \|A\|_2. \tag{2.1.8}$$

Other matrix norms are possible, such as

$$\|A\| = \sum_i \max_j |a_{ij}|; \tag{2.1.9}$$

or instead (choosing a vector norm)

$$\|A\| = \inf\{\beta > 0 : \|A\mathbf{w}\| \leq \beta\|\mathbf{w}\| \text{ for all } \mathbf{w}\}. \tag{2.1.10}$$

For the norm (2.1.10), for each $\mathbf{w} \in \mathbb{R}^n$,

$$\|(AB)\mathbf{w}\| = \|A(B\mathbf{w})\| \leq \|A\| \, \|B\mathbf{w}\| \leq \|A\| \, \|B\| \, \|\mathbf{w}\|;$$

hence (2.1.10) satisfies, whenever $A, B \in \mathbb{R}^{m\times n}$,

$$\|AB\| \leq \|A\| \, \|B\|. \tag{2.1.11}$$

The linear map A is *continuous* if, for some function $\delta(\cdot)$ of $\varepsilon > 0$, $\|A\mathbf{w} - A\mathbf{s}\| < \varepsilon$ whenever $\|\mathbf{w} - \mathbf{s}\| < \delta(\varepsilon)$. This follows from (2.1.7), taking $\delta(\varepsilon) = \varepsilon/(1 + \|A\|)$.

Suppose now that the matrix A is a function of a parameter $\mathbf{c} \in \mathbb{R}^r$; we write $A(\mathbf{c})\mathbf{w}$ for the action of the matrix $A(\mathbf{c})$ on the vector $\mathbf{w}$. Then $A(\mathbf{c})$ is a *continuous* function of $\mathbf{c}$ at $\mathbf{c}_0$ if, for some function $\delta(\cdot)$ of $\varepsilon > 0$, $\|A(\mathbf{c}) - A(\mathbf{c}_0)\| < \varepsilon$ whenever $\|\mathbf{c} - \mathbf{c}_0\| < \delta(\varepsilon)$. This assumes some choice of matrix norm. If $\|\cdot\|_2$ is chosen, then each component $a_{ij}(\mathbf{c})$ of $A(\mathbf{c})$ is a continuous function of $\mathbf{c}$ (using Equation (2.1.8)).

Now let $\mathbf{w}_1, \mathbf{w}_2, \ldots, \mathbf{w}_k, \ldots$ be an infinite sequence of vectors in $\mathbb{R}^n$. (*Caution*: $\mathbf{w}_k$ sometimes denotes the kth component of a vector $\mathbf{w}$, but here $\mathbf{w}_k$ denotes the kth vector in a sequence.) The sequence *converges* to a vector $\mathbf{w}_0 \in \mathbb{R}^n$ if $\|\mathbf{w}_k - \mathbf{w}_0\| \to 0$ as $k \to \infty$. Suppose instead that, for each $\varepsilon > 0$,

$$\|\mathbf{w}_k - \mathbf{w}_j\| < \varepsilon \text{ whenever } j \text{ and } k > N(\varepsilon). \tag{2.1.12}$$

(The sequence $\{\mathbf{w}_k\}$ is then called a *Cauchy sequence.*) Assume the $\|\cdot\|_2$ norm. From Equation (2.1.8), the ith components of these vectors satisfy

$$|w_{k,i} - w_{j,i}| < \varepsilon \text{ whenever } j \text{ and } k > N(\varepsilon).$$

By the completeness property of real numbers, the sequence $\{w_{k,i}\}$ tends, as $k \to \infty$, to a limit, $w_{0,i}$ say. Let $\mathbf{w}_0$ be the vector whose components are $w_{0,i}$. Since $|w_{k,i} - w_{0,i}| < \varepsilon$ whenever k is sufficiently large, and for each i, it follows that $\|\mathbf{w}_k - \mathbf{w}_0\| < \varepsilon$ whenever k is sufficiently large. Thus the Cauchy sequence converges (to $\mathbf{w}_0$).

Example

In $\mathbb{R}^2$, define $\mathbf{w}_k = \begin{bmatrix} 1+k^{-1/2} \\ 2+(-1)^k k^{-1} \end{bmatrix} (k = 1, 2, \ldots)$, and $\mathbf{w} = \begin{bmatrix} 1 \\ 2 \end{bmatrix}$. Then the sequence $\mathbf{w}_k$ converges to $\mathbf{w}$.

Defining the *distance* between $\mathbf{w}$ and $\mathbf{s}$ in $\mathbb{R}^n$ as

$$d(\mathbf{w}, \mathbf{s}) = \|\mathbf{w} - \mathbf{s}\|,$$

(2.1.12) states that $d(\mathbf{w}_k, \mathbf{w}_j) < \varepsilon$ whenever $j, k > N(\varepsilon)$. Note that, from (N3), $d(\mathbf{w}, \mathbf{t}) \leq d(\mathbf{w}, \mathbf{s}) + d(\mathbf{s}, \mathbf{t})$ holds for all $\mathbf{w}, \mathbf{s}, \mathbf{t}$.

From (2.1.5), a sequence in $\mathbb{R}^n$ is Cauchy in terms of $\|\cdot\|_2$ if and only if it is Cauchy in terms of $\|\cdot\|_1$.

Exercise 2.1.1 Verify the norm properties (N1), (N2), (N3) for Equation (2.1.9). Also verify Equation (2.1.7) for this matrix norm, giving $\mathbb{R}^n$ and $\mathbb{R}^m$ the norm $\|\cdot\|_1$.

Exercise 2.1.2 For Equation (2.1.10), verify (N1), (N2), (N3), and also $\|A\| \leq \|A\|_2$.

Exercise 2.1.3 Show that $\langle \mathbf{w}, \mathbf{s} \rangle = \|\mathbf{w}\|_2 \cdot \|\mathbf{s}\|_2$ if and only if $\mathbf{w}$ and $\mathbf{s}$ are *linearly dependent*. (The latter means that $\beta\mathbf{w} + \gamma\mathbf{s} = \mathbf{0}$ for some constant numbers β and γ, not both zero. Note also that $\langle \mathbf{w}, \mathbf{s} \rangle = \mathbf{w}^T\mathbf{s}$, where $\mathbf{w}^T$ denotes the *transpose* of the column vector $\mathbf{w}$.)

2.2 FRÉCHET DERIVATIVES

Let $\mathbf{f}$ map a ball $X_0 = \{\mathbf{w} \in \mathbb{R}^n : \|\mathbf{w} - \mathbf{c}\| < \gamma\}$ (with centre $\mathbf{c}$) into $\mathbb{R}^m$. From Section 1.3, $\mathbf{f}$ is *differentiable* at $\mathbf{c} \in \mathbb{R}^n$ if there is a linear map $\mathbf{f}'(\mathbf{c}) : \mathbb{R}^n \to \mathbb{R}^m$ (represented by a $m \times n$ matrix) satisfying (for $\mathbf{w} \in X_0$)

$$\mathbf{f}(\mathbf{w}) = \mathbf{f}(\mathbf{c}) + \mathbf{f}'(\mathbf{c})(\mathbf{w}-\mathbf{c}) + \boldsymbol{\theta}(\mathbf{w}), \tag{2.2.1}$$

where (for some function $\delta(\cdot)$ of $\varepsilon > 0$)

$$\|\boldsymbol{\theta}(\mathbf{w})\| < \varepsilon\|\mathbf{w}-\mathbf{c}\| \text{ whenever } \|\mathbf{w}-\mathbf{c}\| < \delta(\varepsilon). \tag{2.2.2}$$

The map, or matrix, $\mathbf{f}'(\mathbf{c})$ is called the *derivative* of $\mathbf{f}$ at $\mathbf{c}$. We speak of *Fréchet differentiable* and the *Fréchet derivative* when the concepts just defined have to be distinguished from other sorts of differentiation. For examples, see Section 1.6.

Note that the derivative is a *local* concept; only points arbitrarily close to $\mathbf{c}$ are needed in its definition.

The statement (2.2.2) is often symbolized by writing

$$\theta(\mathbf{w}) = o(\|\mathbf{w}-\mathbf{c}\|). \tag{2.2.3}$$

If the (Fréchet) derivative $\mathbf{f}'(\mathbf{c})$ exists, then it is unique. To show this, first shift the origins to make $\mathbf{c} = \mathbf{0}$ and $\mathbf{f}(\mathbf{c}) = \mathbf{0}$. Suppose, if possible, that $\mathbf{f}(\mathbf{w}) = A\mathbf{w} + \theta_1(\mathbf{w}) = B\mathbf{w} + \theta_2(\mathbf{w})$. Then

$$\|(A-B)\mathbf{w}\| = \|A\mathbf{w} - B\mathbf{w}\| \leq \|\theta_1(\mathbf{w}) - \theta_2(\mathbf{w})\|.$$

Hence, using Equation (2.2.2), $\|(A-B\mathbf{w}\|/\|\mathbf{w}\| \to 0$ as $\|\mathbf{w}\| \to 0$. Hence $\|A-B\| = 0$, using the norm (2.1.10), and so $A-B = 0$.

The function $\mathbf{f} : X_0 \to \mathbb{R}^m$ is called *continuously differentiable* on X_0 (in symbols, $\mathbf{f} \in C^1(X_0, \mathbb{R}^m)$) if $\mathbf{f}$ is *Fréchet* differentiable at each point of X_0, and also $\mathbf{f}'(\mathbf{w})$ is a continuous function of $\mathbf{w}$ on X_0. (Thus $\|\mathbf{f}'(\mathbf{w}) - \mathbf{f}'(\mathbf{s})\| < \varepsilon$ whenever $\mathbf{w} \in X_0$, $\mathbf{s} \in X_0$, and $|\mathbf{w}-\mathbf{s}| < \delta(\varepsilon)$.) Denote by f_i ($i = 1, 2, \ldots, m$) the components of $\mathbf{f}$.

Theorem 2.1
The function $\mathbf{f} : X_0 \to \mathbb{R}^m$ is continuously differentiable on X_0 if and only if all the partial derivatives $\partial f_i/\partial w_j$ exist and are continuous on X_0.

Proof Assume that each $\partial f_i/\partial w_j$ is continuous on X_0. Let $\mathbf{w} \in X_0$ and $\mathbf{w}+\mathbf{h} \in X_0$; then $\mathbf{h} = h_1\mathbf{e}_1 + \ldots + h_n\mathbf{e}_n$ where $\mathbf{e}_1, \ldots, \mathbf{e}_n$ are basis vectors $(1, 0, \ldots, 0), (0, 1, 0, \ldots, 0)$, etc.; let $\mathbf{v}_k = h_1\mathbf{e}_1 + \ldots + h_k\mathbf{e}_k$ for $1 \le k \le n$, and $\mathbf{v}_0 = \mathbf{0}$. Then

$$f_i(\mathbf{w}+\mathbf{h}) - f_i(\mathbf{w}) = \sum_{k=1}^{n} [f_i(\mathbf{w}+\mathbf{v}_k) - f_i(\mathbf{w}+\mathbf{v}_{k-1})]$$

$$= \sum_{k=1}^{n} \frac{\partial}{\partial x_k} f_i(\mathbf{w}+\mathbf{v}_{k-1}+\gamma_k h_k \mathbf{e}_k) h_k \quad (2.2.4)$$

where $0 < \gamma_k < 1$, by the mean-value theorem for real differentiable functions of one real variable. By the assumption that the partial derivatives are continuous, there is $\delta > 0$ so that, when $\|\mathbf{h}\| < \delta$, the right side of Equation (2.2.4) differs by less than $\varepsilon\|\mathbf{h}\|$ from

$$\sum_{k=1}^{n} \frac{\partial}{\partial x_k} f_i(\mathbf{w}) h_k,$$

and this is the ith component of $\mathbf{f}'(\mathbf{w})\mathbf{h}$. Thus

$$\|\mathbf{f}(\mathbf{w}+\mathbf{h}) - \mathbf{f}(\mathbf{w}) - f'(\mathbf{w})\mathbf{h}\| < \varepsilon\|\mathbf{h}\| \text{ whenever } \|\mathbf{h}\| < \delta = \delta(\varepsilon).$$

Thus $\mathbf{f}$ is Fréchet differentiable at $\mathbf{w}$. But the matrix $\mathbf{f}'(\mathbf{w})$ has the continuous functions $\partial f_i/\partial w_j$ as its elements, so $\mathbf{f}'(\mathbf{w})$ is a continuous function of $\mathbf{w}$. Hence $\mathbf{f}$ is continuously differentiable.

Conversely, if $\mathbf{f}$ is continuously differentiable, then $\mathbf{f}$ is differentiable, and since $\mathbf{f}'(\mathbf{w})$ is a continuous function of w, $\partial f_i/\partial x_j$ is a continuous function of $\mathbf{w}$ for each i and j. □

The following example shows that *existence* of partial derivatives, without continuity, is not enough to ensure Fréchet differentiability. Consider the function $f(x, y) = xy/(x+y)$ when $(x, y) \in \mathbb{R}^2$ and $(x, y) \neq (0, 0)$, and $f(0, 0) = 0$. Then $\frac{\partial}{\partial x} f(0, 0) = 0 = \frac{\partial}{\partial y} f(0, 0)$. In polar coordinates $x = r \cos \theta$, $y = r \sin \theta$, the directional derivative of f at $(0, 0)$ in the polar direction θ is

$$\lim_{r \downarrow 0} \frac{1}{r} \frac{(r \cos \theta)(r \sin \theta)}{r \cos \theta + r \sin \theta} = \frac{\cos \theta \sin \theta}{\cos \theta + \sin \theta}.$$

This directional derivative does *not* equal

$$\frac{\partial}{\partial x} f(0, 0)\cos\theta + \frac{\partial}{\partial y} f(0, 0)\sin\theta,$$

as it would have to (see Section 1.4) if the Fréchet derivative $f'(0, 0)$ existed. Therefore f is *not* Fréchet differentiable at (0, 0). Note also that $\frac{\partial}{\partial x} f(x, y) = \frac{y^2}{(x+y)^2} = \frac{\sin^2\theta}{(\cos\theta + \sin\theta)^2}$ does not tend to $0 = \frac{\partial}{\partial x} f(0, 0)$ as $r \downarrow 0$. Thus $\frac{\partial}{\partial x} f(x, y)$ is *not* continuous at (0, 0).

The alternative notation $D_x f(a, b)$ for $\frac{\partial}{\partial x} f(a, b)$ is often convenient. The symbol $\mathbf{f} \in C^k(X_0, \mathbb{R}^m)$ means that $\mathbf{f}$ has continuous partial derivatives up to order k. C^∞ means partial derivatives of *all* orders; C^ω means functions expansible as Taylor series; note that the function $f(x) = e^{-1/x^2}$ is in $C^\infty(\mathbb{R}, \mathbb{R})$ but not in $C^\omega(\mathbb{R}, \mathbb{R})$.

Example
Define $f : \mathbb{R} \to \mathbb{R}$ by $f(x) = e^{-1/x^2}$ for $x \neq 0$, $f(0) = 0$. Then

$$x^{-1}[f(x) - f(0)] = x^{-1}e^{-x^2} \to 0 \text{ as } x \to 0,$$

so $f'(0) = 0$. Continuing,

$$x^{-1}[f'(x) - f'(0)] = x^{-1}f'(x) = 2x^{-4}e^{-1/x^2} \to 0 \text{ as } x \to 0,$$

noting that $P(x^{-1})e^{-1/x^2} \to 0$ as $x \to 0$, for any polynomial $P(\cdot)$. Thus $f''(0) = 0$. We may continue on these lines, to prove that $f^{(k)}(0) = 0$ for $k = 0, 1, 2, \ldots$. Thus this $f \in C^\infty$, but f is *not* expansible in a Taylor series about $x = 0$ (the series is identically zero, but f is not), so this $f \notin C^\omega$.

If $F(x, y) = \begin{bmatrix} f(x, y) \\ g(x, y) \end{bmatrix}$, the determinant of the matrix representing the derivative of $F(x, y)$ with respect to (x, y) is often called the *Jacobian*. Its traditional symbol is $\frac{\partial F(x, y)}{\partial(x, y)}$.

In differential geometry, the notation $\mathbf{df}(\mathbf{c})$ is often used for a quantity equivalent to the Fréchet derivative $\mathbf{f}'(\mathbf{c})$.

The following remark leads to another approach to the Fréchet derivative. Let X_0 be a ball in $\mathbb{R}^n$ with centre a (thus $X_0 = \{x \in \mathbb{R}^n : d(x, a) < \delta\}$): if $\mathbf{f}$ is differentiable at $\mathbf{c}$, then $\mathbf{f}(\mathbf{c}+\mathbf{s})-\mathbf{f}(\mathbf{c}) = \mathbf{f}'(\mathbf{c})\mathbf{s}+\boldsymbol{\theta}(\mathbf{s})$ where $\|\boldsymbol{\theta}(\mathbf{s})\|/\|\mathbf{s}\| \to 0$ as $\|\mathbf{s}\| \to 0$. Define $A(\mathbf{s}) \in \mathbb{R}^{m\times n}$ by $A(\mathbf{s})\mathbf{x} = \mathbf{f}'(\mathbf{c})\mathbf{x}+\boldsymbol{\theta}(\mathbf{s})\langle\mathbf{s}, \mathbf{x}\rangle/\|\mathbf{s}\|^2$. Then

$$\mathbf{f}(\mathbf{c}+\mathbf{s})-\mathbf{f}(\mathbf{c}) = A(\mathbf{s})\mathbf{s}, \text{ where } A(\mathbf{s}) \in \mathbb{R}^{m\times n}, \|A(\mathbf{s})-\mathbf{f}'(\mathbf{c})\| \to 0 \text{ as } \mathbf{s} \to \mathbf{0}. \tag{2.2.5}$$

Conversely, it is clear that (2.2.5) implies that $\mathbf{f}$ is differentiable at $\mathbf{c}$.

For exercises on Fréchet derivatives, refer also to Sections 1.6 and 1.7.

Exercise 2.2.1 Let $\mathbf{f}$ be Fréchet differentiable at $\mathbf{c}$. Use

$$\|\mathbf{f}(\mathbf{w})-\mathbf{f}(\mathbf{c})\| \leq \|\mathbf{f}'(\mathbf{c})\|\,\|\mathbf{w}-\mathbf{c}\|+\|\boldsymbol{\theta}(\mathbf{w})\|,$$

in terms of some suitable matrix norm $\|\mathbf{f}'(\mathbf{c})\|$, to show that $\mathbf{f}$ is *continuous* at $\mathbf{c}$, thus that $\|\mathbf{f}(\mathbf{w})-\mathbf{f}(\mathbf{c})\| < \varepsilon$ whenever $\|\mathbf{w}-\mathbf{c}\| < \delta(\varepsilon)$.

Exercise 2.2.2 Suppose that $\mathbf{f}$ and $\mathbf{g}$ are both differentiable at $\mathbf{c}$; let α and β be any constants. Show that also $\alpha\mathbf{f}+\beta\mathbf{g}$ is differentiable at $\mathbf{c}$, and that

$$(\alpha\mathbf{f}+\beta\mathbf{g})'(\mathbf{c}) = \alpha\mathbf{f}'(\mathbf{c})+\beta\mathbf{g}'(\mathbf{c}).$$

(This means that the map which takes each function $\mathbf{f}$, which is Fréchet differentiable at $\mathbf{c}$, to its derivative $\mathbf{f}'(\mathbf{c})$, is a *linear* map.)

Exercise 2.2.3 Let $f : \mathbb{R}^n \to \mathbb{R}$ and $g : \mathbb{R}^n \to \mathbb{R}$ be Fréchet differentiable functions. Define $h : \mathbb{R}^n \to \mathbb{R}$ by $h(\mathbf{x}) = f(\mathbf{x})g(\mathbf{x})$ for each $\mathbf{x}$. (It is natural to denote $h = fg$, but remember that the symbol fg can sometimes have other meanings.) Show that h is Fréchet differentiable, with $h'(\mathbf{s}) = g(\mathbf{s})f'(\mathbf{s})+f(\mathbf{s})g'(\mathbf{s})$.

Exercise 2.2.4 Define $\mathbf{f} : \mathbb{R}^n \to \mathbb{R}^m$ by $\mathbf{f}(\mathbf{x}) = B\mathbf{x}$, where $B \in \mathbb{R}^{m\times n}$. Show that, for each $\mathbf{x} \in \mathbb{R}^n$, $\mathbf{f}'(\mathbf{x}) = B$.

Exercise 2.2.5 Let $A \in \mathbb{R}^{n\times n}$ be a real symmetric matrix; define $f : \mathbb{R}^n \to \mathbb{R}$ by $f(\mathbf{x}) = \mathbf{x}^{\mathrm{T}}A\mathbf{x}$. Show that

$$f(\mathbf{c}+\mathbf{w})-f(\mathbf{c}) = \mathbf{w}^{\mathrm{T}}A\mathbf{c}+\mathbf{c}^{\mathrm{T}}A\mathbf{w}+\mathbf{w}^{\mathrm{T}}A\mathbf{w} = 2\mathbf{c}^{\mathrm{T}}A\mathbf{w}+\mathbf{w}^{\mathrm{T}}A\mathbf{w},$$

and deduce that $f'(\mathbf{c}) = 2\mathbf{c}^{\mathrm{T}}A$.

2.3 CHAIN RULE

Theorem 2.2
Let $\mathbf{f} : \mathbb{R}^m \to \mathbb{R}^n$ and $\mathbf{g} : \mathbb{R}^n \to \mathbb{R}^p$ be Fréchet differentiable functions, let $\mathbf{c} \in \mathbb{R}^m$ and let $\mathbf{b} = \mathbf{f}(\mathbf{c})$. Then the composite function $\mathbf{g} \circ \mathbf{f}$ is Fréchet differentiable at $\mathbf{c}$, and

$$(\mathbf{g} \circ \mathbf{f})'(\mathbf{c}) = \mathbf{g}'(\mathbf{b}) \circ \mathbf{f}'(\mathbf{c}). \tag{2.3.1}$$

Proof Shift the origins in the three spaces to make $\mathbf{c} = \mathbf{0}$, $\mathbf{b} = \mathbf{0}$, $\mathbf{g}(\mathbf{b}) = \mathbf{0}$. Denote $A = \mathbf{f}'(\mathbf{c})$ and $B = \mathbf{g}'(\mathbf{b})$. Let $\mathbf{s} = \mathbf{f}(\mathbf{w})$. Then $\mathbf{f}(\mathbf{w}) = A\mathbf{w} + \boldsymbol{\theta}(\mathbf{w})$ where $\|\boldsymbol{\theta}(\mathbf{w})\| < \varepsilon\|\mathbf{w}\|$ when $\|\mathbf{w}\| < \delta_f(\varepsilon)$, and $\mathbf{g}(\mathbf{s}) = B\mathbf{s} + \boldsymbol{\rho}(\mathbf{s})$ where $\|\boldsymbol{\rho}(\mathbf{s})\| < \varepsilon\|\mathbf{s}\|$ when $\|\mathbf{s}\| < \delta_g(\varepsilon)$. Then

$$(\mathbf{g} \circ \mathbf{f})(\mathbf{w}) = \mathbf{g}(\mathbf{s}) = B\mathbf{s} + \boldsymbol{\rho}(\mathbf{s}) = B(A\mathbf{w} + \boldsymbol{\theta}(\mathbf{w})) + \boldsymbol{\rho}(\mathbf{s}) \equiv BA\mathbf{w} + \boldsymbol{\psi}(\mathbf{w}). \tag{2.3.2}$$

For $0 < \varepsilon < 1$, choose $\|\mathbf{w}\| < \min\{\delta_f(\varepsilon), [1 + \|A\|]^{-1}\delta_g(\varepsilon)\}$. Then $\|\mathbf{s}\| \leq \|A\|\ \|\mathbf{w}\| + 1\|\mathbf{w}\| < \delta_g(\varepsilon)$, so $\|\boldsymbol{\rho}(\mathbf{s})\| < \varepsilon\|\mathbf{s}\| \leq (1 + \|A\|)\|\mathbf{w}\|$. Also $\|B\boldsymbol{\theta}(\mathbf{w})\| \leq \|B\|\ \|\boldsymbol{\theta}(\mathbf{w})\| < \|B\|\varepsilon\|\mathbf{w}\|$. Hence $\|\boldsymbol{\psi}(\mathbf{w})\| \leq [1 + \|A\| + \|B\|]\varepsilon\|\mathbf{w}\|$ whenever $\|\mathbf{w}\|$ is sufficiently small. Then, from Equation (2.3.2), $\mathbf{g} \circ \mathbf{f}$ is differentiable, with $(\mathbf{g} \circ \mathbf{f})'(\mathbf{0}) = BA$. □

The function which takes x to $f(x, h(x))$ is the composite of two functions, the first taking x to $\begin{bmatrix} x \\ h(x) \end{bmatrix}$, and the second taking $\begin{bmatrix} u \\ v \end{bmatrix}$ to $f(u, v)$. Their Fréchet derivatives are $\begin{bmatrix} 1 \\ h'(x) \end{bmatrix}$ and $[\mathrm{D}_u f'(u, v), \mathrm{D}_v f(u, v)]$. By the chain rule, if f and h are differentiable,

$$\frac{\mathrm{d}}{\mathrm{d}x} f(x, h(x)) = [\mathrm{D}_u f \quad \mathrm{D}_v f]\begin{bmatrix} 1 \\ h'(x) \end{bmatrix}.$$

More conventionally, regarding $f(x, v)$ as a function of x and v,

$$\frac{\mathrm{d}}{\mathrm{d}x} f(x, h(x)) = \frac{\partial}{\partial x} f(x, h(x)) + \frac{\partial}{\partial v} f(x, h(x))h'(x).$$

In such cases, the conventional notation can be ambiguous.

In the chain rule, $\mathbf{f}$ need only be defined on some ball with centre $\mathbf{c}$, provided that $\mathbf{g}$ is defined on some ball with centre $\mathbf{f}(\mathbf{c})$.

Theorem 2.3 (Mean-value theorem)
Let $f : X_0 \to \mathbb{R}^m$ be Fréchet differentiable at each point of $X_0 = \{\mathbf{w} \in \mathbb{R}^n : \|\mathbf{w}\| < \gamma\}$; let $\mathbf{x} \in X_0$ and $\mathbf{y} \in X_0$. Then

$$\|\mathbf{f}(\mathbf{x}) - \mathbf{f}(\mathbf{y})\| \leq M\|\mathbf{x} - \mathbf{y}\|,$$

where M is the supremum of $\|\mathbf{f}'(\mathbf{t})\|$ as $\mathbf{t}$ runs over the line segment $[\mathbf{x}, \mathbf{y}]$ joining $\mathbf{x}$ to $\mathbf{y}$.

Proof Let $0 \leq \alpha \leq 1$, and let $\mathbf{v} = \alpha\mathbf{x} + (1-\alpha)\mathbf{y} = \mathbf{y} + \alpha(\mathbf{x} - \mathbf{y})$; then $\mathbf{v} \in X_0$. Define $\mathbf{h} : [0, 1] \to \mathbb{R}^m$ by $\mathbf{h}(\alpha) = \mathbf{f}(\mathbf{v})$. By the chain rule, $\mathbf{h}$ is also differentiable, and $\mathbf{h}'(\alpha) = \mathbf{f}'(\mathbf{y} + \alpha(\mathbf{x} - \mathbf{y}))(\mathbf{x} - \mathbf{y})$. By applying the mean-value theorem for differentiable real functions to each component of $\mathbf{h}$, it follows that

$$\|\mathbf{f}(\mathbf{x}) - \mathbf{f}(\mathbf{y})\| = \|\mathbf{h}(1) - \mathbf{h}(0)\| m(1-0),$$

where $m = \sup_{0 < \alpha < 1} \|\mathbf{h}'(\alpha)\| \leq M\|\mathbf{x} - \mathbf{y}\|$. □

A direct proof that $\|\mathbf{h}(1) - \mathbf{h}(0)\| \leq m(1-0)$ is as follows. Choose any $\varepsilon > 0$. Denote by J the set of those $\xi \in [0, 1]$ for which $\|\mathbf{h}(\lambda) - \mathbf{h}(0)\| \leq (m + \varepsilon)\lambda$ whenever $0 \leq \lambda < \xi$. Then $0 \in J$. Let $\gamma = \sup J$; since $\mathbf{h}$ is continuous (because differentiable), $\gamma \in J$ also. Suppose that $\gamma < 1$; a contradiction will be deduced, showing that, in fact, $\gamma = 1$, which proves the result. If $\gamma < 1$, the definition of derivative shows that, for some $\eta > \gamma$, $\|\mathbf{h}(\eta) - \mathbf{h}(\gamma) - \mathbf{h}'(\eta)(\gamma - \eta)\| < \varepsilon(\eta - \gamma)$. From the triangle inequality, $\|\mathbf{h}(\eta) - \mathbf{h}(\gamma)\| \leq (m + \varepsilon)(\eta - \gamma)$. But also, since $\gamma \in J$, $\|\mathbf{h}(\gamma) - \mathbf{h}(0)\| \leq (m + \varepsilon)\gamma$. Combining the last two inequalities shows that $\|\mathbf{h}(\eta) - \mathbf{h}(0)\| \leq (m + \varepsilon)(\eta - \gamma) + (m + \varepsilon)\gamma = (m + \varepsilon)\eta$, contradicting $\eta \notin J$.

For exercises on the chain rule, see also Section 1.7.

Exercise 2.3.1 Use the chain rule to calculate the Fréchet derivatives of the following functions. (Note any restrictions needed on the domains.)

(i) $f(x, y) = [g(x)]^y$ (where $g : \mathbb{R}^n \to \mathbb{R}$ is differentiable, and y is real).
(ii) $F(x, y) = f(g(x)h(y), g(x) + h(y))$ (assume $f : \mathbb{R} \times \mathbb{R} \to \mathbb{R}^m$).
(iii) $f(x, y) = \sin(x \sin y)$.
(iv) $f(x, y) = \int_a^{x+y} g(t)\, \mathrm{d}t$ (where g is a real continuous function; note that $f(x, y)$ has the form $\varphi(x+y)$).

Exercise 2.3.2 Use the chain rule to evaluate the partial derivative with respect to x of the function $f(x, g(x, y), h(x, y))$, assuming that the (real) functions f, g, h are all Fréchet differentiable. (Note that here there are two kinds of '$\partial f/\partial x$'; the function asked for is, by some authors, denoted $\dfrac{\mathrm{D}f}{\mathrm{D}x}$, but there is no agreement on symbols.)

Exercise 2.3.3 The differentiable function f is called *homogeneous* of degree k if $f(\alpha x) = \alpha^k f(x)$ for each x and each $\alpha > 0$. Prove Euler's formula:

$$f'(x)x = kf(x).$$

Exercise 2.3.4 Suppose that $f(x, y)$ is a real differentiable function of (x, y), and that $\dfrac{\partial}{\partial x} f(x, y) = 0$ for each (x, y) in a convex set $E \subset \mathbb{R}^2$. (Convex means that, whenever $p \in E$ and $q \in E$, then the line segment joining p to q is also in E.) Use the mean-value theorem to show that, when $(x, y) \in E$, the value of $f(x, y)$ is independent of x. More precisely, if $(x, y) \in E$ and $(x^*, y) \in E$, then $f(x, y) = f(x^*, y)$.

Exercise 2.3.5 Let $\mathbf{f}$ map a ball in $\mathbb{R}^n$, with centre zero, into $\mathbb{R}^n$; let $\mathbf{f}(\mathbf{0}) = \mathbf{0}$. Suppose that, whenever $\|\mathbf{y}\| < \delta$, the equation $\mathbf{f}(\mathbf{x}) = \mathbf{y}$ has a unique solution $\mathbf{x} = \mathbf{g}(\mathbf{y})$. Assuming also that both $\mathbf{f}$ and $\mathbf{g}$ are Fréchet differentiable, use the chain rule to show that $\mathbf{g}'(\mathbf{y})$ is the inverse of $\mathbf{f}'(\mathbf{g}(\mathbf{y}))$, when $\|\mathbf{y}\|$ is sufficiently small. (Conditions for $\mathbf{g}$ to be unique and differentiable are obtained later in Section 2.4.)

Exercise 2.3.6 Let $f : \mathbb{R} \to \mathbb{R}$ be continuously differentiable, and satisfy $f(0) = 0$ and $a = f'(0) \neq 0$. We consider when the equation $f(x) = y$ can be solved for x, assuming $|y|$ small. Show first that $f(x) = y$ if and only if $A^{-1}f(x) = v$ where $v = A^{-1}y$, and $A^{-1}f(x) = x + \theta(x)$ where $|\theta(x)| < \varepsilon|x|$ whenever $|x| < \Delta(\varepsilon)$. Deduce that $f(x) = y$ has a solution x, for given y, exactly when $F(x) \equiv x + \theta(x) - v = 0$. Suppose now that $0 < v < \frac{1}{2}\Delta(\frac{1}{2})$. Show then that $F(\frac{2}{3}v) \leq 0 \leq F(2v)$, and deduce that the equation $F(v) = 0$ has a solution $\bar{x}$, with $\frac{2}{3}v \leq \bar{x} \leq 2v$. (These ideas, developed in Section 2.4, lead to the *inverse function theorem.* If f is *continuously* differentiable, then $|\theta'(x)| < 1$ for small enough $|x|$, and then $F(\cdot)$ is a monotone function, so that the solution $\bar{x}$ is unique. Note that $\theta'(0) = 0$ by definition of $f'(0)$.)

Exercise 2.3.7 Use Equation (2.3.2) to prove the chain rule, as follows. There are matrices $A(\mathbf{s})$ and $B(\mathbf{w})$ such that $\mathbf{s} = A(\mathbf{w})\mathbf{w}$, $A(\mathbf{w}) \to A$ as $\|\mathbf{w}\| \to 0$, $\mathbf{g}(\mathbf{s}) = B(\mathbf{s})\mathbf{s}$, $B(\mathbf{s}) \to B$ as $\|\mathbf{s}\| \to 0$. Then $(\mathbf{g} \circ \mathbf{f})(\mathbf{w}) = \mathbf{g}(\mathbf{s}) = B(\mathbf{s})A(\mathbf{w})\mathbf{w}$. The conclusion will follow if $B(\mathbf{s})A(\mathbf{w}) \to BA$ as $\|\mathbf{w}\| \to 0$.

2.4 INVERSE FUNCTION THEOREM

Let $\mathbf{f}$ be a differentiable function from $X_0 = \{\mathbf{x} \in \mathbb{R}^n : \|x\| < \gamma\}$ into $\mathbb{R}^n$, such that $\mathbf{f}(\mathbf{0}) = \mathbf{0}$. When is the equation $\mathbf{f}(\mathbf{x}) = \mathbf{y}$ solvable for a unique $\mathbf{x}$ near $\mathbf{0}$, for each $\mathbf{y} \in \mathbb{R}^n$ with $\|\mathbf{y}\|$ small enough? Such a solution, say $\mathbf{x} = \mathbf{g}(\mathbf{y})$, would be an inverse function to $\mathbf{f}$. If $\mathbf{g}$ exists, when is $\mathbf{g}$ differentiable? (If it is, then $\mathbf{g}'(\mathbf{y})$ is calculable – see Exercise 2.3.5 above). Some restriction is certainly needed. For example, define $f: \mathbb{R} \to \mathbb{R}$ by $f(x) = x^2$; then $f(x) = y$ has no solution if $y < 0$, however small $|y|$ may be. Observe in this example that $\partial f/\partial x = 0$ at $x = 0$ (see Fig. 2.1).

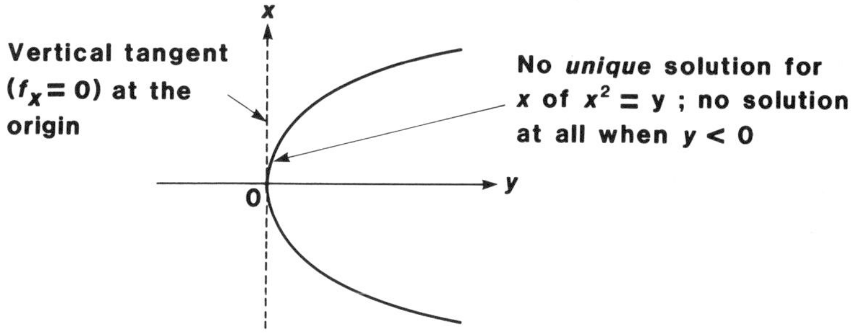

Figure 2.1 Inverse function?

In particular, if $\mathbf{f}$ is linear, thus if $\mathbf{f}(\mathbf{x}) = A\mathbf{x}$ where $A \in \mathbb{R}^{m \times n}$, then $\mathbf{g}$ exists if and only if the matrix A is invertible. This, and Exercise 2.3.6 above, motivate the following theory. A preliminary theorem is required, which is also useful in many other places, to show that solutions exist. Let d denote the *distance* in $\mathbb{R}^n$, defined by $d(\mathbf{w}, \mathbf{s}) = \|\mathbf{w} - \mathbf{s}\|$.

Theorem 2.4 (Contraction mapping theorem)
Let the function $\varphi : \mathbb{R}^n \to \mathbb{R}^n$ and the constant λ satisfy $0 < \lambda < 1$ and

$$d(\varphi(\mathbf{x}), \varphi(\mathbf{y})) \leq \lambda d(\mathbf{x}, \mathbf{y}) \qquad (2.4.1)$$

for all $\mathbf{x}, \mathbf{y} \in \mathbb{R}^n$. Then the equation $\varphi(\mathbf{u}) = \mathbf{u}$ possesses a unique solution $\mathbf{u} = \bar{\mathbf{u}} \in \mathbb{R}^n$, called a *fixed point* of φ. Moreover, $\bar{\mathbf{u}}$ is the limit of the sequence $\{\mathbf{u}_j\}$ defined by $\mathbf{u}_{j+1} = \varphi(\mathbf{u}_j)$ for $j = 0, 1, 2, \ldots$, and arbitrary $\mathbf{u}_0 \in \mathbb{R}^n$; and then

$$d(\bar{\mathbf{u}}, \mathbf{u}_1) \leq c\lambda/(1-\lambda), \text{ where } c = d(\mathbf{u}_0, \mathbf{u}_1). \qquad (2.4.2)$$

Proof

$$\begin{aligned} d(\mathbf{u}_{j+1}, \mathbf{u}_j) &= d(\varphi(\mathbf{u}_j), \varphi(\mathbf{u}_{j-1})) \leq \lambda d(\mathbf{u}_j, \mathbf{u}_{j-1}) \\ &\leq \lambda^2 d(\mathbf{u}_{j-1}, \mathbf{u}_{j-2}) \leq \ldots \leq \lambda^j d(\mathbf{u}_1, \mathbf{u}_0) = \lambda^j c. \end{aligned}$$

Hence, for $0 \leq i < j$,

$$\begin{aligned} d(\mathbf{u}_i, \mathbf{u}_j) &\leq d(\mathbf{u}_i, \mathbf{u}_{i+1}) + d(\mathbf{u}_{i+1}, \mathbf{u}_{i+2}) + \ldots + d(\mathbf{u}_{j-1}, \mathbf{u}_j) \\ &\leq \lambda^i c + \lambda^{i+1} c + \ldots + \lambda^{j-1} c < \lambda^i c/(1-\lambda) \\ &\to 0 \text{ as } i, j \to \infty, \text{ since } 0 < \lambda < 1. \end{aligned} \qquad (2.4.3)$$

Hence $\{\mathbf{u}_j\}$ is a Cauchy sequence in $\mathbb{R}^n$; hence there exists $\bar{\mathbf{u}} \in \mathbb{R}^n$ such that $\|\mathbf{u}_j - \bar{\mathbf{u}}\| \to 0$ as $j \to \infty$. Then, letting $j \to \infty$ in $\varphi(\mathbf{u}_j) = \mathbf{u}_{j+1}$ and noting that φ is continuous, $\varphi(\bar{\mathbf{u}}) = \bar{\mathbf{u}}$. If also $\varphi(\mathbf{v}) = \mathbf{v}$, then $d(\bar{\mathbf{u}}, \mathbf{v}) = d(\varphi(\bar{\mathbf{u}}), \varphi(\bar{\mathbf{v}})) \leq \lambda d(\bar{\mathbf{u}}, \mathbf{v})$; since $0 < \lambda < 1$, $d(\bar{\mathbf{u}}, \mathbf{v}) = 0$, hence $\bar{\mathbf{u}} = \mathbf{v}$. Using Equation (2.4.3) with $i = 1$ and $j \to \infty$ gives Equation (2.4.2). □

Because of Equation (2.4.1), the function φ is called a *contraction mapping*. For each j, Equation (2.4.3) shows that $d(\mathbf{u}_0, \mathbf{u}_j) < c/(1-\lambda)$. Hence the hypothesis that $d(\varphi(\mathbf{x}), \varphi(\mathbf{y})) \leq \lambda d(\mathbf{x}, \mathbf{y})$ need not be assumed for all $\mathbf{x}, \mathbf{y} \in \mathbb{R}^n$; it is enough to assume it for all $\mathbf{x}, \mathbf{y}$ in the ball $\{\mathbf{w} \in \mathbb{R}^n : d(\mathbf{u}_0, \mathbf{w}) \leq c/(1-\lambda)\}$, having chosen $\mathbf{u}_0$. The fixed point $\bar{\mathbf{u}}$ of the contraction mapping φ then lies in this ball.

Theorem 2.5 (Inverse function theorem)
Let $X_0 = \{x \in \mathbb{R}^n : \|x\| < \gamma\}$; let the function $\mathbf{f} : X_0 \to \mathbb{R}^n$ be continuously differentiable in X_0; let $\mathbf{f}(\mathbf{0}) = \mathbf{0}$; let $\mathbf{f}'(\mathbf{0}) : \mathbb{R}^n \to \mathbb{R}^n$ be

invertible. Then, for some $\Delta > 0$, the equation $\mathbf{f}(\mathbf{x}) = \mathbf{y}$ has a unique solution $\mathbf{x} = \mathbf{g}(\mathbf{y})$, whenever $\|\mathbf{y}\| < \Delta$ and $\|\mathbf{x}\| < \Delta$; and $\mathbf{g}$ is continuously differentiable.

Remark Suppose, instead, that $\mathbf{f}(\mathbf{x}_0) = \mathbf{y}_0$ and $\mathbf{f}'(\mathbf{x}_0)$ is invertible. Let $\xi = \mathbf{x}-\mathbf{x}_0$ and $\eta = \mathbf{y}-\mathbf{y}_0$, and define $\mathbf{F}(\xi) = \mathbf{f}(\mathbf{x}_0+\xi)-\mathbf{f}(\mathbf{x}_0)$. Then the equation $\mathbf{f}(\mathbf{x}) = \mathbf{y}$ can be rewritten as $\mathbf{F}(\xi) = \eta$, where now $\mathbf{F}'(\mathbf{0}) = \mathbf{f}'(\mathbf{x}_0)$ is invertible. From the theorem, $\mathbf{F}(\xi) = \eta$ is solvable uniquely for ξ, assuming that $\|\xi\|$ and $\|\eta\|$ are sufficiently small. Hence $\mathbf{y} = \mathbf{f}(\mathbf{x})$ is solvable uniquely for $\mathbf{x} = \mathbf{g}(\mathbf{y})$, assuming that both $\|\mathbf{x}-\mathbf{x}_0\|$ and $\|\mathbf{y}-\mathbf{y}_0\|$ are sufficiently small.

Proof Let $A = \mathbf{f}'(\mathbf{0})$. Since A is invertible, $\mathbf{f}(\mathbf{x}) = \mathbf{y} \Leftrightarrow \mathbf{v} = A^{-1}\mathbf{f}(\mathbf{x})$, where $\mathbf{v} = A^{-1}\mathbf{y}$. By the chain rule, the function $A^{-1}\mathbf{f}$ is differentiable, with $(A^{-1}\mathbf{f})'(\mathbf{0}) = A^{-1}\mathbf{f}'(\mathbf{0}) = I$, the identity matrix. Thus

$$\mathbf{f}(\mathbf{x}) = \mathbf{y} \Leftrightarrow A^{-1}\mathbf{f}(\mathbf{x}) = \mathbf{v} \Leftrightarrow \mathbf{x}+\boldsymbol{\theta}(\mathbf{x}) = \mathbf{v} \Leftrightarrow \varphi(\mathbf{x}) = \mathbf{x},$$

where $\|\boldsymbol{\theta}(\mathbf{x})\| < \varepsilon\|\mathbf{x}\|$ whenever $\|\mathbf{x}\|$ is small enough, and $\varphi(\mathbf{x}) = \mathbf{v}-\boldsymbol{\theta}(\mathbf{x})$. Now $\boldsymbol{\theta}'(\mathbf{0}) = \mathbf{0}$, and $\boldsymbol{\theta}'(\mathbf{x})$ is a continuous function of $\mathbf{x}$ since $\mathbf{f}$ is *continuously* differentiable. Hence, for some function $\delta(\cdot)$ of $\varepsilon > 0$, $\|\boldsymbol{\theta}'(\mathbf{x})\| < \varepsilon$ whenever $\|\mathbf{x}\| \leq \delta(\varepsilon) < \gamma$. From the mean-value theorem, $\|\varphi(\mathbf{x})-\varphi(\mathbf{z})\| = \|\theta(\mathbf{x})-\theta(\mathbf{z})\| \leq \varepsilon\|\mathbf{x}-\mathbf{z}\|$ whenever $\|\mathbf{x}\|, \|\mathbf{z}\| \leq \delta(\varepsilon)$.

Assume $0 < \varepsilon \leq \frac{1}{2}$ and $\|\mathbf{y}\| < \frac{1}{2}\|A^{-1}\|^{-1}\delta(\varepsilon)$; then $\|\mathbf{v}\| = \|A^{-1}\mathbf{y}\| < \frac{1}{2}\delta(\varepsilon)$. Set $\mathbf{u}_0 = \mathbf{0}$ and $\lambda = \varepsilon$; then $\varphi(\mathbf{u}_0) = \mathbf{v} = A^{-1}\mathbf{y}$ and $c \equiv d(\varphi(\mathbf{u}_0), \mathbf{u}_0) = \|\mathbf{v}\|$, so that $c/(1-\lambda) \leq 2\|\mathbf{v}\| < \delta(\varepsilon)$. Since φ is a contraction mapping when $\|\mathbf{x}\| \leq \delta(\varepsilon)$, the contraction mapping theorem (and the remark following it), show that φ has a unique fixed point, $\mathbf{x} = \mathbf{g}(\mathbf{y})$ say, with $\|\mathbf{g}(\mathbf{y})\| \leq \delta(\varepsilon)$. Moreover, from Equation (2.4.2),

$$\|\mathbf{g}(\mathbf{y})-A^{-1}\mathbf{y}\| \leq \|\mathbf{v}\|\varepsilon/(1-\varepsilon) \leq 2\varepsilon\|\mathbf{v}\| \leq 2\|A^{-1}\|\varepsilon\|\mathbf{y}\|$$

whenever $\|\mathbf{y}\| < \frac{1}{2}\|A^{-1}\|^{-1}\delta(\varepsilon)$. Hence $\mathbf{g}$ is differentiable at $\mathbf{0}$, with $\mathbf{g}'(\mathbf{0}) = A^{-1} = \mathbf{f}'(\mathbf{0})^{-1}$.

Choose any $\Delta < \delta(\frac{1}{2}) \min\{1, \frac{1}{2}\|A^{-1}\|^{-1}\}$. Then $\mathbf{f}(\mathbf{x}) \equiv \mathbf{y}$ has been solved uniquely when $\|\mathbf{y}\| < \Delta$, yielding $\|\mathbf{x}\| < \Delta$. It remains to show that $\mathbf{g}$ is continuously differentiable on $\|\mathbf{y}\| < \Delta$.

Let $\|\mathbf{y}_0\| < \Delta$. Then $\mathbf{x}_0 = \mathbf{g}(\mathbf{y}_0)$ has $\|\mathbf{x}\| < \delta(\frac{1}{2})$, hence $\|\boldsymbol{\theta}'(\mathbf{x}_0)\| < 1$. By Exercise 2.4.1 below, the matrix $A^{-1}\mathbf{f}'(\mathbf{x}_0) = I+\boldsymbol{\theta}'(\mathbf{x}_0)$ is invertible. The result of the previous paragraph then finds a solution to $\mathbf{y} = \mathbf{f}(\mathbf{x})$, rewritten as $\mathbf{y}-\mathbf{y}_0 = \mathbf{f}(\mathbf{x})-\mathbf{f}(\mathbf{x}_0)$, when $\|\mathbf{y}-\mathbf{y}_0\|$ (and $\|\mathbf{x}-\mathbf{x}_0\|$) are small enough. This solution is differentiable at $\mathbf{y}_0$; but since the solution is unique, it must agree with $\mathbf{x} = \mathbf{g}(\mathbf{y})$. Hence $\mathbf{g}$ is differentiable whenever $\|\mathbf{y}\| < \Delta$ (and $\|\mathbf{x}\| < \Delta$). Then $\mathbf{g}$ is continuously differentiable, since $\mathbf{g}'(\mathbf{y}) = \mathbf{f}'(\mathbf{g}(\mathbf{y}))^{-1}$, the inverse of a continuous function of $\mathbf{y}$. □

Example

Define $\mathbf{f} : \mathbb{R}^2 \to \mathbb{R}^2$ by

$$\mathbf{f}\left(\begin{bmatrix} x \\ y \end{bmatrix}\right) = \begin{bmatrix} x^2-4y^2 \\ x+y-3 \end{bmatrix}; \text{ at } \begin{bmatrix} x \\ y \end{bmatrix} = \begin{bmatrix} 2 \\ 1 \end{bmatrix},$$

$$\mathbf{f}\left(\begin{bmatrix} 2 \\ 1 \end{bmatrix}\right) = \begin{bmatrix} 0 \\ 0 \end{bmatrix} \text{ and } \mathbf{f}'\left(\begin{bmatrix} 2 \\ 1 \end{bmatrix}\right) = \begin{bmatrix} 4 & -8 \\ 1 & 1 \end{bmatrix}.$$

Since $\mathbf{f}'\left(\begin{bmatrix} 2 \\ 1 \end{bmatrix}\right)$ is a nonsingular matrix, the equation $\mathbf{f}\left(\begin{bmatrix} x \\ y \end{bmatrix}\right) = \begin{bmatrix} u \\ v \end{bmatrix}$ can be solved for $\begin{bmatrix} x \\ y \end{bmatrix}$, provided that u and v are sufficiently small. Set $x = 2+\xi$ and $y = 1+\eta$. The equations to be solved are then

$$\begin{bmatrix} (2+\xi)^2-4(1+\eta)^2 \\ (2+\xi)+(1+\eta)-3 \end{bmatrix} = \begin{bmatrix} 4\xi-8\eta+\xi^2-4\eta^2 \\ \xi+\eta \end{bmatrix} = \begin{bmatrix} u \\ v \end{bmatrix}.$$

If terms in ξ^2 and η^2 are neglected, then

$$\begin{bmatrix} 4 & -8 \\ 1 & 1 \end{bmatrix}\begin{bmatrix} \xi \\ \eta \end{bmatrix} \approx \begin{bmatrix} u \\ v \end{bmatrix}, \text{ so } \begin{bmatrix} \xi \\ \eta \end{bmatrix} \approx (1/12)\begin{bmatrix} 1 & 8 \\ -4 & 4 \end{bmatrix}\begin{bmatrix} u \\ v \end{bmatrix},$$

on substituting the inverse matrix. In this case, the inverse function theorem states that an inverse function exists, given approximately by this expression, provided that $|u|$ and $|v|$ are small enough. In this example, the quadratics could be solved exactly, but in more complicated instances, there are no exact formulas for the inverse function.

Under the hypotheses of the inverse function theorem, the map of x to y is one-to-one *locally*, meaning in a sufficiently small region. But the theorem does *not* guarantee a function which is *globally* one-to-one, meaning over the whole domain of the function $\mathbf{f}$. The next example shows this.

Example

Define $f : \mathbb{R}^2 \to \mathbb{R}^2$ by $f\left(\begin{bmatrix} x \\ y \end{bmatrix}\right) = \begin{bmatrix} e^x \cos y \\ e^x \sin y \end{bmatrix}$. At each point, $f'\left(\begin{bmatrix} x \\ y \end{bmatrix}\right)$ is invertible, so f is locally one-to-one. But this f is *not* one-to-one over all of $\mathbb{R}^2$, since $f\left(\begin{bmatrix} x \\ y+2\pi \end{bmatrix}\right) = f\left(\begin{bmatrix} x \\ y \end{bmatrix}\right)$.

Exercise 2.4.1 Let I be the unit matrix in $\mathbb{R}^{n\times n}$; let $M \in \mathbb{R}^{n\times n}$ satisfy $\|M\| < 1$ (in terms of some matrix norm). Show that the function $\varphi(\mathbf{w}) = \mathbf{s} - M\mathbf{w}$ is a contraction mapping, and deduce that the equation $(I+M)\mathbf{w} = \mathbf{s}$ has a unique solution $\mathbf{w} \in \mathbb{R}^n$ for each $\mathbf{s} \in \mathbb{R}^n$. Deduce that $I+M$ is an invertible matrix.

Exercise 2.4.2 Define $\varphi : \mathbb{R} \to \mathbb{R}$ by $\varphi(x) = y - cx^2$. Show that φ becomes a contraction mapping if the domain of f is restricted to **a** sufficiently small interval $(-\delta, \delta)$. Deduce that the equation $x + cx^2 = y$ is uniquely solvable for x as a function of y, provided that $|y|$ is sufficiently small. Compare the approximate solution $x \approx y - c(y - cy^2)^2$, obtained from the contraction mapping, with the solution obtained by solving the quadratic equation.

Exercise 2.4.3 Define $f : \mathbb{R}^2 \to \mathbb{R}^2$ by $f\left(\begin{bmatrix} x \\ y \end{bmatrix}\right) = \begin{bmatrix} x^2+y^2 \\ 2xy \end{bmatrix}$. Show that the equation $f\left(\begin{bmatrix} x \\ y \end{bmatrix}\right) = \begin{bmatrix} u \\ v \end{bmatrix}$ is uniquely solvable, for $\begin{bmatrix} x \\ y \end{bmatrix}$ sufficiently near to $\begin{bmatrix} x_0 \\ y_0 \end{bmatrix}$ and $\begin{bmatrix} u \\ v \end{bmatrix}$ sufficiently near to $f\left(\begin{bmatrix} x_0 \\ y_0 \end{bmatrix}\right)$, provided that the points $\begin{bmatrix} x_0 \\ y_0 \end{bmatrix}$ lying on two particular lines are excluded from $\mathbb{R}^2$. If the solution is $\begin{bmatrix} x \\ y \end{bmatrix} = g\left(\begin{bmatrix} u \\ v \end{bmatrix}\right)$, calculate $g'(\cdot)$ in terms of partial derivatives of f.

Exercise 2.4.4 Similarly discuss $f\left(\begin{bmatrix} x \\ y \end{bmatrix}\right) = \begin{bmatrix} e^{-x} \cos y \\ e^{-x} \sin y \end{bmatrix}$.

2.5 IMPLICIT FUNCTIONS

When is an equation $f(x, y) = 0$ solvable (given $f(0, 0) = 0$) by $y = g(x)$, valid whenever $|x|$ is small enough? Such a solution g is called an *implicit function* (the equation determines y as a function of x, but does not give it by an explicit formula.) If g exists, and if f and g are differentiable, then $g'(x)$ can be obtained by the chain rule. But an implicit function does not always exist. The function $f(x, y) = x^2+y^2$ $(x, y \in \mathbb{R})$ satisfies $f(0, 0) = 0$, but has no other (real) zeros, so there is no implicit function $y = g(x)$.

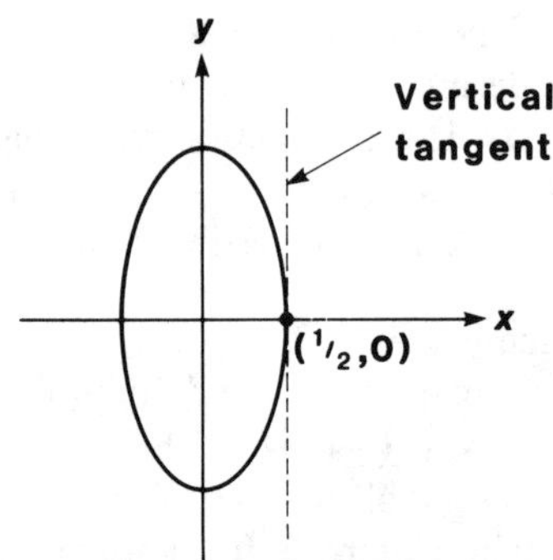

Figure 2.2 Implicit function

Consider the function $f(x, y) = 4x^2+y^2-1$, near the point $(\frac{1}{2}, 0)$ (see Fig. 2.2). Solving $f(x, y) = 0$ near this point, gives $y = \pm(1-4x^2)^{1/2}$; so there is not a *unique* solution, and moreover, neither of the two solutions has a derivative at $x = \frac{1}{2}$; the slope is vertical. This is linked with the fact that $\partial f/\partial y$ (at $(\frac{1}{2}, 0)$) is zero, and is therefore *not* invertible. However, $f(2/5, 3/5) = 0$, and $\partial f/\partial y(2/5, 3/5) = 6/5 \neq 0$. The slope here is *not* vertical, and the tangent to the ellipse at this point has the equation

$$\frac{16}{5}\left(x - \frac{2}{5}\right)+\frac{6}{5}\left(y-\frac{3}{5}\right) = 0,$$

which solves (since $\partial f/\partial y \neq 0$) to $y = \frac{3}{5}+\frac{16}{5}\left(x-\frac{2}{5}\right)$, which gives a linear approximation to the implicit function.

Theorem 2.6 (Implicit function theorem)
Let $\mathbf{f} : \mathbb{R}^m \times \mathbb{R}^n \to \mathbb{R}^n$ be continuously differentiable, and let $\mathbf{f}(\mathbf{0}, \mathbf{0}) = \mathbf{0}$. Let the partial Fréchet derivative $\mathbf{f}_y(\mathbf{0}, \mathbf{0}) : \mathbb{R}^n \to \mathbb{R}^n$ be invertible. Then there exists a continuously differentiable function

$\mathbf{g} : E \to \mathbb{R}^n$, where $E = \{\mathbf{x} \in \mathbb{R}^m : \|\mathbf{x}\| < \Delta\}$ for some $\Delta > 0$, such that $\mathbf{f}(\mathbf{x}, \mathbf{g}(\mathbf{x})) = \mathbf{0}$ identically for each $\mathbf{x} \in E$.

Remark The function $\mathbf{f}$ need only be defined, and continuously differentiable, for sufficiently small $\|\mathbf{x}\|$ and $\|\mathbf{y}\|$. By a shift of origin, we could assume instead that $\mathbf{f}(\mathbf{a}, \mathbf{b}) = \mathbf{0}$, and require $\mathbf{g}(\mathbf{a}) = \mathbf{b}$ in place of $\mathbf{g}(\mathbf{0}) = \mathbf{0}$. For convenience, we write $\mathbf{f}(\mathbf{x}, \mathbf{y})$ instead of $\mathbf{f}\left(\begin{bmatrix} \mathbf{x} \\ \mathbf{y} \end{bmatrix}\right)$. The partial Fréchet derivative $\mathbf{f}_y(\mathbf{0}, \mathbf{0})$ is the Fréchet derivative at $\mathbf{0}$ of $\mathbf{f}(\mathbf{0}, \mathbf{y})$ with respect to $\mathbf{y}$.

Proof The function F which takes $\begin{bmatrix} \mathbf{x} \\ \mathbf{y} \end{bmatrix} \in \mathbb{R}^{m+n}$ to $\begin{bmatrix} \mathbf{x} \\ \mathbf{f}(\mathbf{x}, \mathbf{y}) \end{bmatrix} \in \mathbb{R}^{m+n}$ has, at $\begin{bmatrix} \mathbf{0} \\ \mathbf{0} \end{bmatrix}$, the Fréchet derivative

$$H = \begin{bmatrix} I & 0 \\ \mathbf{f}_x(\mathbf{0}, \mathbf{0}) & \mathbf{f}_y(\mathbf{0}, \mathbf{0}) \end{bmatrix},$$

where I is the identity map (which takes each $\mathbf{x}$ to $\mathbf{x}$). Since $\mathbf{f}_y(\mathbf{0}, \mathbf{0})$ is, by hypothesis, invertible, $H : \mathbb{R}^{m+n} \to \mathbb{R}^{m+n}$ is also invertible. The inverse function theorem shows, therefore, that for sufficiently small $\|\mathbf{x}\|$, say $\|\mathbf{x}\| < \Delta$, $\mathbf{F}\left(\begin{bmatrix} \mathbf{x} \\ \mathbf{y} \end{bmatrix}\right) = \begin{bmatrix} \mathbf{x} \\ \mathbf{0} \end{bmatrix}$ has a continuously differentiable, solution for $\begin{bmatrix} \mathbf{x} \\ \mathbf{y} \end{bmatrix}$ as a function of $\begin{bmatrix} \mathbf{x} \\ \mathbf{0} \end{bmatrix}$, and hence of $\mathbf{x}$. This is unique when $\|\mathbf{x}\| < \Delta$, $\|\mathbf{y}\| < \Delta$, and gives the required function $\mathbf{y} = \mathbf{g}(\mathbf{x})$. □

Example

Define $\mathbf{f} : \mathbb{R}^3 \to \mathbb{R}^2$ by $\mathbf{f}(x, y, z) = (x^2 - y^2 + z^2,\ 2xy - 2)$, or, in matrix terms,

$$\mathbf{f}\left(\begin{bmatrix} x \\ y \\ z \end{bmatrix}\right) = \begin{bmatrix} x^2 - y^2 + z^2 \\ 2xy - 2 \end{bmatrix}.$$

Can the equation $\mathbf{f}(x, y, z) = 0$ be solved uniquely for (x, y) in terms of z, near the point solution $(x, y, z) = (1, 1, 0)$? Clearly, $\mathbf{f}$ is continuously differentiable, and

$$\mathbf{f}'\left(\begin{bmatrix} x \\ y \\ z \end{bmatrix}\right) = \left[\begin{array}{cc:c} 2x & -2y & 2z \\ 2y & 2x & 0 \end{array}\right].$$

The first two columns of this matrix form the partial Fréchet derivative $\mathbf{f}_{(x,y)}$, and this is nonsingular, since its determinant is $4(x^2+y^2) \neq 0$ at $(x, y) = (1, 1)$. Hence the desired (local) solution, $\begin{bmatrix} x \\ y \end{bmatrix} = \mathbf{h}(z)$ say, exists uniquely. The Fréchet derivative of $\mathbf{h}$ may then be calculated by applying the chain rule to the identity $\mathbf{f}(\mathbf{h}(z), z) = 0$. This gives (compare Exercise 2.5.1 below) that

$$\begin{bmatrix} 2x & -2y \\ 2y & 2x \end{bmatrix} \mathbf{h}'(z) + \begin{bmatrix} 2z \\ 0 \end{bmatrix} = \begin{bmatrix} 0 \\ 0 \end{bmatrix},$$

for (x, y, z) satisfying $\mathbf{f}(x, y, z) = 0$ and (x, y, z) near to $(1, 1, 0)$.

Example

In thermodynamics, the entropy S of a suitable system is related to the temperature T and the volume V by some function, say $S = \mathbf{S}(T, V)$, assumed continuously differentiable. If the implicit function theorem can be applied to solve this equation locally for V, say by $V = \mathbf{V}(T, S)$, then $S = \mathbf{S}(T, \mathbf{V}(S, T))$ holds identically in a region. Using the chain rule, $0 = \mathbf{S}_T + \mathbf{S}_V \mathbf{V}_T$ and $1 = \mathbf{S}_V \mathbf{V}_S$. Hence $\mathbf{S}_T = -\mathbf{V}_S{}^{-1} \mathbf{V}_T$. Observe that the hypothesis that $\mathbf{S}_V \neq 0$ is required twice here (first for the implicit function theorem). Thus derivatives of $\mathbf{S}$ are obtained in terms of derivatives of $\mathbf{V}$.

Note that a careful distinction is made here between the *variables* S and V, and the *functions* $\mathbf{S}$ and $\mathbf{V}$, and this is needed to avoid confusion. (The *variable* S might also be expressed as $\hat{S}(T, P)$, where P denotes pressure, and $\hat{S}$ is a different function from $\mathbf{S}$). However, in physics books, it is common to make no difference of notation between S, $\mathbf{S}$ and $\hat{S}$. The formula for $\mathbf{S}_T$ is then written as

$$(\partial S/\partial T)_V = -(\partial V/\partial T)_S/(\partial V/\partial S)_T,$$

in which $(\quad)_V$ means a partial derivative in which V is held constant, and analogously for $(\quad)_S$ and $(\quad)_T$. This can be confusing!

Exercise 2.5.1 Assume that $f : \mathbb{R}^2 \to \mathbb{R}$ is differentiable, $f(a, b) = 0$, and that $f(x, g(x)) = 0$ holds identically for small enough $|x-a|$, where g is a differentiable function with $g(a) = b$. Apply the chain rule to obtain $f_x + f_y g'(x) = 0$, and hence obtain $g'(x)$ in terms of derivatives of f. What assumption has been made?

Exercise 2.5.2 Apply the implicit function theorem to the function $f(x, y) = 4x^2 + y^2 - 1$ near the point $(0, -1)$. Calculate $g'(0)$ using the chain rule, as in Exercise 2.5.1, and also from an explicit formula for $g(x)$.

Exercise 2.5.3 Define $f : \mathbb{R}^3 \to \mathbb{R}^2$ by $f(x, y, z) = (x+y+z, x-y-2xz)$. Show that $f(x, y, z) = 0$ can be solved for $(x, y) = \psi(z)$ near $z = 0$, and that $\psi'(0) = [-\frac{1}{2}, -\frac{1}{2}]^T$. (Use the implicit function theorem, *without* solving the linear equations. Superscript T denotes *matrix transpose*.)

Exercise 2.5.4 Consider the system of simultaneous equations:

$$\begin{aligned} 3x+y-z+u^2 &= 0, \\ x-y+2z+u &= 0, \\ 2x+2y-3z+2u &= 0, \end{aligned}$$

noting that they are satisfied when $(x, y, z, u) = (0, 0, 0, 0)$. Discuss whether this system of equations can be solved: (i) for (x, y, z) in terms of u; (ii) for (x, y, u) in terms of z; (iii) for (x, z, u) in terms of y.

Exercise 2.5.5 Let $\mathbf{f} : \mathbb{R}^k \to \mathbb{R}^n$ be continuously differentiable, with $k > n$. Let $\mathbf{f}(\mathbf{0}) = \mathbf{0}$, and assume that the derivative $\mathbf{f}'(\mathbf{0})$ has *full rank* (meaning the largest possible rank, which here is n, since $\mathbf{f}'(\mathbf{0})$ is an $n \times k$ matrix and $n < k$). It follows that a certain n columns of $\mathbf{f}'(\mathbf{0})$ form a nonsingular matrix M. Suppose (by re-ordering the coordinates in $\mathbb{R}^k$) that they are the first n columns; then $\mathbf{f}'(\mathbf{0})$ may be partitioned as $\mathbf{f}'(\mathbf{0}) = [M, B]$ where the submatrix B is $n \times (k-n)$; correspondingly, $\mathbf{z} \in \mathbb{R}^k$ partitions into $\mathbf{x} \in \mathbb{R}^n$ and $\mathbf{y} \in \mathbb{R}^{k-n}$. Then $\mathbf{f}'(\mathbf{0})\mathbf{z} = M\mathbf{x}+B\mathbf{y}$, and $\mathbf{f}(\mathbf{z}) = \mathbf{s}$ may be rewritten as $\mathbf{f}(\mathbf{x}, \mathbf{y}) = \mathbf{s}$. Show now that the implicit function theorem can be applied to solving $\mathbf{f}(\mathbf{x}, \mathbf{y}) = \mathbf{s}$ for $\mathbf{x}$.

Remark This idea may be treated more formally as follows. Suppose that $\mathbf{f}'(\mathbf{0})$ has full rank. Then the null space N of $\mathbf{f}'(\mathbf{0})$ has dimension $k-n$, and there is a subspace S of $\mathbb{R}^k$, with dimension n, such that each $\mathbf{z} \in \mathbb{R}^k$ can be uniquely represented as $\mathbf{z} = \mathbf{x}+\mathbf{y}$ with $\mathbf{x} \in S$ and $\mathbf{y} \in N$. Then $\mathbf{f}(\mathbf{z}) = \mathbf{f}(\mathbf{x}+\mathbf{y}) \equiv \mathbf{F}(\mathbf{x}, \mathbf{y})$, say, where $\mathbf{f}'(\mathbf{0})\mathbf{z} = A\mathbf{x}$, for some nonsingular matrix A. The implicit function theorem, applied to $\mathbf{F}(\mathbf{x}, \mathbf{y}) = \mathbf{0}$, then shows that there is a differentiable function $\mathbf{x} = \mathbf{q}(\mathbf{y})$, for which $\mathbf{F}(\mathbf{q}(\mathbf{y}), \mathbf{y}) = \mathbf{0}$ for all sufficiently small

$\|\mathbf{y}\|$, with $\mathbf{y} \in N$. The chain rule then shows that $A\mathbf{q}'(\mathbf{y})+\mathbf{0} = \mathbf{0}$, whence $\mathbf{q}'(\mathbf{y}) = \mathbf{0}$. Hence $\mathbf{f}(\mathbf{z}) = \mathbf{0}$, and $\|\mathbf{z}\|$ sufficiently small, imply that $\mathbf{z} = \mathbf{q}(\mathbf{y})+\mathbf{y}$ where $\mathbf{y} \in N$ and $\|\mathbf{q}(\mathbf{y})\| < \varepsilon\|\mathbf{y}\|$ when $\|\mathbf{y}\| < \delta(\varepsilon)$. (The function $\mathbf{y} \to \mathbf{z}$ maps a piece of the 'flat' subspace N one-to-one onto a piece of the curved 'surface' defined by $\mathbf{f}(\mathbf{z}) = \mathbf{0}$.)

2.6 FUNCTIONAL DEPENDENCE

Suppose that several functions of $\mathbf{z} \in \mathbb{R}^n$ are related by an identity, for example, when $n = 2$, $u = F_1(x, y) = x+y$ and $v = F_2(x, y) = (x+y)^2$ are related by $v = u^2$. If $F = \begin{bmatrix} F_1 \\ F_2 \end{bmatrix}$, then $F'(z) = \begin{bmatrix} 1 & 1 \\ 2(x+y) & 2(x+y) \end{bmatrix}$ has rank less than 2. This property, where the rank of the derivative is less than the number of functions, nearly characterizes functional dependence between the functions.

Let $F_1, F_2, \ldots, F_p$ be continuously differentiable functions of $\mathbf{z} \in \mathbb{R}^n$, with $p \leq n$; let $\mathbf{F}(\mathbf{z})$ be the column with components $F_1(\mathbf{z}), \ldots, F_p(\mathbf{z})$; then $\mathbf{F} : \mathbb{R}^n \to \mathbb{R}^p$ is continuously differentiable. Assume (by shifting origins) that $\mathbf{F}(\mathbf{0}) = \mathbf{0}$. *Assume that* $\mathbf{F}'(\mathbf{z})$ *has constant rank* $r < p$ *whenever* $\|\mathbf{z}\| < \delta$. Then, by renumbering the components of $\mathbf{F}$ and $\mathbf{z}$, $\mathbf{F} = \begin{bmatrix} \mathbf{f} \\ \mathbf{g} \end{bmatrix}$ and $\mathbf{z} = \begin{bmatrix} \mathbf{x} \\ \mathbf{y} \end{bmatrix}$, where $\mathbf{f}$ and $\mathbf{x}$ each have r components, and $\mathbf{F}'(\mathbf{z}) = \begin{bmatrix} \mathbf{f}_x(\mathbf{x}, \mathbf{y}) & \mathbf{f}_y(\mathbf{x}, \mathbf{y}) \\ \mathbf{g}_x(\mathbf{x}, \mathbf{y}) & \mathbf{g}_y(\mathbf{x}, \mathbf{y}) \end{bmatrix}$, with the $r \times r$ matrix $\mathbf{f}_x(\mathbf{x}, \mathbf{y})$ nonsingular. By the implicit function theorem, the equation $\mathbf{f}(\mathbf{x}, \mathbf{y}) = \mathbf{w}$ has a unique differentiable solution $\mathbf{x} = \mathbf{h}(\mathbf{w}, \mathbf{y})$, for $\|\mathbf{w}\|$ small enough. Then $\mathbf{g}(\mathbf{x}, \mathbf{y}) = \mathbf{g}(\mathbf{h}(\mathbf{w}, \mathbf{y}), \mathbf{y})$; *if* the latter function has the form $\varphi(\mathbf{w})$, independent of $\mathbf{y}$, then $\mathbf{g}(\mathbf{x}, \mathbf{y}) = \varphi[\mathbf{f}(\mathbf{x}, \mathbf{y})]$; *thus* $p-r$ *of the functions* F_j *are functionally dependent on the remaining* r *functions, when* $\left\|\begin{bmatrix} \mathbf{x} \\ \mathbf{y} \end{bmatrix}\right\| < \delta$.

To show that $\mathbf{g}(\mathbf{h}(\mathbf{w}, \mathbf{y}), \mathbf{y})$ is independent of $\mathbf{y}$, the chain rule, applied to $\mathbf{f}(\mathbf{h}(\mathbf{w}, \mathbf{y}), \mathbf{y}) = \mathbf{w}$ shows that (differentiating with respect to $\mathbf{y}$), $\mathbf{f}_x\mathbf{h}_y+\mathbf{f}_y = \mathbf{0}$, noting that $\mathbf{w}$ is a variable independent of $\mathbf{y}$. But the rank hypothesis requires that, for some matrix $\mathbf{q}$, $\mathbf{g}_x = \mathbf{q}\mathbf{f}_x$ and $\mathbf{g}_y = \mathbf{q}\mathbf{f}_y$. Hence $\mathbf{g}_x\mathbf{h}_y+\mathbf{g}_y = \mathbf{0}$. But, from the chain rule again, $\frac{\partial}{\partial \mathbf{y}}\mathbf{g}(\mathbf{h}(\mathbf{w}, \mathbf{y}), \mathbf{y}) = \mathbf{g}_x\mathbf{h}_y+\mathbf{g}_y = \mathbf{0}$, whenever $\|(\mathbf{x}, \mathbf{y})\| < \delta$. It follows, by Exercise 2.3.4, that $\mathbf{g}(\mathbf{h}(\mathbf{w}, \mathbf{y}), \mathbf{y})$ does not depend on $\mathbf{y}$.

Exercise 2.6.1 The three functions $u = x^3+y^3+z^3-3xyz$, $v = x+y+z$, and $w = x^2+y^2+z^2-xy-yz-zx$ are related by the identity $u = vw$. Without assuming this identity, set $F = \begin{bmatrix} u \\ v \\ w \end{bmatrix}$, and show that the derivative of F has rank less than 3. Deduce that u, v, w are functionally dependent, and use the above theory to calculate the function relating u, v, w.

2.7 HIGHER DERIVATIVES

Let $U = \{\mathbf{x} \in \mathbb{R}^n : \|\mathbf{x}\| < \gamma\}$. If $f \in C^1(U, \mathbb{R})$ and $\mathbf{a} \in U$, then, for each $\mathbf{u} \in \mathbb{R}^n$ with $a+u \in U$, $f(\mathbf{a}+\mathbf{u})-f(\mathbf{a})$ has linear part

$$f'(\mathbf{a})\mathbf{u} = \sum_{i=1}^{n} \mathrm{D}_i f(\mathbf{a}) u_i. \tag{2.7.1}$$

Here $\mathrm{D}_i f(\mathbf{a})$ denotes $\dfrac{\partial f}{\partial x_i}(a)$. If $f \in C^2(U, \mathbb{R})$ then, for each $\mathbf{v} \in \mathbb{R}^n$ with $\mathbf{a}+\mathbf{v} \in U$, the linear part of

$$[f'(\mathbf{a}+\mathbf{v})-f'(\mathbf{a})]\mathbf{u} = \sum_{i=1}^{n} [\mathrm{D}_i f(\mathbf{a}+\mathbf{v})-\mathrm{D}_i f(\mathbf{a})]u_i$$

is

$$f''(\mathbf{a})(\mathbf{u}, \mathbf{v}) = \sum_{i,j=1}^{n} \mathrm{D}_{ij} f(\mathbf{a}) u_i v_j, \tag{2.7.2}$$

where $\mathrm{D}_{ij} f(\mathbf{a})$ denotes $\dfrac{\partial}{\partial x_j}\dfrac{\partial f}{\partial x_i}(a)$.

This process may be continued. If $f \in C^k(U, \mathbb{R})$, denote

$$\mathrm{D}_{i_1 i_2 \ldots i_k} f(\mathbf{a}) = \frac{\partial}{\partial x_{i_k}} \frac{\partial}{\partial x_{i_{k-1}}} \cdots \frac{\partial}{\partial x_{i_1}} f(a). \tag{2.7.3}$$

Define then, for $\mathbf{w}_1, \mathbf{w}_2, \ldots, \mathbf{w}_k \in \mathbb{R}^n$,

$$f^{(k)}(\mathbf{a})(\mathbf{w}_1, \mathbf{w}_2, \ldots, \mathbf{w}_k) = \sum_{i_1, i_2, \ldots, i_k = 1}^{n} \mathrm{D}_{i_1 i_2 \ldots i_k} f(\mathbf{a}) \mathbf{w}_{1, i_1} \mathbf{w}_{2, i_2} \ldots \mathbf{w}_{k, i_k} \tag{2.7.4}$$

where $\mathbf{w}_{1, i_1}$ denotes the i_1 component of $\mathbf{w}_1$. If all $\mathbf{w}_i = \mathbf{w}$, abbreviate $f^{(k)}(\mathbf{a})(\mathbf{w}, \mathbf{w}, \ldots, \mathbf{w})$ to $f^{(k)}(\mathbf{a})(\mathbf{w})^n$.

The derivative $f'(\mathbf{a})$ is represented by a $1 \times n$ matrix, whose components are $\mathrm{D}_i f(\mathbf{a})$. Also $f''(\mathbf{a})$ is represented by an $n \times n$ matrix, M say, whose i, j element is $\mathrm{D}_{i,\ j} f(\mathbf{a})$; if $\mathbf{u}$ and $\mathbf{v}$ are regarded as columns, then

$$f''(\mathbf{a})(\mathbf{u}, \mathbf{v}) = \mathbf{v}^{\mathrm{T}} M \mathbf{u}. \tag{2.7.5}$$

It is shown below that M is a symmetric matrix. (Thus M equals its transpose.)

Example

Define $f : \mathbb{R}^2 \to \mathbb{R}$ by the polynomial

$$f(x, y) = 3 + 7x + 4y + x^2 + 3xy + 2y^2 + 6x^2 y.$$

Then

$$f'(\mathbf{0} + \mathbf{v}) - f'(\mathbf{0}) = [2v_1 + 3v_2 + 12v_1 v_2,\ 3v_1 + 4v_2 + 6v_1^2].$$

Taking the linear part of this expression, and applying it to $u = \begin{bmatrix} u_1 \\ \hline u_2 \end{bmatrix}$,

$$f''(\mathbf{0})(\mathbf{u}, \mathbf{v}) = [2v_1 + 3v_2,\ 3v_1 + 4v_2] \begin{bmatrix} u_1 \\ u_2 \end{bmatrix} = [v_1 \quad v_2] \begin{bmatrix} 2 & 3 \\ 3 & 4 \end{bmatrix} \begin{bmatrix} u_1 \\ u_2 \end{bmatrix},$$

where the 2×2 matrix consists of second partial derivatives.

In more abstract terms, let $\mathbf{L}(\mathbb{R}^n, \mathbb{R})$ denote the vector space of (continuous) linear maps from $\mathbb{R}^n$ into $\mathbb{R}$. Then, in terms of (continuous) linear maps, $f'(\mathbf{a}) \in \mathbf{L}(\mathbb{R}^n, \mathbb{R})$, $f''(\mathbf{a}) \in \mathbf{L}(\mathbf{L}(\mathbb{R}^n, \mathbb{R}), \mathbb{R})$, and so on. Also, $f''(\mathbf{a})$ is a *bilinear* map from $\mathbb{R}^n \times \mathbb{R}^n$ into $\mathbb{R}$; this means that $f''(\mathbf{a})(\mathbf{u}, \mathbf{v})$ is linear in $\mathbf{u}$ for each fixed $\mathbf{v}$, and also linear in $\mathbf{v}$ for each fixed $\mathbf{u}$.

Theorem 2.7 (Taylor's theorem)
Let $f \in C^k(U, \mathbb{R})$; let $\mathbf{a} \in U$ and let $\mathbf{a}+\mathbf{x} \in U$. Then

$$f(\mathbf{a}+\mathbf{x}) = f(\mathbf{a})+\frac{1}{1!}f'(\mathbf{a})\mathbf{x}+\frac{1}{2!}f''(\mathbf{a})(\mathbf{x})^2+\ \dots$$

$$+\frac{1}{(k-1)!}f^{(k-1)}(\mathbf{a})(\mathbf{x})^{k-1}+\frac{1}{k!}f^{(k)}(\mathbf{c})(\mathbf{x})^k, \qquad (2.7.6)$$

where $\mathbf{c} = \mathbf{a}+\beta\mathbf{x}$ for some β in $0 < \beta < 1$.

Proof Define $F : [0, 1] \to \mathbb{R}$ by $F(\alpha) = f(a+\alpha x)$. Then the usual Taylor's theorem, for a real function of one real variable, shows that

$$F(1) = F(0)+\frac{1}{1!}F'(0)+\frac{1}{2!}F''(0)+\ \dots\ +\frac{1}{(k-1)!}F^{(k-1)}(0)$$

$$+\frac{1}{k!}F^{(k)}(a+\beta x) \qquad (2.7.7)$$

for some β in $0 < \beta < 1$. Now $F^{(r)}(\alpha) = f^{(r)}(a+\alpha x)(x)^r$ holds trivially for $r = 0$; if it holds for some r then, by the chain rule,

$$F^{(r+1)}(\alpha) = [f^{(r+1)}(a+\alpha x)x](x)^r = f^{(r+1)}(a+\alpha x)(x)^{r+1};$$

so the expression holds, by induction, for $r = 0, 1, 2, \dots$. Substitution for F and its derivatives then proves Taylor's theorem. □

Example
For the previous polynomial example,

$$f\left(\begin{bmatrix}0\\0\end{bmatrix}\right)+f'\left(\begin{bmatrix}0\\0\end{bmatrix}\right)\begin{bmatrix}x\\y\end{bmatrix}+\tfrac{1}{2}f''\left(\begin{bmatrix}0\\0\end{bmatrix}\right)\left(\begin{bmatrix}x\\y\end{bmatrix}\right)^2$$

$$= 3+[7, 4]\begin{bmatrix}x\\y\end{bmatrix}+\tfrac{1}{2}[x, y]\begin{bmatrix}2 & 3\\3 & 4\end{bmatrix}\begin{bmatrix}x\\y\end{bmatrix},$$

which agrees with the given polynomial function up to quadratic terms.

Remark Consider Taylor's theorem with $k = 3$. Since $f \in C^3(U, \mathbb{R})$, each component of $f^{(3)}(\cdot)$ is a continuous function, and hence is bounded on the segment $\{\mathbf{a}+\alpha\mathbf{x} : 0 \leq \alpha \leq 1\}$. Hence the *remainder term* in the Taylor expansion satisfies a bound $|f^{(3)}(\mathbf{a})(\mathbf{x})^3/3!| \leq b\|\mathbf{x}\|^3$, where b is some constant.

The next theorem shows that $f''(\mathbf{a})$ is represented by a *symmetric* matrix, assuming that f has continuous second partial derivatives.

Theorem 2.8
Let $f \in C^2(U, \mathbb{R})$, where $U = \{\mathbf{x} \in \mathbb{R}^n : \|\mathbf{x}\| < \gamma\}$; let $\mathbf{a} \in U$. Then $f''(\mathbf{a})$ is represented by a symmetric matrix M.

Proof In order to show that M is a symmetric matrix, it is enough to consider a function f of two real variables x and y, and then to show that $f_{xy} = f_{yx}$; here $f_{xy} = \dfrac{\partial}{\partial y}\left(\dfrac{\partial f}{\partial x}\right)$ and $f_{yx} = \dfrac{\partial}{\partial x}\left(\dfrac{\partial f}{\partial y}\right)$. Hence let $f \in C^2(U_0, \mathbb{R})$ where $U_0 = \left\{\begin{bmatrix} x \\ y \end{bmatrix} \in \mathbb{R}^2 : \left\|\begin{bmatrix} x \\ y \end{bmatrix}\right\| < \gamma\right\}$, and take $\mathbf{a} = \mathbf{0}$. Define

$$\psi(x, y) = \frac{f(x, y) - f(0, y) - f(x, 0) + f(0, 0)}{xy} \tag{2.7.8}$$

and, for fixed y, let $\varphi(x) = f(x, y) - f(x, 0)$. Then the mean-value theorem shows that, for fixed y,

$$\psi(x, y) = \frac{\varphi(x) - \varphi(0)}{xy} = \frac{\varphi'(\alpha x)x}{xy} = \frac{f_x(\alpha x, y) - f_x(x, 0)}{y}$$

for some α in $0 < \alpha < 1$. A second application of the mean-value theorem shows that $\psi(x, y) = f_{xy}(\alpha x, \beta y)$ for some β in $0 < \beta < 1$. Since $f_{xy}(\cdot, \cdot)$ is assumed continuous,

$$|\psi(x, y) - f_{xy}(0, 0)| < \varepsilon \text{ whenever } |x| < \delta(\varepsilon) \text{ and } |y| < \delta(\varepsilon). \tag{2.7.9}$$

Let $y \to 0$; from Equation (2.7.8),

$$\begin{aligned} \lim_{y \to 0} \psi(x, y) &= \lim_{y \to 0} \frac{1}{x}\left[\frac{f(x, y) - f(x, 0)}{y} - \frac{f(0, y) - f(0, 0)}{y}\right] \\ &= x^{-1}[f_y(x, 0) - f_y(0, 0)]. \end{aligned} \tag{2.7.10}$$

From Equations (2.7.9) and (2.7.10),

$$\left|\frac{f_y(x,0)-f_y(0,0)}{x}-f_{xy}(0,0)\right| < \varepsilon \text{ whenever } |x| < \delta(\varepsilon).$$

Therefore $f_{yx}(0,0) = f_{xy}(0,0)$. □

Note that this proof only assumes the existence of f_x and f_y, together with the existence of f_{xy}, and the continuity of f_{xy} at (0, 0). This continuity means, precisely, that, for some function $\delta(\cdot)$ and positive ε, $|f_{xy}(x,y)-f_{xy}(0,0)| < \varepsilon$ whenever $|x| < \delta(\varepsilon)$ and $|y| < \delta(\varepsilon)$. The proof of the theorem then shows that f_{yx} also exists, and equals f_{xy} at (0, 0). Note also that, in order that $f_{xy}(\cdot,\cdot)$ is continuous at (0, 0), it is *not* enough to assume that $f_{xy}(x, y)$ is continuous in x for each fixed y, and continuous in y for each fixed x (see Exercise 2.7.4).

Exercise 2.7.1 Show, using Taylor's theorem for a function of two variables, that

$$e^{x+y} = 1+[1,1]\begin{bmatrix}x\\y\end{bmatrix}+\tfrac{1}{2}[x,y]\begin{bmatrix}1&1\\1&1\end{bmatrix}\begin{bmatrix}x\\y\end{bmatrix}+\text{higher order terms.}$$

Compare with $1+(x+y)+(x+y)^2/2!+\dots$.

Exercise 2.7.2 For the function $f(x,y) = xy(x^2-y^2)/(x^2+y^2)$ for $(x,y) = (0,0)$, $f(0,0) = 0$, show that f_{xy} and f_{yx} both exist at (0, 0), but are unequal. Why?

Exercise 2.7.3 Let $f \in C^3(U, \mathbb{R})$, where $U = \{\mathbf{x} \in \mathbb{R}^n : \|\mathbf{x}\| < \gamma\}$; assume that $\mathbf{a} \in U$, $f'(\mathbf{a}) = \mathbf{0}$, but $f''(\mathbf{a}) \neq 0$. Show from Taylor's theorem that

$$f(\mathbf{x})-f(\mathbf{a}) = \tfrac{1}{2}\mathbf{x}^{\mathrm{T}}M\mathbf{x}+\theta(\mathbf{x})$$

for $\mathbf{x} \in U$, where $M = f''(\mathbf{a})$, and $|\theta(\mathbf{x})| < \varepsilon\|\mathbf{x}-\mathbf{a}\|^2$ whenever $\|\mathbf{x}-\mathbf{a}\|$ is sufficiently small (depending on ε). Now assume also that the matrix M is *positive definite*; this means that $\mathbf{v}^{\mathrm{T}}M\mathbf{v} > 0$ for every nonzero vector $\mathbf{v}$. Show that in this case there is a positive constant c such that $\mathbf{v}^{\mathrm{T}}M\mathbf{v} \geq c\|\mathbf{v}\|^2$, first if $\|\mathbf{v}\| = 1$, and hence for every nonzero vector $\mathbf{v}$. Hence deduce that $f(\mathbf{x}) > f(\mathbf{a})$ whenever $\mathbf{x} \neq \mathbf{a}$ and $\|\mathbf{x}-\mathbf{a}\|$ is sufficiently small (so $f(\cdot)$ is *minimized* at $\mathbf{a}$).

Exercise 2.7.4 Define $f : \mathbb{R}^2 \to \mathbb{R}$ by $f(x, y) = \dfrac{xy}{x^2+y^2}$ for $(x, y) \neq (0, 0)$, $f(0, 0) = 0$, show that f is continuous in x for each fixed y, and f is continuous in y for each fixed x, but that f is *not* continuous at $(0, 0)$. This example shows that continuity in (x, y) is *not* implied by the two special cases of $y = 0$, x varying and $x = 0$, y varying.

Exercise 2.7.5 Prove the bilinear property of $f''(\mathbf{a})$ from Equation (2.7.5). Consider an extension to a vector-valued function $\mathbf{f} \in C^2(U, \mathbb{R}^2)$.

3. Maxima and minima

3.1 EXTREMA AND STATIONARY POINTS

Let U be an *open* set in $\mathbb{R}^n$; this means that to every point $\mathbf{u} \in U$ there corresponds a ball $N(\mathbf{u}) = \{\mathbf{y} \in \mathbb{R}^n : \|\mathbf{y}-\mathbf{u}\| < \gamma(\mathbf{u})\}$, for some $\gamma(\mathbf{u}) > 0$, such that $N(\mathbf{u}) \subset U$. This concept is illustrated in Fig. 3.1. Let $f : U \to \mathbb{R}$ be a (Fréchet) differentiable function. (Note that the

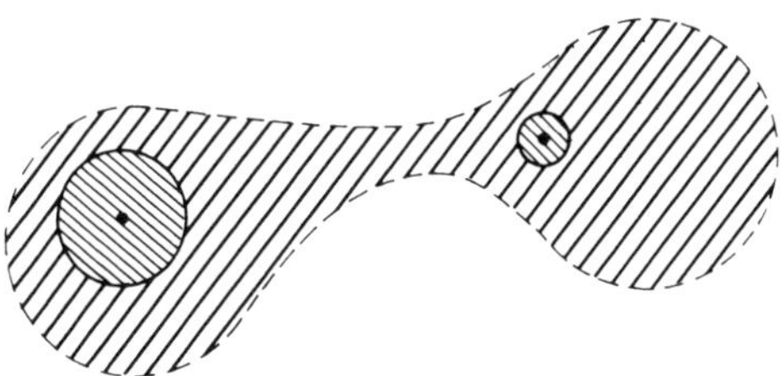

Figure 3.1 Open set, showing two balls $N(\mathbf{u})$

definition of $f'(\mathbf{u})$ at $\mathbf{u} \in U$ requires that the domain of f contains some ball $N(\mathbf{u})$. An open set U, from the definition, does not contain the points of its boundary.)

Definitions

The function f attains a *local maximum* at $\mathbf{u}_0 \in U$ if, for some $\delta > 0$,

$$\mathbf{u} \in U \text{ and } \|\mathbf{u}-\mathbf{u}_0\| < \delta \Rightarrow f(\mathbf{u}) \leq f(\mathbf{u}_0). \qquad (3.1.1)$$

The function f attains a *global maximum* at $\mathbf{u}_0 \in U$ if

$$u \in U \Rightarrow f(\mathbf{u}) \leq f(\mathbf{u}_0). \tag{3.1.2}$$

The function f attains a *local minimum* at $\mathbf{u}_0 \in U$ if, for some $\delta > 0$,

$$\mathbf{u} \in U \text{ and } \|\mathbf{u}-\mathbf{u}_0\| < \delta \Rightarrow f(\mathbf{u}) \geq f(\mathbf{u}_0). \tag{3.1.3}$$

The point $\mathbf{u}_0 \in U$ is a *stationary point* of f if $\mathbf{u} \in U \Rightarrow f(\mathbf{u}) - f(\mathbf{u}_0) = \psi(\mathbf{u})$ where $\psi(\mathbf{u}) = o(\|\mathbf{u}-\mathbf{u}_0\|)$, meaning that, for some function $\Delta(\cdot)$ of positive ε,

$$|\psi(\mathbf{u})| < \varepsilon\|\mathbf{u}-\mathbf{u}_0\| \text{ whenever } \|\mathbf{u}-\mathbf{u}_0\| < \Delta(\varepsilon). \tag{3.1.4}$$

A stationary point $\mathbf{u}_0$ is a *saddlepoint* if $f(\mathbf{u}) > f(\mathbf{u}_0)$ for some points $\mathbf{u} \in U$, arbitrarily close to $\mathbf{u}_0$, and also $f(\mathbf{u}) < f(\mathbf{u}_0)$ for some other points $\mathbf{u} \in U$, arbitrarily close to $\mathbf{u}_0$.

These definitions apply whether or not U is open; for the present, we shall consider only an open domain for f. *Maximum* will mean *local maximum*, and *minimum* will mean *local minimum*; an *extremum* means a local maximum or minimum. (Some other authors use *maximum* to mean *global maximum*; here, we shall say *global* when we mean it.) A global maximum is necessarily a local maximum, but the converse does not hold. The graph in Fig. 3.2 illustrates the difference, in case U is a real open interval (a, b).

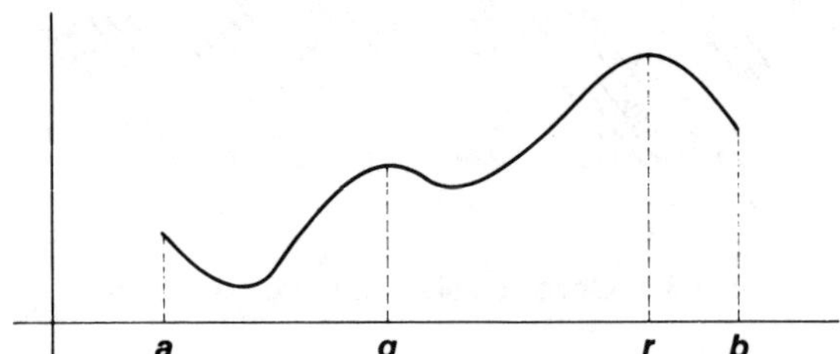

Figure 3.2 Local and global maxima

In this example, q and r are local maxima; r is the global maximum. Note that if f is defined instead on the *closed* interval $[a, b]$, then the *boundary point* a is also a local maximum.

Theorem 3.1

Let the differentiable function $f: U \to \mathbb{R}$ (where U is open) attain a maximum at $\mathbf{u}_0 \in U$. Then $f'(\mathbf{u}_0) = 0$.

Proof Since U is open, there is a ball $N(\mathbf{u}_0) \subset U$. If $f'(\mathbf{u}_0) \neq 0$, then $f'(\mathbf{u}_0)\mathbf{q} \neq 0$ for some direction $\mathbf{q}$. If $f'(\mathbf{u}_0)\mathbf{q} > 0$, set $\mathbf{v} = \mathbf{q}/\|\mathbf{q}\|$; if $f'(\mathbf{u}_0)\mathbf{q} < 0$, set $\mathbf{v} = -\mathbf{q}/\|\mathbf{q}\|$. Then $\|\mathbf{v}\| = 1$ and $f'(\mathbf{u}_0)\mathbf{v} > 0$. For sufficiently small $\alpha > 0$, thus for $0 < \alpha < \gamma(\mathbf{u}_0)$, $\mathbf{u}_0 + \alpha\mathbf{v} \in N(\mathbf{u}_0) \subset U$. Therefore

$$f(\mathbf{u}_0 + \alpha\mathbf{v}) - f(\mathbf{u}_0) = f'(\mathbf{u}_0)(\alpha\mathbf{v}) + \theta(\alpha\mathbf{v})$$

where $|\theta(\alpha\mathbf{v})| < \varepsilon\|\alpha\mathbf{v}\| = \varepsilon\alpha$ whenever $\|\alpha\mathbf{v}\| = \alpha < \Delta(\varepsilon)$. Hence

$$f(\mathbf{u}_0 + \alpha\mathbf{v}) - f(\mathbf{u}_0) = \alpha[f'(\mathbf{u}_0)\mathbf{v} + \theta(\alpha\mathbf{v})/\alpha] > 0$$

for sufficiently small $\alpha > 0$, taking $\varepsilon = f'(\mathbf{u}_0)\mathbf{v}$. But this contradicts the maximum of f at $\mathbf{u}_0$. Consequently, $f'(\mathbf{u}_0) = \mathbf{0}$. □

Observe that, from the definition of $f'(\mathbf{u}_0)$, $\mathbf{u}_0$ is a stationary point of $f : U \to \mathbb{R}$ if and only if $f'(\mathbf{u}_0) = 0$. Thus (when U is open) each local maximum of f is a stationary point. Since a local minimum of f is a local maximum of $-f$, it is also a stationary point of f.

Example

$f(x, y) = x^2 + y^4$ has a minimum at (0, 0). $f(x, y) = -x^2 - y^2$ has a maximum at (0, 0). $f(x, y) = x^2 - y^2$ has a saddlepoint at (0, 0). But note that $g : [0, 1] \to \mathbb{R}$, given by $g(x) = 2x + x^2$, has a minimum at the boundary point 0, with $g'(0) \neq 0$; here, however, the domain of f is not open.

Assume now that $f \in C^3(U, \mathbb{R})$, with U open. Let $\mathbf{u}_0 \in U$ be a stationary point of f. From Taylor's theorem (Theorem 2.7: compare Exercise 2.7.3), noting that $f'(\mathbf{u}_0) = 0$,

$$f(\mathbf{u}_0 + \mathbf{x}) - f(\mathbf{u}_0) = \tfrac{1}{2}\mathbf{x}^{\mathrm{T}}M\mathbf{x} + \theta(\mathbf{x})$$

where M is a symmetric matrix representing $f''(\mathbf{u}_0)$, $\|\mathbf{x}\|$ is taken small enough that $\mathbf{u}_0 + \mathbf{x} \in U$, and $|\theta(\mathbf{x})| < \varepsilon\|\mathbf{x}\|^2$ whenever $\|\mathbf{x}\| < \delta(\varepsilon)$. A theorem in linear algebra states that M has n real eigenvalues $\lambda_1 \geq \lambda_2 \geq \ldots \geq \lambda_n$. (Thus $M\mathbf{v}_i = \lambda_i\mathbf{v}_i$ for some non-zero vector $\mathbf{v}_i$; note that the λ_i need not be all different). Moreover, for all $\mathbf{x} \neq \mathbf{0}$,

$$\lambda_1 \geq (\mathbf{x}^{\mathrm{T}}M\mathbf{x})/(\mathbf{x}^{\mathrm{T}}\mathbf{x}) \geq \lambda_n, \tag{3.1.5}$$

where λ_1 and λ_n are the largest and smallest eigenvalues of M. Assuming this theorem, M is *positive definite*, meaning that

$\mathbf{x}^T M\mathbf{x} > 0$ whenever $\mathbf{x} \neq \mathbf{0}$, if and only if $\lambda_n > 0$, and in this case,

$$\tfrac{1}{2}\mathbf{x}^T M\mathbf{x} + \theta(\mathbf{x}) \geq \tfrac{1}{2}\lambda_n\|\mathbf{x}\|^2 - \varepsilon\|\mathbf{x}\|^2 > 0 \text{ whenever } 0 < \|\mathbf{x}\| < \delta(\varepsilon),$$

choosing ε positive and less than $\frac{1}{2}\lambda_n$. It follows then that f attains a *minimum* at $\mathbf{u}_0$. A similar argument shows that if M is *negative definite*, meaning that $\mathbf{x}^T M\mathbf{x} < 0$ whenever $\mathbf{x} \neq \mathbf{0}$, then f attains a *maximum* at $\mathbf{u}_0$. If M has both positive and negative eigenvalues, then $\mathbf{u}_0$ is a *saddlepoint*.

Concerning calculation of eigenvalues of M, see Exercise 3.1.7 below. However, a shorter method is available for functions of two variables. For $n = 2$, let $M = \begin{bmatrix} A & H \\ H & B \end{bmatrix}$; let $D = AB - H^2$. By writing, when $A \neq 0$, $Ax^2 + 2Hxy + By^2$ as $A(x + Hy/A)^2 + (D/A)y^2$, it follows that:

if $A > 0$ and $D > 0$ then the stationary point is a minimum;
if $A < 0$ and $D > 0$ then the stationary point is a maximum;
if $D < 0$ then the stationary point is a saddlepoint.

Note that the minimum occurring here is *strict*, meaning that $f(\mathbf{u}) > f(\mathbf{u}_0)$ strictly when $\|\mathbf{u} - \mathbf{u}_0\|$ is small enough; a similar remark applies to the maximum.

Example
$f : \mathbb{R}^2 \to \mathbb{R}$, given by $f(x, y) = x^2 - y^2$. At $(0, 0)$, $f_x = 0 = f_y$, and $M = \begin{bmatrix} 2 & 0 \\ 0 & -2 \end{bmatrix}$. Here $D = -4 < 0$, so $(0, 0)$ is a saddlepoint.

Example
Consider $g : \mathbb{R}^2 \to \mathbb{R}$ and $h : \mathbb{R}^2 \to \mathbb{R}$, given by $g(x, y) = x^2 + y^4$ and $h(x, y) = x^2 - y^4$. For both functions, $(0, 0)$ is stationary. Since $x^2 + y^4 \geq 0$ always, $(0, 0)$ is a minimum for g. Since $x^2 - y^4 > 0$ when $y = 0$, $x \neq 0$, but < 0 when $x = 0$, $y \neq 0$, $(0,0)$ is a saddlepoint for h. However, for both functions, $M = \begin{bmatrix} 2 & 0 \\ 0 & 0 \end{bmatrix}$, so that $D = 0$, and M has eigenvalues 2 and 0. In such a case, the quadratic terms alone do not determine the nature of the stationary point, and higher-order terms (as here $\pm y^4$) must be studied.

Let M have components M_{ij} where $i, j = 1, 2, \ldots, n$. Let Δ_j be the determinant of the matrix

$$\begin{bmatrix} M_{11} & \cdots & M_{1j} \\ M_{12} & \cdots & M_{2j} \\ \cdot & \cdots & \cdot \\ M_{j1} & \cdots & M_{jj} \end{bmatrix}.$$

If all the Δ_j are $> 0, j = 1, 2, \ldots, n$, then a criterion due to Routh and Hurwicz shows that M is positive definite. If the Δ_j are alternatively < 0 and > 0, then M is negative definite. This criterion may be used to discriminate maxima and minima.

Suppose that $E \subset \mathbb{R}^n$ is a closed bounded set, and $f : E \to \mathbb{R}$ is a continuous function. Then a theorem of analysis shows that the greatest lower bound, $\inf_{\mathbf{x} \in E} f(\mathbf{x})$ is finite, and that it equals $f(\bar{\mathbf{x}})$ for some $\bar{\mathbf{x}} \in E$. Thus the global minimum of f on E is attained at $\bar{\mathbf{x}}$. A similar remark applies to the least upper bound, $\sup_{\mathbf{x} \in E} f(\mathbf{x})$; thus the global maximum of f on E is also attained.

A set $E \subset \mathbb{R}^n$ is *convex* if, whenever $\mathbf{u} \in E$ and $\mathbf{v} \in E$ and $0 < \lambda < 1$, it follows that $\lambda\mathbf{u}+(1-\lambda)\mathbf{v} \in E$. (Thus E contains the line segments joining each pair of its points.) A function $f : E \to \mathbb{R}$ is *convex* if, whenever $\mathbf{u}, \mathbf{v} \in E$ and $0 < \lambda < 1$,

$$f(\lambda\mathbf{u}+(1-\lambda)\mathbf{v}) \leq \lambda f(\mathbf{u})+(1-\lambda) f(\mathbf{v}). \tag{3.1.6}$$

(Geometrically, this means that each chord lies above the graph – see Fig. 3.3.)

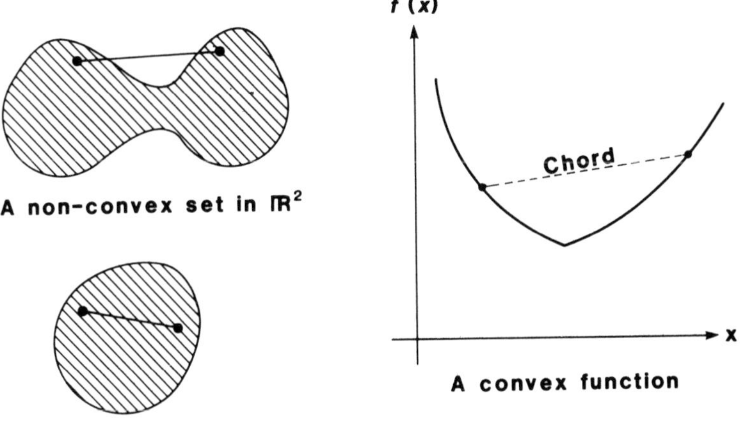

Figure 3.3 Convex sets and functions

A convex function need not be differentiable at all points.

Theorem 3.2
Let $E \subset \mathbb{R}^n$ be convex; let the function $f : E \to \mathbb{R}$ attain a local minimum at $\mathbf{p} \in E$. Then $\mathbf{p}$ is also a global minimum of f on E.

Proof Suppose not; then $f(\mathbf{x}) < f(\mathbf{p})$ for some $\mathbf{x} \in E$. For all $0 < \lambda < 1$, $\mathbf{p}+\lambda(\mathbf{x}-\mathbf{p}) = \lambda\mathbf{x}+(1-\lambda)\mathbf{p} \in E$ since E is convex. Since f is a convex function,

$$f(\mathbf{p}+\lambda(\mathbf{x}-\mathbf{p}))-f(\mathbf{p}) \leq \lambda f(\mathbf{x})+(1-\lambda)f(\mathbf{p})-f(\mathbf{p}) = \lambda[f(\mathbf{x})-f(\mathbf{p})] < 0$$

for λ arbitrarily small, contradicting the local minimum. □

Theorem 3.3
Let $f : \mathbb{R}^n \to \mathbb{R}$ be a differentiable function. Then f is convex if and only if, for each $a, b \in \mathbb{R}^n$,

$$f(b)-f(a) \geq f'(a)(b-a) \tag{3.1.7}$$

Proof Let f be convex; then Equation (3.1.6) holds. Rearranging this formula gives, when $0 < \alpha < 1$,

$$f(b)-f(a) \leq \alpha^{-1}[f(a+\alpha(b-a))-f(a)];$$

and Equation (3.1.7) follows, as $\alpha \downarrow 0$. Conversely, let Equation (3.1.7) hold; denote $\zeta = \alpha b+(1-\alpha)a$, for $0 < \alpha < 1$; then Equation (3.1.6) follows since

$$\begin{aligned}\alpha f(b)+(1-\alpha)f(a)-f(\zeta) &= \alpha[f(b)-f(\zeta)]+(1-\alpha)[f(a)-f(\zeta)]\\ &\geq \alpha f'(\zeta)(1-\alpha)(b-a)+(1-\alpha)f'(\zeta)\alpha(b-a) = 0.\end{aligned}$$ □

Geometrically, Equation (3.1.7) means that a tangent line to the graph of a convex function lies below the graph of the function (see Fig. 3.4).

A search for stationary points leads to local maxima and minima (and saddlepoints). There is usually no guarantee that these are also *global*, except under some kind of convex assumptions.

Exercise 3.1.1 Let $U \subset \mathbb{R}^n$ be open, and $f : U \to \mathbb{R}$ differentiable. Suppose that the maximum of f on a subset $E \subset U$ occurs at a boundary point $\mathbf{a}$ of E. Does it follow that $f'(\mathbf{a}) = 0$? If not, why not?

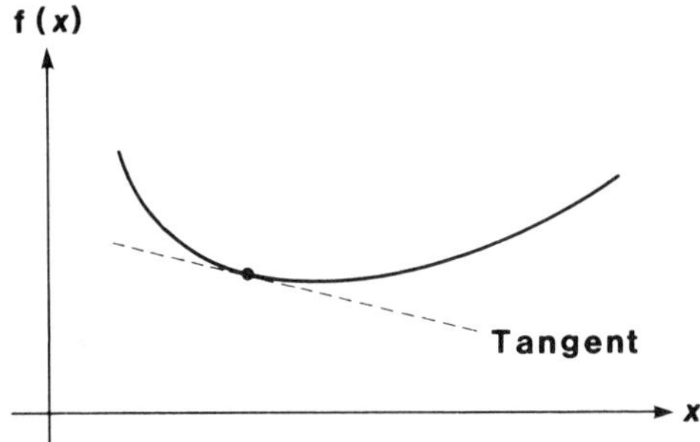

Figure 3.4 The tangent to a convex function

Exercise 3.1.2 For the stationary point (0, 0) of $f(x, y) = x^2 - y^2$, find the directions in which f increases, as (x, y) moves away from (0, 0), and also the directions in which f decreases. (It is convenient here to substitute $x = r \cos \theta$ and $y = r \sin \theta$.)

Exercise 3.1.3 Find the stationary points of the following functions of two variables, and discuss the nature of each stationary point, using any applicable methods. (i) $f(x, y) = x^2 + 4xy + 2y^2 - 2y$; (ii) $f(x, y) = x^4 - 4xy$; (iii) $f(x, y) = x^3 + y^2$; (iv) $f(x, y) = x^3 - 3xy^2$; (v) $f(x, y) = ye^{-x^2}$; (vi) $f(x, y) = (ax^2 + by^2)e^{-x^2-y^2}(0 < a < b)$; (vii) $f(x, y) = x^2y^2 + 8xy + x^2 + y^2$.

Exercise 3.1.4 By considering the functions from $\mathbb{R}^2$ into $\mathbb{R}$ given by $f(x, y) = x^2 + y^4$ and $g(x, y) = x^2 - y^4$, show that a minimum may, but need not, occur when all eigenvalues of M are only assumed to be ≥ 0.

Exercise 3.1.5 Define $f : \mathbb{R}^2 \to \mathbb{R}$ by $f(0, 0) = 0$ and

$$f(x, y) = y^2 - \frac{8x^4y^4}{(x^4 + y^2)^2} \text{ for } (x, y) \neq (0, 0).$$

Use $2x^4y^2 \leq (x^4 + y^2)^2$ to show that f is continuous at (0, 0). Is f differentiable there? Show that $f(x, x^2) = -x^4$, so that (0, 0) is *not* a minimum of f. Show, however, that for each fixed angle $\theta \neq 0, \pi$, substituting $x = r \cos \theta$ and $y = r \sin \theta$,

$$f(x, y) \cdot (x^4 + y^2)^2 = (r \sin \theta)^6 + \text{higher powers of } r.$$

Deduce that $f(r\cos\theta, r\sin\theta)$ is minimized at $r = 0$ along each radial line θ = constant.

Exercise 3.1.6 Define $f: \mathbb{R}^2 \to \mathbb{R}$ by $f(x, y) = x^3 - y^3$, and consider the stationary point (0, 0). Show that $f(x, y)$ increases from $f(0, 0)$ as (x, y) moves from (0, 0) with θ (defined by $x = r\cos\theta$, $y = r\sin\theta$) in a certain interval, and $f(x, y)$ decreases when θ is in a complementary interval. (Such a saddlepoint may be called an *inflection*, since it generalizes to $\mathbb{R}^2$ the inflection at $x = 0$ of $\varphi(x) = x^3$. However, the possible kinds of saddlepoint in higher dimensions are many, and they do not all have names.)

Exercise 3.1.7 Show that the matrix

$$M = \begin{bmatrix} 2 & 1 & 1 \\ 1 & 2 & 0 \\ 1 & 0 & 1 \end{bmatrix}$$

is positive definite: (a) by considering the eigenvalues of M, as the zeros of the determinant

$$\begin{vmatrix} 2-\lambda & 1 & 1 \\ 1 & 2-\lambda & 0 \\ 1 & 0 & 0-\lambda \end{vmatrix};$$

and also (b) by using the Routh–Hurwicz criterion.

Exercise 3.1.8 Define $f: \mathbb{R}^n \to \mathbb{R}$ by $f(\mathbf{x}) = \mathbf{c}^T\mathbf{x} + \mathbf{x}^T A\mathbf{x}$, where $\mathbf{c}$ is a constant vector, and A is a positive definite matrix. Show that f is convex.

Exercise 3.1.9 Let $f \in C^2(U, \mathbb{R})$ be stationary at $\mathbf{u}_0 \in U$, where U is open; let $M = f''(\mathbf{u}_0)$ be positive definite. Use Taylor's theorem, in the form

$$f(\mathbf{u}_0 + \mathbf{x}) - f(\mathbf{u}_0) = \tfrac{1}{2} f''(\mathbf{u}_0 + \beta\mathbf{x})(\mathbf{x})^2,$$

where β (dependent on $\mathbf{x}$) lies in $0 < \beta < 1$, to prove that f attains a minimum at $\mathbf{u}_0$. (*Hint*: Since $f''(\cdot)$ is continuous, $f''(\mathbf{u}_0 + \beta\mathbf{x})$ is also positive definite, provided that $\|\mathbf{x}\|$ is small enough.)

3.2 CONSTRAINED MINIMA AND LAGRANGE MULTIPLIERS

Consider now the *constrained minimization problem*:

$$\text{Minimize } \mathbf{f}(\mathbf{z}) \text{ subject to } \mathbf{g}(\mathbf{z}) = \mathbf{0}. \tag{3.2.1}$$

Here $\mathbf{z} \in \mathbb{R}^n$, and $f : \mathbb{R}^n \to \mathbb{R}$ and $\mathbf{g} : \mathbb{R}^n \to \mathbb{R}^m$ are differentiable functions, with $m < n$. (There are thus n variables z_i, and m ($< n$) *constraints* $g_j(z) = 0$ on the values which $\mathbf{z}$ may take.) Since g is continuous, the *constraint set* $Q = \{\mathbf{z} \in \mathbb{R}^n : \mathbf{g}(\mathbf{z}) = \mathbf{0}\}$ is a closed subset of $\mathbb{R}^n$. A minimum is attained if also Q is bounded, and also in some other cases.

Suppose that a minimum of (3.2.1) is attained at $\mathbf{z} = \mathbf{c} \in Q$. Assume (hopefully) that $\mathbf{z} \in \mathbb{R}^n$ can be partitioned into $\mathbf{x} \in \mathbb{R}^{n-m}$ and $\mathbf{y} \in \mathbb{R}^m$ (write $\mathbf{z} = (\mathbf{x}, \mathbf{y})$, and correspondingly $\mathbf{c} = (\mathbf{a}, \mathbf{b})$), so that $\mathbf{g}(\mathbf{z}) = \mathbf{g}(\mathbf{x}, \mathbf{y}) = \mathbf{0}$ can be solved, say by $\mathbf{y} = \mathbf{q}(\mathbf{x})$, for $(\mathbf{x}, \mathbf{y})$ near $(\mathbf{a}, \mathbf{b})$. Then (3.2.1) reduces to minimizing $\mathbf{f}(\mathbf{x}, \mathbf{q}(\mathbf{x}))$, where $\mathbf{x}$ runs over some open ball with centre $\mathbf{a}$. But this unconstrained problem is usually not useful to calculate with, because the implicit function $\mathbf{q}(\cdot)$ has generally no explicit formula to work with.

Equating to zero the derivative of $\mathbf{f}(\mathbf{x}, \mathbf{q}(\mathbf{x}))$, using the chain rule (Theorem 2.2), gives $f_\mathbf{x} + f_\mathbf{y}\mathbf{q}' = \mathbf{0}$. Differentiating $\mathbf{g}(\mathbf{x}, \mathbf{q}(\mathbf{x})) = \mathbf{0}$ (which holds for all $\mathbf{x}$ near $\mathbf{a}$) gives similarly that $\mathbf{g}_\mathbf{x} + \mathbf{g}_\mathbf{y}\mathbf{q}' = \mathbf{0}$. Define $\lambda = -f_\mathbf{y}\mathbf{g}_\mathbf{y}^{-1}$. Then $f_\mathbf{y} + \lambda\mathbf{g}_\mathbf{y} = \mathbf{0}$ (by definition), and

$$f_\mathbf{x} + \lambda\mathbf{g}_\mathbf{x} = f_\mathbf{x} + (-f_\mathbf{y}\mathbf{g}_\mathbf{y}^{-1})\mathbf{g}_\mathbf{x} = f_\mathbf{x} + f_\mathbf{y}\mathbf{q}' = 0.$$

Hence

$$f'(\mathbf{c}) + \lambda\mathbf{g}'(\mathbf{c}) = [f_\mathbf{x}(\mathbf{c}), f_\mathbf{y}(\mathbf{c})] + \lambda[\mathbf{g}_\mathbf{x}(\mathbf{c}), \mathbf{g}_\mathbf{y}(\mathbf{c})] = \mathbf{0}. \tag{3.2.2}$$

Hence necessary conditions for a minimum of (3.2.1) at $\mathbf{z} = \mathbf{c}$ are obtained as

$$f'(\mathbf{c}) + \lambda\mathbf{g}'(\mathbf{c}) = 0; \qquad \mathbf{g}(\mathbf{c}) = \mathbf{0}; \tag{3.2.3}$$

for some $\lambda \in \mathbb{R}^m$. Here λ (written as a row vector) is called a *Lagrange multiplier*. Observe that the Lagrangian conditions (3.2.3) do not require $\mathbf{q}$, or the partitioning $\mathbf{z} = (\mathbf{x}, \mathbf{y})$, to be stated. The function $L(\mathbf{z}, \lambda) = f(\mathbf{z}) + \lambda\mathbf{g}(\mathbf{z})$ is called the *Lagrangian*. These calculations apply, in fact, whenever $\mathbf{c}$ is a *stationary point* (not necessarily a minimum) of (3.2.1), thus when

$$f(\mathbf{z}) - f(\mathbf{c}) = o(\|\mathbf{z} - \mathbf{c}\|), \text{ restricting } \mathbf{z} \text{ to satisfy } \mathbf{g}(\mathbf{z}) = \mathbf{0}.$$

In order to state a precise result, recall that the *rank* of a matrix M is the number of rows of the largest invertible submatrix of M (thus made from rows and columns of M). If the $m \times n$ matrix $\mathbf{g}'(\mathbf{c})$ has *full rank* (meaning the largest possible rank), then this rank is m (since $m < n$). Consequently, if the columns of $\mathbf{g}'(\mathbf{c})$ are suitably reordered, then $\mathbf{g}'(\mathbf{c})$ is partitioned as $\mathbf{g}'(\mathbf{c}) = [A \quad B]$, where $A \in \mathbb{R}^{m\times(n-m)}$, and $B \in \mathbb{R}^{m\times m}$, *with B invertible*. Correspondingly, $\mathbf{z} \in \mathbb{R}^n$ is partitioned into $\mathbf{x} \in \mathbb{R}^{n-m}$ and $\mathbf{y} \in \mathbb{R}^m$, and then $A = \mathbf{g}_\mathbf{x}(\mathbf{c})$ and $B = \mathbf{g}_\mathbf{y}(\mathbf{c})$.

Theorem 3.4

Let $f : \mathbb{R}^n \to \mathbb{R}$ and $\mathbf{g} : \mathbb{R}^n \to \mathbb{R}^m$ be continuously differentiable, with $m < n$. Let $\mathbf{g}'(\mathbf{c})$ have full rank. Then $f(\mathbf{z})$ is stationary at $\mathbf{c}$, subject to $\mathbf{g}(\mathbf{z}) = \mathbf{0}$, if and only if the Lagrangian conditions (3.2.3) hold for some Lagrange multiplier $\lambda \in \mathbb{R}^m$.

Proof From the full rank, it follows as above that $\mathbf{g}_\mathbf{y}(\mathbf{c})$ is invertible. Then, from the implicit function theorem, there exists a differentiable function $\mathbf{q}$, satisfying $\mathbf{g}(\mathbf{x}, \mathbf{q}(\mathbf{x})) = \mathbf{0}$ whenever $\|\mathbf{x}-\mathbf{a}\|$ is sufficiently small, and $\mathbf{q}(\mathbf{a}) = \mathbf{b}$ (where $\mathbf{c} = (\mathbf{a}, \mathbf{b})$). The calculations above, leading to Equations (3.2.2) and (3.2.3), then follow from the chain rule. Conversely, assume (3.2.3). Let $\mathbf{z}$ satisfy $\mathbf{g}(\mathbf{z}) = \mathbf{0}$, and denote $\mathbf{L}(\mathbf{z}) = f(\mathbf{z})+\lambda\mathbf{g}(\mathbf{z})$, with λ as in (3.2.3). Then

$$f(\mathbf{z})-f(\mathbf{c}) = \mathbf{L}(\mathbf{z})-\mathbf{L}(\mathbf{c}) = \mathbf{L}'(\mathbf{c})(\mathbf{z}-\mathbf{c})+o(\|\mathbf{z}-\mathbf{c}\|) = 0+o(\|\mathbf{z}-\mathbf{c}\|)$$

since $\mathbf{L}'(\mathbf{c}) = 0$ from (3.2.3). Thus $\mathbf{c}$ is a stationary point. □

Example

Minimize $f(x, y) = \cos \pi(x+y)$ subject to $x^2+y^2 = 1$. Here $g(x, y) = x^2+y^2-1$, so $g'(x, y) = [2x \quad 2y]$. This matrix has always at least one nonzero element, since $x^2+y^2 = 1$, so it has full rank (here, rank $= 1$). So the Lagrangian necessary conditions (3.2.3) for a stationary point apply. These are

$$[-\pi \sin \pi(x+y) \quad -\sin \pi(x+y)]+\lambda[2x \quad 2y] = [0 \quad 0];\; x^2+y^2 = 1.$$

If $\lambda = 0$, then $\pi \sin \pi(x+y) = 0$, so $x+y$ is an integer. From $x^2+y^2 = 1$, the only possibilities are $(x, y) = (2^{-1/2}, \; -2^{-1/2})$, $(-2^{-1/2}, 2^{1/2})$, for which $x+y = 0$ and $f(x, y) = 1$, and $(x, y) = (0, \pm 1)$, $(\pm 1, 0)$, for which $x+y = \pm 1$ and $f(x, y) = -1$. If

$\lambda \neq 0$, then $x = (2\lambda)^{-1}\pi \sin \pi(x+y) = y$; from $x^2+y^2 = 1$, $x = y = \pm 2^{-1/2}$; for $(x, y) = (2^{-1/2}, 2^{-1/2})$ and $(-2^{-1/2}, -2^{-1/2})$, $f(x, y) = \cos 2^{1/2}\pi$, so $-1 < f(x, y) < 1$. Until Section 3.3, we have no formal way to discriminate between *constrained* maxima and minima. However, consideration of the values of f shows, in this instance, that those (x, y) giving $f(x, y) = -1$ are minima, and those giving $f(x, y) = 1$ are maxima.

Example
Consider stationary points of $f(\mathbf{z}) = \mathbf{z}^{\mathrm{T}}A\mathbf{z}$ subject to $\mathbf{z}^{\mathrm{T}}\mathbf{z} = 1$; here $\mathbf{z} \in \mathbb{R}^n$ and A is a symmetric $n \times n$ matrix. The Lagrangian here is $L(\mathbf{z}, \lambda) = \mathbf{z}^{\mathrm{T}}A\mathbf{z} + \lambda(\mathbf{z}^{\mathrm{T}}\mathbf{z} - 1) = \mathbf{z}^{\mathrm{T}}(A + \lambda I)\mathbf{z} - \lambda$, where I is the $n \times n$ unit matrix. The Lagrangian conditions (3.2.3) are then $2\mathbf{z}^{\mathrm{T}}(A + \lambda I) = 0$, $\mathbf{z}^{\mathrm{T}}\mathbf{z} = 1$, referring to Exercise 2.2.5 for the derivative of a quadratic expression. Consequently, $A\mathbf{z} = -\lambda\mathbf{z}$ and $\mathbf{z} \neq 0$, so $-\lambda$ is an eigenvalue of A. Also $\mathbf{z}^{\mathrm{T}}A\mathbf{z} = -\lambda\mathbf{z}^{\mathrm{T}}\mathbf{z} = -\lambda$ at a stationary point. Here a minimum is obtained at the smallest eigenvalue of A; the largest eigenvalue gives a maximum.

Example
Let $A \in \mathbb{R}^{m\times r}$, $B \in \mathbb{R}^{m\times m}$, $a \in \mathbb{R}^r$, $b \in \mathbb{R}^m$, $k \in \mathbb{R}^m$; let B be invertible. Denote by $F(k)$ the minimum of $a^{\mathrm{T}}x + b^{\mathrm{T}}y$ over $x \in \mathbb{R}^r$, $y \in \mathbb{R}^m$, subject to $Ax + By = k$. Since B is invertible, $[A \quad B]$ has full rank m. The Lagrangian conditions give

$$a^{\mathrm{T}} + \lambda^{\mathrm{T}}A = 0,\ b^{\mathrm{T}} + \lambda^{\mathrm{T}}B = 0,\ A\bar{x} + B\bar{y} = k.$$

where $(\bar{x}, \bar{y})$ is the minimum, assumed to exist, and the Lagrange multiplier λ is written here as a column. Therefore

$$F(k) = a^{\mathrm{T}}\bar{x} + b^{\mathrm{T}}\bar{y} = -\lambda^{\mathrm{T}}(A\bar{x} + B\bar{y}) = -\lambda^{\mathrm{T}}k.$$

Hence $F'(0) = -\lambda^{\mathrm{T}}$; the Lagrange multiplier measures the rate of change of the minimum function value $F(k)$ as k changes.

A similar calculation may be made for a nonlinear problem:

$$\text{Minimize } f(x, y) \text{ subject to } g(x, y) = k.$$

Here $g(x, y) = k$ may be thought of as a perturbation of a given constraint $g(x, y) = 0$. The above calculation, replacing a, b, A, B by f_x, f_y, g_x, g_y at the minimum for $k = 0$, leads to $F'(0) = -\lambda^{\mathrm{T}}$, where λ is the Lagrange multiplier when $k = 0$.

Exercise 3.2.1 Discuss the minimization of $f(x, y) = x+y$ on the ellipse $(x^2/4)+(y^2/9) = 1$.

Exercise 3.2.2 Find the maximum of $f(x, y, z) = x^2y^2z^2$ given that $x^2+y^2+z^2 = c^2$.

Exercise 3.2.3 Find those points on the intersection of the cylinder $\{(x, y, z) \in \mathbb{R}^3 : x^2+y^2 = 1\}$ and the plane $\{(x, y, z) : 2x+3y+z = 1\}$ which are nearest to the origin, and which are farthest from the origin. (Note that, for this problem, $f+\lambda g$ takes the form

$$(x^2+y^2+z^2)+\rho(x^2+y^2-1)+\sigma(2x+3y+z-1).$$

Here ρ and σ are the components of the Lagrange multiplier vector λ.)

Exercise 3.2.4 Show that the volume of the largest box that can be inscribed in the ellipsoidal region

$$\left\{(x, y, z) \in \mathbb{R}^3 : \frac{x^2}{a^2}+\frac{y^2}{b^2}+\frac{z^2}{c^2} \leq 1\right\}$$

is $8abc/3^{3/2}$. (Take $a, b, c > 0$).

Exercise 3.2.5 By considering the maximum of $f(x) = (x_1x_2 \ldots x_n)^{1/n}$ subject to $\sum_{i=1}^{n} x_i = nk$, where k is constant, show that the geometric mean $(x_1x_2 \ldots x_n)^{1/n}$ of n positive real numbers x_i does not exceed their arithmetic mean.

Exercise 3.2.6 In statistical physics, the problem arises of maximizing

$$S = \sum_{k=1}^{N} \log \frac{(g_k+x_k-1)!}{n_k!(g_k-1)!}$$

subject to the constraints

$$\sum_{k=1}^{N} e_k x_k = E \text{ and } \sum_{k=1}^{N} x_k = N.$$

Here N is a larger integer, and the g_k and e_k are given positive numbers; E is constant. If the integer variables x_k are approximated by real variables, and the factorials are approximated by Stirling's formula:

$$n! \approx (2\pi)^{1/2}e^{-n}n^{n+1/2} \qquad (n \text{ large}),$$

show that the given problem is approximately equivalent to minimizing

$$\sum_{k=1}^{N} [(g_k+x_k)\log(g_k+x_k)-x_k \log x_k],$$

subject to the constraints, and assuming all x_k are large numbers. For the approximate problem, show that the optimum x_k are given by

$$x_k = g_k[e^{-(e_k-\mu)/\theta}-1]^{-1},$$

where $1/\theta$ and μ/θ are Lagrange multipliers. (In the physical application, the x_k represent numbers of particles, e_k and E represent energies, and θ represents temperature.)

3.3 DISCRIMINATING CONSTRAINED STATIONARY POINTS

Assume that f and g in problem (3.2.1) are C^2 functions (twice continuously differentiable). Assume that this problem has a stationary point at $\mathbf{c}$, and assume that $\mathbf{g}'(\mathbf{c})$ has full rank. Then the Lagrangian conditions (3.2.3) hold at $\mathbf{c}$, with some Lagrange multiplier λ. Denote $\mathbf{L}(\mathbf{z}) = f(\mathbf{z})+\lambda\mathbf{g}(\mathbf{z})$; let $M = \mathbf{L}''(\mathbf{c})$. When $\mathbf{g}(\mathbf{c}+\mathbf{w}) = \mathbf{0}$,

$$f(\mathbf{c}+\mathbf{w})- f(\mathbf{c}) = \mathbf{L}(\mathbf{c}+\mathbf{w})-\mathbf{L}(\mathbf{c}) = \tfrac{1}{2}\mathbf{L}''(\mathbf{c}+\beta\mathbf{w})(\mathbf{w})^2 \qquad (3.3.1)$$

for some β in $0 < \beta < 1$, by Taylor's theorem, since $\mathbf{L}'(\mathbf{c}) = \mathbf{0}$. Hence

$$f(\mathbf{c}+\mathbf{w})- f(\mathbf{c}) = \tfrac{1}{2}\mathbf{w}^{\mathrm{T}}M\mathbf{w}+\theta(\mathbf{w}), \qquad (3.3.2)$$

where $|\theta(\mathbf{w})| < \|\mathbf{w}\|^2$ when $\|\mathbf{w}\| < \delta(\varepsilon)$. But also

$$\mathbf{g}(\mathbf{c}+\mathbf{w}) = \mathbf{g}(\mathbf{c})+\mathbf{g}'(\mathbf{c})\mathbf{w}+ \psi(\mathbf{w}), \qquad (3.3.3)$$

where $\psi(\mathbf{w}) < \varepsilon\|\mathbf{w}\|$ whenever $\|\mathbf{w}\| < \delta_1(\varepsilon)$. Since $\mathbf{g}(\mathbf{c}) = \mathbf{0}$ and $\mathbf{g}(\mathbf{c}+\mathbf{w}) = \mathbf{0}$, $\mathbf{g}'(\mathbf{c})\mathbf{w} = -\psi(\mathbf{w})$. These results suggest, if the 'small' terms θ and ψ are neglected, that the behaviour of the stationary point is determined by the behaviour of the quadratic function $\mathbf{w}^{\mathrm{T}}M\mathbf{w}$, subject to the linear constraint $B\mathbf{w} = \mathbf{0}$, where $B = \mathbf{g}'(\mathbf{c})$.

Theorem 3.5

In problem (3.2.1), let f and $\mathbf{g}$ be C^2 functions; let the problem have a stationary point at $\mathbf{c}$; let $B = \mathbf{g}'(\mathbf{c})$ have full rank; let $M = \mathbf{L}''(\mathbf{c})$ have no zero eigenvalues. Then the stationary point $\mathbf{c}$ of (3.2.1) has the same nature (maximum, minimum, or saddlepoint) as the stationary point $\mathbf{0}$ of

$$\mathbf{u}^{\mathrm{T}}M\mathbf{u} \text{ subject to } B\mathbf{u} = \mathbf{0}. \tag{3.3.4}$$

Proof As in Section 3.2, the implicit function theorem, given $\mathbf{g}'(\mathbf{c})$ of full rank, generates a differentiable solution $\mathbf{c}+\mathbf{w}(\mathbf{d}) = (\mathbf{a}+\mathbf{d}, \mathbf{q}(\mathbf{a}+\mathbf{d}))$ to $\mathbf{g}(\mathbf{c}+\mathbf{w}(\mathbf{d})) = \mathbf{0}$; here $\mathbf{c} = (\mathbf{a}, \mathbf{b})$, and the vector $\mathbf{d}$ is arbitrary, provided that $\|\mathbf{d}\|$ is sufficiently small. Let $\mathbf{u} = \mathbf{w}'(\mathbf{0})\mathbf{d}$; here $\mathbf{w}'(\mathbf{0}) = (I, \mathbf{q}'(\mathbf{a}))$, I is the identity, and $\mathbf{g}'(\mathbf{c})\mathbf{u} = \mathbf{0}$ by the chain rule. In fact, since $\mathbf{q}' = -\mathbf{g}_{\mathbf{y}}^{-1}\mathbf{g}_{\mathbf{x}}$ by the chain rule, every $\mathbf{u}$ satisfying $\mathbf{g}'(\mathbf{c})\mathbf{u} = \mathbf{0}$ is of this form. Now substitute $\mathbf{w} = \mathbf{w}(\mathbf{d})$ into Equation (3.3.2); this gives

$$f(\mathbf{c}+\mathbf{w}(\mathbf{d}))-f(\mathbf{c}) = \tfrac{1}{2}\mathbf{u}^{\mathrm{T}}M\mathbf{u}+\text{terms of higher order in } \mathbf{u}. \tag{3.3.5}$$

By hypothesis, all the eigenvalues λ_i of M are nonzero. By a theorem of linear algebra, if the coordinate axes for $\mathbf{u}$ are suitably rotated, $\mathbf{u}^{\mathrm{T}}M\mathbf{u}$ takes the form $\sum\lambda_i u_i^2$, where (the rotated) $\mathbf{u} = (u_1, u_2, \ldots)$. Since each $\lambda_i \neq 0$, each higher-order term in Equation (3.3.5) is negligible, whenever $\|\mathbf{u}\|$ is sufficiently small, in comparison with one of the terms $\lambda_i u_i^2$. Consequently, the nature of the stationary point $\mathbf{c}$ is the same as that of $\mathbf{0}$ for $\mathbf{u}^{\mathrm{T}}M\mathbf{u}$, subject to the constraint $\mathbf{g}'(\mathbf{c})\mathbf{u} = \mathbf{0}$. □

Remark Since B has full rank, the columns of B may be partitioned, and the rows of $\mathbf{w}$ reordered, so that

$$B\mathbf{w} = [B_1 \quad B_2]\begin{bmatrix} w_1 \\ w_2 \end{bmatrix},$$

with the submatrix B_1 nonsingular. And M may be similarly partitioned as

$$M = \begin{bmatrix} M_{11} & M_{12} \\ M_{21} & M_{22} \end{bmatrix}.$$

Hence, if $\mathbf{w}$ satisfies $B\mathbf{w} = \mathbf{0}$, then calculation gives $\mathbf{w}^{\mathrm{T}}M\mathbf{w} = w_2{}^{\mathrm{T}}Sw_2$, where

$$S = M_{22}+K^{\mathrm{T}}M_{11}K-2K^{\mathrm{T}}M_{12}$$

with $K = B_1{}^{-1}B_2$. It follows that the behaviour of the stationary point depends on the eigenvalues of S, assuming that S has no zero eigenvalues.

Remark Let $[\alpha, \beta]$ denote the range of values assumed by $\mathbf{u}^{\mathrm{T}}M\mathbf{u}/\mathbf{u}^{\mathrm{T}}\mathbf{u}$, subject to the linear constraint $B\mathbf{u} = \mathbf{0}$. It is equivalent to consider the stationary values of $\mathbf{u}^{\mathrm{T}}M\mathbf{u}$, subject to the two constraints $2B\mathbf{u} = \mathbf{0}$ and $\mathbf{u}^{\mathrm{T}}\mathbf{u} = 1$. The Lagrangian conditions for the latter problem are

$$2\mathbf{u}^{\mathrm{T}}M+2\rho^{\mathrm{T}}B+2\theta\mathbf{u}^{\mathrm{T}} = \mathbf{0},\ 2B\mathbf{u} = \mathbf{0},\ \mathbf{u}^{\mathrm{T}}\mathbf{u} = 1.$$

If the multiplier $\rho = 0$, then $\mathbf{u}^{\mathrm{T}}M\mathbf{u} = -\theta$, $\sigma \equiv -\theta$ is an eigenvalue of M, with $\mathbf{u}$ as the corresponding eigenvector, and $B\mathbf{u} = 0$. If σ is not an eigenvalue of M, then $\rho \neq 0$, $(M-\sigma I)\mathbf{u}+B^{\mathrm{T}}\rho = \mathbf{0}$, so $\mathbf{0} = -B\mathbf{u} = B(M-\sigma I)^{-1}B^{\mathrm{T}}\rho$. Since $\rho \neq 0$, the determinant $\det B(M-\sigma I)^{-1}B^{\mathrm{T}}$ must vanish, yielding an equation for σ. Then α and β are the least and greatest values of σ. Now let M have eigenvalues $\mu_1 \leq \mu_2 \leq \ldots \leq \mu_n$. It can be shown that $\mu_1 \leq \alpha \leq \mu_m$ and $\mu_{n-m} \leq \beta \leq \mu_n$, when the constraint $B\mathbf{u} = \mathbf{0}$ represents m linearly independent equations.

We may ask when the Lagrangian conditions (3.2.3) are also *sufficient* for a minimum of the problem (3.2.1). One such answer is given by the following theorem (in which $\mathbf{L}(\mathbf{z}) \equiv f(\mathbf{z})+\lambda\mathbf{g}(\mathbf{z})$).

Theorem 3.6
Assume that $\mathbf{L}$ is twice continuously differentiable, and that $\mathbf{L}''(\mathbf{c})$ is positive definite on the null space of $\mathbf{g}'(\mathbf{c})$; this means that

$$[\mathbf{g}'(\mathbf{c})\mathbf{d} = \mathbf{0} \text{ and } \mathbf{d} \neq \mathbf{0}] \Rightarrow \mathbf{d}^{\mathrm{T}}\mathbf{L}''(\mathbf{c})\mathbf{d} > 0.$$

Assume that the Lagrangian conditions, $\mathbf{L}'(\mathbf{c}) = \mathbf{0}$ and $\mathbf{g}(\mathbf{c}) = \mathbf{0}$, hold. Then $\mathbf{c}$ is a local minimum for (3.2.1).

Proof Suppose, if possible, that $\mathbf{c}$ is *not* a minimum; a contradiction will be deduced. For if $\mathbf{c}$ is not a minimum, $f(\mathbf{z}_k) < f(\mathbf{c})$ for some sequence $\{\mathbf{z}_k\} \to \mathbf{c}$ for which $\mathbf{g}(\mathbf{z}_k) = 0$. Set $\mathbf{z}_k = \mathbf{c}+\alpha_k\mathbf{d}_k$ with $\alpha_k > 0$ and $\|\mathbf{d}_k\| = 1$; by choosing a subsequence, assume that $\{\mathbf{d}_k\} \to \mathbf{d}$.

Then $\mathbf{g}'(\mathbf{c})\mathbf{d} = \mathbf{0}$. By Taylor's theorem (Theorem 2.7), for some ζ_k on the line segment joining $\mathbf{c}$ to $\mathbf{z}_k$,

$$\alpha_k^{-2}[f(\mathbf{z}_k) - f(\mathbf{c})] = \alpha_k^{-2}[\mathbf{L}(\mathbf{z}_k) - \mathbf{L}(\mathbf{c})] = \alpha_k^{-2}[\tfrac{1}{2}\mathbf{d}_k^T\mathbf{L}''(\zeta_k)\mathbf{d}_k]$$
$$\rightarrow \tfrac{1}{2}\mathbf{d}_k^T\mathbf{L}''(\mathbf{c})\mathbf{d}_k > 0 \text{ as } k \rightarrow \infty$$

by the positive definite assumption. So the minimum is contradicted.

□

Remark Since $\{\mathbf{d} : \|\mathbf{d}\| = 1\}$ is a closed bounded set in $\mathbb{R}^n$, any sequence $\{\mathbf{d}_k\}$ in this set possesses a convergent subsequence (as assumed in this proof), by a theorem of analysis.

Exercise 3.3.1 Apply the S criterion, above, to Exercises 3.2.3 and 3.2.4.

Exercise 3.3.2 Formulate also, for these two problems, the criterion in terms of σ.

Exercise 3.3.3 Show that $f(x, y) = 2xy + 2^{1/2}y^3$ has a critical point, subject to $-\frac{1}{2}x^2 + y^2 = 1$, at $(x, y) = (-2^{1/2}, -2^{1/2})$, with Lagrange multiplier $\lambda = 2$. Discuss the nature of this critical point. (Note that $M = \mathbf{L}''(\mathbf{c})$ is *not* necessarily positive definite, or negative definite; and that convexity cannot be assumed here.)

3.4 INEQUALITY CONSTRAINTS

The minimization problem (3.2.1) had an equality constraint $\mathbf{g}(\mathbf{z}) = \mathbf{0}$. Consider now a problem with both an equality constraint $\mathbf{h}(\mathbf{z}) = \mathbf{0}$, and an inequality constraint $\mathbf{g}(\mathbf{z}) \leq \mathbf{0}$. The latter represents the system of inequalities $g_i(\mathbf{z}) \leq 0$ $(i = 1, 2, \ldots, m)$; in writing $\mathbf{g}(\mathbf{z}) \leq \mathbf{0}$, the inequality $\leq$ is taken componentwise; that is, applying separately to each vector component. The minimization problem now considered is then:

$$\text{Minimize } f(\mathbf{z}) \text{ subject to } \mathbf{g}(\mathbf{z}) \leq \mathbf{0},\ \mathbf{h}(\mathbf{z}) = \mathbf{0}, \qquad (3.4.1)$$

where $\mathbf{z} \in \mathbb{R}^n$, and $f : \mathbb{R}^n \rightarrow \mathbb{R}$, $\mathbf{g} : \mathbb{R}^n \rightarrow \mathbb{R}^m$ and $\mathbf{h} : \mathbb{R}^m \rightarrow \mathbb{R}^s$ are differentiable functions, with $m + s < n$. The constraints of (3.4.1), written out in components, are

$$g_1(\mathbf{z}) \leq 0,\ g_2(\mathbf{z}) \leq 0, \ldots, g_m(\mathbf{z}) \leq 0;$$
$$h_1(\mathbf{z}) = 0,\ h_2(\mathbf{z}) = 0, \ldots, h_s(\mathbf{z}) = 0. \qquad (3.4.2)$$

We look for necessary conditions for (3.4.1) to attain a (local) minimum at $\mathbf{z} = \mathbf{c}$. Renumbering the g_i if necessary, we may assume that $g_i(\mathbf{c}) = 0$ for $i = 1, 2, \ldots, r$, whereas $g_i(c) < 0$ for $i = r+1, \ldots, m$. We then call the constraints $g_1(\mathbf{z}) \leq 0, g_2(\mathbf{z}) \leq 0, \ldots,$ $g_r(\mathbf{z}) \leq 0$, together with the equality constraints $h_1(\mathbf{z}) = 0, \ldots,$ $h_s(\mathbf{z}) = 0$, the *active* (or *binding*) constraints, whereas $g_{r+1}(\mathbf{z}) \leq 0, \ldots,$ $g_m(\mathbf{z}) \leq 0$ are *inactive* constraints. The distinction between active and inactive depends on the point $\mathbf{c}$, and may be different at another point. Since an inactive constraint still satisfies $g_i(\mathbf{z}) < 0$ whenever $\|\mathbf{z}-\mathbf{c}\|$ is small enough, and there are only a finite number of constraints, the problem (3.4.1) modified by omitting the inactive constraints (at $\mathbf{c}$) still reaches a minimum at $\mathbf{c}$. The *constraint set* Q is the region satisfying the constraints.

Example (a)
Consider the constraints $z_1 \geq 0$, $z_2 \geq 0$, with $\mathbf{c} = (1, 0)$ (see Fig. 3.5). Then $z_2 \geq 0$ is active, whereas $z_1 \geq 0$ is inactive – it still holds

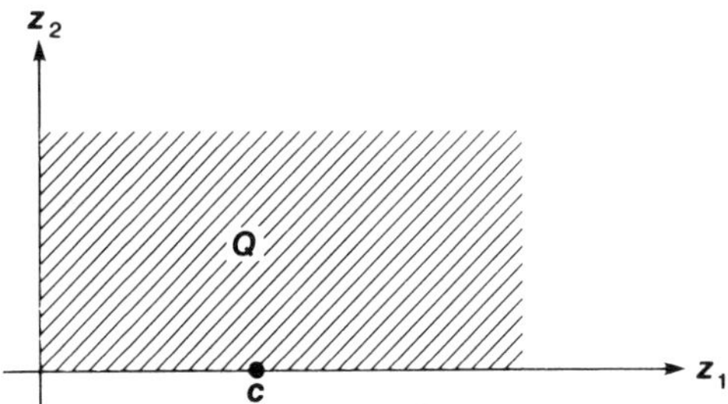

Figure 3.5 Active and inactive constraints

if $\mathbf{z}$ is moved a small distance away from (1, 0). (Note that these constraints can be put into the form of (3.4.1) by rewriting them as $g_1(\mathbf{z}) \equiv -z_1 \leq 0$, $g_2(\mathbf{z}) \equiv -z_2 \leq 0$.)

Example (b)
Consider the constraint $g(x) \leq 0$, where $x \in \mathbb{R}$, and $g(x) = x^2$ when $x \geq 0$, $g(x) = 0$ when $x < 0$. Then $Q = \{x \in \mathbb{R}: g(x) \leq 0\} = (-\infty, 0]$. Observe that g is differentiable, with $g'(0) = 0$.

Theorem 3.7 (Kuhn-Tucker theorem)
For the problem (3.4.1), let f, $\mathbf{g}$ and $\mathbf{h}$ be continuously differentiable, and let the problem attain a (local) minimum at $\mathbf{z} = \mathbf{c}$. Assume that the gradients of the active constraints (thus $g_i'(\mathbf{c})$ $(i = 1, 2, \ldots, r)$ and $h_j(\mathbf{c})(j = 1, 2, \ldots, s)$) are linearly independent. Then there exist Lagrange multipliers $\lambda_1, \lambda_2, \ldots, \lambda_m$ and $\mu_1, \ldots, \mu_s$ satisfying,

$$\left.\begin{aligned} &f'(\mathbf{c})+\sum_{i=1}^{m}\lambda_i g_i'(\mathbf{c})+\sum_{j=1}^{s}\mu_j h_j'(\mathbf{c}) = \mathbf{0};\\ &\text{and, for } i = 1, 2, \ldots, m,\ \lambda_i \geq 0 \text{ and } \lambda_i g_i(\mathbf{c}) = 0. \end{aligned}\right\} \quad (3.4.3)$$

Remarks The system (3.4.3) is called the *Kuhn–Tucker conditions* for the problem (3.4.1). The first line may be written as $f'(\mathbf{c})+\lambda^T\mathbf{g}'(\mathbf{c})+\mu^T\mathbf{h}'(\mathbf{c}) = \mathbf{0}$, in matrix terms, or as $\mathbf{L}'(\mathbf{c}) = \mathbf{0}$ in terms of the *Lagrangian*

$$\mathbf{L}(\mathbf{z}) = f(\mathbf{z})+\sum_{i=1}^{m}\lambda_i g_i(\mathbf{z})+\sum_{j=1}^{s}\mu_j h_j(\mathbf{z}). \quad (3.4.4)$$

Note that $\lambda_i g_i(\mathbf{c}) = 0$ implies that $\lambda_i = 0$ for an *inactive* constraint $(g_i(\mathbf{c}) < 0)$.

Proof Consider the modified problem, with the constraints inactive at $\mathbf{c}$ removed; let $\mathbf{k}$ be the vector with components $g_1, g_2, \ldots, g_r$, corresponding to the active inequality constraints only. For temporary theoretical purposes, we rewrite the constraint $\mathbf{k}(\mathbf{z}) \leq \mathbf{0}$ as $\mathbf{K}(\mathbf{z}, \mathbf{u}) = \mathbf{0}$, where $\mathbf{u} \in \mathbb{R}^r$, and $\mathbf{K}(\mathbf{z}, \mathbf{u})$ has components $g_i(\mathbf{z})+u_i^2$, for $i = 1, 2, \ldots, r$. The modified problem then becomes:

$$\text{Minimize } F(\mathbf{z}, \mathbf{u}) \equiv f(\mathbf{z}) \text{ subject to } \begin{bmatrix}\mathbf{K}(\mathbf{z}, \mathbf{u})\\ \mathbf{h}(\mathbf{z})\end{bmatrix} = \begin{bmatrix}0\\0\end{bmatrix}. \quad (3.4.5)$$

The Fréchet derivatives, with respect to $\begin{bmatrix}\mathbf{z}\\ \mathbf{u}\end{bmatrix}$, of $F(\mathbf{z}, \mathbf{u})$ and $\begin{bmatrix}\mathbf{K}(\mathbf{z}, \mathbf{u})\\ \mathbf{h}(\mathbf{z})\end{bmatrix}$, are respectively

$$[f'(\mathbf{c}) \quad \mathbf{0}] \text{ and } T \equiv \begin{bmatrix}\mathbf{k}'(\mathbf{c}) & 2\Theta\\ \mathbf{h}'(\mathbf{c}) & \mathbf{0}\end{bmatrix}, \text{ where } \Theta = \begin{bmatrix}u_1 & 0 & 0 & \ldots & 0\\ 0 & u_2 & 0 & \ldots & 0\\ 0 & 0 & u_3 & \ldots & 0\\ \cdot & \cdot & \cdot & \ldots & \cdot\\ 0 & 0 & 0 & \ldots & u_r\end{bmatrix}.$$

The assumption about linear independence ensures that the matrix T has full rank. Hence the Lagrangian theorem (Theorem 3.4) can be applied to the problem (3.4.5). Necessary conditions for a minimum of (3.4.5) at $(\mathbf{z}, \mathbf{u}) = (\mathbf{c}, \mathbf{0})$ are that Lagrange multipliers $\rho \in \mathbb{R}^r$ and $\mu \in \mathbb{R}^s$ exist, which satisfy

$$[f'(\mathbf{c}) \quad 0] + [\rho^{\mathrm{T}} \quad \mu^{\mathrm{T}}] \begin{bmatrix} \mathbf{k}'(\mathbf{c}) & \mathbf{0} \\ \mathbf{h}'(\mathbf{c}) & \mathbf{0} \end{bmatrix} = [0 \quad 0]. \qquad (3.4.6)$$

(Note here that the Lagrange multiplier of the theorem appears as $\begin{bmatrix} \rho \\ \mu \end{bmatrix}$, to correspond to the two rows of T; and that $\Theta = \mathbf{0}$ at $\mathbf{u} = \mathbf{0}$.)
From (3.4.6),

$$f'(\mathbf{c}) + \rho^{\mathrm{T}}\mathbf{k}'(\mathbf{c}) + \mu^{\mathrm{T}}\mathbf{h}'(\mathbf{c}) = \mathbf{0}. \qquad (3.4.7)$$

Since $\begin{bmatrix} \mathbf{k}'(\mathbf{c}) \\ \mathbf{h}'(\mathbf{c}) \end{bmatrix}$ has full rank, the implicit function theorem 3.6 shows that $\mathbf{k}(\mathbf{z}) + \alpha\mathbf{p} = \mathbf{0}$, $\mathbf{h}(\mathbf{z}) = \mathbf{0}$ (where $\mathbf{p}$ is a fixed vector with all components positive) can be solved in terms of the real positive parameter α, provided that α is sufficiently small. This gives a solution $\mathbf{z} = \mathbf{c} + \alpha\mathbf{w} + o(\alpha)$, for some vector $\mathbf{w}$. Differentiating $\mathbf{k}(\mathbf{c} + \alpha\mathbf{w} + o(\alpha)) + \alpha\mathbf{p} = \mathbf{0}$ and $\mathbf{h}(\mathbf{c} + \alpha\mathbf{w} + o(\alpha)) = \mathbf{0}$ with respect to α shows that $\mathbf{k}'(\mathbf{c})\mathbf{w} + \mathbf{p} = \mathbf{0}$ and $\mathbf{h}'(\mathbf{c})\mathbf{w} = \mathbf{0}$. Since $\mathbf{k}(\mathbf{z}) \leq \mathbf{0}$ and $\mathbf{h}(\mathbf{z}) = \mathbf{0}$, $f(\mathbf{z})$ is minimized, with respect to such $\mathbf{z}$, at $\mathbf{z} = \mathbf{c}$. Hence

$$\begin{aligned} 0 \leq \alpha^{-1}[f(\mathbf{z}) - f(\mathbf{c})] &= \alpha^{-1}[f'(\mathbf{c})\alpha\mathbf{w} + o(\alpha)] \\ &= -[\rho^{\mathrm{T}}\mathbf{k}'(\mathbf{c}) + \mu^{\mathrm{T}}\mathbf{h}'(\mathbf{c})]\mathbf{w} + o(\alpha)/\alpha \qquad \text{from (3.4.7)} \\ &\to \rho^{\mathrm{T}}\mathbf{p} + 0 + 0 \qquad (3.4.8) \end{aligned}$$

as $\alpha \to 0$ through positive values. Since $\mathbf{p}$ has positive components, each component of ρ is nonnegative. Define $\lambda_i = \rho_i$ for $i = 1, 2, \ldots, r$, and $\lambda_i = 0$ for $i = r+1, \ldots, m$. Then Equation (3.4.7), with all $\lambda_i \geq 0$, is equivalent to (3.4.3), noting that the *complementary slackness* conditions $\lambda_i g_i(\mathbf{c}) = 0$ imply, when $g_i(\mathbf{c}) < 0$, that the corresponding $\lambda_i = 0$. □

Remark The Lagrange multiplier μ_j corresponding to an *equality* constraint $h_j(\mathbf{z}) = 0$ may have either sign. But the Lagrange multiplier λ_i corresponding to an *inequality* constraint $g_j(\mathbf{z}) \leq 0$ must (for a minimization problem) satisfy $\lambda_i \geq 0$. If the problem is, instead, to maximize $f(\mathbf{z})$, this may be considered as minimizing $-f(\mathbf{z})$. The hypothesis of linear independence for the gradients of the active constraints can be checked by computation, for given functions. In fact, Kuhn and Tucker assumed a somewhat weaker (though less convenient) hypothesis, for which (3.4.3) still holds.

Example

$$\underset{(x,\, y) \in \mathbb{R}^2}{\text{Minimize}}\ f(x, y) = \tfrac{1}{3}x^3 - y^2, \text{ subject to } \tfrac{1}{2}x^2 + y^2 \leq 1.$$

Here there is a single inequality constraint, $g(x, y) \equiv \frac{1}{2}x^2 + y^2 - 1 \leq 0$. The Kuhn–Tucker conditions for this problem are then $\lambda \geq 0$, and

$$x^2 + \lambda x = 0;\ -2y + \lambda(2y) = 0;\ \lambda(\tfrac{1}{2}x^2 + y^2 - 1) = 0. \qquad (3.4.9)$$

All solutions to (3.4.9) should be sought. If $\lambda = 0$ then $(x, y) = (0, 0)$. If $0 \neq \lambda \neq 1$ then $y = 0$; hence either $x = 0$ (contradicting $\frac{1}{2}x^2 + y^2 = 1$), or $-\lambda = x = \pm 2^{1/2}$ (from $y = 0$ and $\frac{1}{2}x^2 + y^2 = 1$). If $\lambda = 1$ then $x = 0$ or -1, for which $y = \pm 1$ or $\pm 2^{1/2}$. Hence the *Kuhn–Tucker points* (those points satisfying (3.4.9), without necessarily $\lambda \geq 0$) are tabulated as follows. (Here $\bar{p} = 1 - \frac{1}{2}\bar{x}^2 - \bar{y}^2$, where the Kuhn–Tucker point is now denoted $(\bar{x}, \bar{y})$.)

$\bar{x}$	$\bar{y}$	λ	$\bar{p}$	$f(\bar{x}, \bar{y})$
0	± 1	1	0	-1
-1	$\pm 2^{-1/2}$	1	0	$-5/6$
0	0	0	1	0
$2^{1/2}$	0	$-2^{1/2}$	0	$2^{3/2}/3$
$-2^{1/2}$	0	$+2^{1/2}$	0	$-2^{3/2}/3$

By considering the values of $f(\bar{x}, \bar{y})$, it is clear that $(0, \pm 1)$ are minima. This example will be further discussed in Section 3.5, where other criteria will be given for discriminating between constrained *critical points* (maxima, minima and saddlepoints).

Exercise 3.4.1 Use the Kuhn–Tucker conditions to establish necessary conditions for a minimum at $\mathbf{z} = \mathbf{c}$ of the *quadratic programming* problem:

$$\underset{\mathbf{z} \in \mathbb{R}^n}{\text{Minimize}}\ \tfrac{1}{2}\mathbf{z}^{\mathrm{T}} A\mathbf{z} + b^{\mathrm{T}}\mathbf{z} \qquad \text{subject to } M\mathbf{z} \geq \mathbf{q}, \qquad (3.4.10)$$

where A and M are suitable matrices, and b and $\mathbf{q}$ are constant vectors. (What must be assumed concerning A for a minimum to be attained? What must be assumed to verify the linear independence hypothesis?)

Exercise 3.4.2 Find the critical points of $f(x, y) = 2y^2 - x^2y$, subject to $\frac{1}{2}x^2 + y^2 \leq 1$.

Exercise 3.4.3 Let $\mathbf{z} = \mathbf{c}$ be an optimal solution of the problem

$$\underset{\mathbf{z} \in \mathbb{R}^n}{\text{Minimize}}\ f(\mathbf{z}) = \sum_{j=1}^{n} f_j(z_j) \text{ subject to } z_j \geq 0 \ (j = 1, 2, \ldots, n)$$

$$\text{and to } z_1 + z_2 + \ldots + z_n = 1.$$

Assume that each function $f_j : \mathbb{R} \to \mathbb{R}$ is differentiable. Show that there exists θ such that $f_j'(c) = \theta$ when $c_j > 0$, and $f_j'(c) \geq \theta$ when $c_j = 0$. Validate the use of the Kuhn–Tucker conditions.

Exercise 3.4.4 For the problem

$$\text{Minimize } f(\mathbf{z}) \text{ subject to } g_i(\mathbf{z}) \leq 0 \ (i = 1, 2, \ldots, m), \quad (3.4.11)$$

assume that each function f and g_i is *convex* (see Section 3.1), and differentiable. Show that the sum of two convex functions is convex (from the definition of convex function). Use this to show that the Lagrangian $\mathbf{L}(\cdot) = f(\cdot) + \sum_{i=1}^{n} \lambda_i g_i(\cdot)$ is a convex function. (*Hint*: What is the role here of $\lambda_i \geq 0$?)

Suppose now that $g_i(\mathbf{c}) \leq 0$ $(i = 1, 2, \ldots, m)$, and that the Kuhn–Tucker conditions for (3.4.11) hold at $\mathbf{c}$. Prove, under the convexity assumptions made, that (3.4.11) attains a minimum at $\mathbf{c}$. (*Hint*: Let $\mathbf{z}$ satisfy the constraints of (3.4.11). Then $f(\mathbf{z}) - f(\mathbf{c}) = \mathbf{L}(\mathbf{z}) - \mathbf{L}(\mathbf{c}) + \ldots \geq \ldots$, using convexity.) (Observe that the *necessary* Kuhn–Tucker conditions become also *sufficient* for a minimum, under extra assumptions of convexity.)

A further exercise relating to constrained minimization and the Kuhn–Tucker theorem may be found in Section 3.5.

3.5 DISCRIMINATING MAXIMA AND MINIMA WITH INEQUALITY CONSTRAINTS

When there are inequality constraints, a constrained *minimum* is not necessarily a *stationary* point, as defined in Section 3.1. For example, $f(x) = x^2$ is minimized, subject to $x \in [2, 3]$, at $x = 2$; however, $f(x) - f(2) = 4(x-2)+(x-2)^2$, for $x \in [2, 3]$; thus $f(x)-f(2) \neq o(|x-2|)$. The phrase *critical point* is therefore used, to include all maxima, minima, saddlepoints, and stationary points. The Kuhn–Tucker conditions (3.4.3) give (under suitable assumptions) *necessary* conditions for a minimum. For a convex problem (see Exercise 3.4.4), they are also *sufficient* for a minimum.

Suppose now that $\mathbf{c}$ is a *Kuhn–Tucker point* for the minimization problem (3.4.1); this means that the Kuhn–Tucker conditions (3.4.3) are satisfied at $\mathbf{c}$, except possibly $\boldsymbol{\lambda} \geq \mathbf{0}$. Some method is needed, to find systematically whether the critical point $\mathbf{c}$ is a maximum, minimum, or saddlepoint of (3.4.1), without assuming convexity.

Example

$$\operatorname*{Minimize}_{(x,\, y)\, \in\, \mathbb{R}^2} f(x, y) = \tfrac{1}{3}x^3 - y^2, \text{ subject to } \tfrac{1}{2}x^2 + y^2 \leq 1. \quad (3.5.1)$$

The Kuhn–Tucker conditions were stated for this problem, in the example in Section 3.4, and the Kuhn–Tucker points were tabulated there. Now rewrite the inequality constraint as $\frac{1}{2}x^2+y^2+p = 1$, $p \geq 0$. Define a *modified* Lagrangian

$$\begin{aligned} L^*(x, y; \lambda; p) &= \tfrac{1}{3}x^3 - y^2 + \lambda(\tfrac{1}{2}x^2 + y^2 - 1 + p) \qquad (3.5.2) \\ &= \tfrac{1}{2}\lambda x^2 + \tfrac{1}{3}x^3 + (\lambda - 1)y^2 + \lambda p - \lambda. \end{aligned}$$

From the Kuhn–Tucker conditions, L^* has zero derivative (with respect to (x, y)) at each Kuhn–Tucker point; hence L^* has no linear terms in x and y. Consider now a Kuhn–Tucker point $(\bar{x}, \bar{y})$, and a small perturbation of (x, y) from $(\bar{x}, \bar{y})$. Since

$$f(x, y) - f(\bar{x}, \bar{y}) = L^*(x, y; \lambda; p) - L^*(\bar{x}, \bar{y}; \lambda; \bar{p}), \quad (3.5.3)$$

where $\bar{p} = 1 - (\frac{1}{2}\bar{x}^2 + \bar{y}^2)$, the change in L^* describes the nature of the Kuhn–Tucker point. (Note that $\bar{p} = 0$ for an active constraint.)

Set $(x, y) = (0, 1) + (\xi, \eta)$; this gives $L^* = -1 + \frac{1}{2}\xi^2 + \frac{1}{3}\xi^3 + p$. The quadratic form $\frac{1}{2}\xi^2$ in L^* is here *degenerate* (it has a zero eigenvalue). In general, higher-order terms (here the cubic $\frac{1}{3}\xi^3$) are not negligible (when $|\xi|$ and $|\eta|$ are small enough) in comparison with a *degenerate* quadratic form. However, in this instance, $\frac{1}{3}\xi^3$ is negligible, in comparison with $\frac{1}{2}\xi^2$, for $|\xi|$ small enough. So the behaviour of the critical point is sufficiently described by the function $-1+\frac{1}{2}\xi^2+p$. Since $p \geq 0$ and $\frac{1}{2}\xi^2 \geq 0$, this critical point is a *minimum*. Similarly $(0, -1)$ is a *minimum*.

If $(x, y) = (-1+\xi, 2^{-1/2}+\eta)$, then $L^* = -\frac{5}{6}-\frac{1}{2}\xi^2+\frac{1}{3}\xi^3+p$. Here the quadratic form $-\frac{1}{2}\xi^2$ is degenerate; however, the cubic term is negligible, in comparison with it, when $|\xi|$ is small enough. So it suffices to consider $-\frac{5}{6}-\frac{1}{2}\xi^2+p$. The constraint $\frac{1}{2}(x^2+y^2)+p = 1$ now gives

$$\tfrac{1}{2}(1-2\xi+\xi^2)+(\tfrac{1}{2}+2^{1/2}\eta+\eta^2)+p = 1,$$

hence $-\xi+2^{1/2}\eta+\frac{1}{2}\xi^2+\eta^2+p = 0$. This may be solved for η, giving $\xi = 2^{-1/2}\eta-2^{-1/2}p+$higher-order terms, and this substituted into L^*, giving $L^* = -\frac{5}{6}-\frac{1}{2}\xi^2+p+$higher-order terms. (The form of L^* is here unaltered by the substitution, since this L^* happened not to contain η.) So we have both positive (p) and negative ($-\frac{1}{2}\xi^2$) terms, hence $(-1, 2^{-1/2})$ is a *saddlepoint*. Similarly $(-1, -2^{-1/2})$ is a saddlepoint.

At $(0, 0)$, the inequality constraint is *inactive* ($p = 1$), as it is *not* appropriate to consider p as small. However, the question now reduces to the *unconstrained* stationary point $(0, 0)$ of $\frac{1}{3}x^3-y^2$, and this is a *saddlepoint*.

If $(x, y) = (2^{1/2}+\xi, 0+\eta)$, then $L^* = 2^{3/2}/3+2^{-1/2}\xi^2+\frac{1}{3}\xi^3-(1+2^{1/2})\eta^2-2^{1/2}p$. The quadratic form $2^{-1/2}\xi^2-(1+2^{1/2})\eta^2$ is nondegenerate, so $\frac{1}{3}\xi^3$ may be neglected in L^*. The constraint gives $2^{1/2}\xi+p+\frac{1}{2}\xi^2+\eta^2 = 0$. Since the quadratic form in L^* is nondegenerate, it suffices to consider only the linear terms (in ξ and η) from the constraint, thus $2^{1/2}\xi+p \approx 0$. Substituting $\xi \approx -2^{-1/2}p$ into L^* then gives $L^* \approx 2^{3/2}/3-(1+2^{1/2})\eta^2-2^{1/2}p(1-\frac{1}{4}p)$, where the terms neglected are of higher order. Since $-(1+2^{1/2})\eta^2 < 0$ and $-2^{1/2}p(1-\frac{1}{4}p) < 0$, for sufficiently small $p \geq 0$, the point $(2^{1/2}, 0)$ is a *maximum*.

If $(x, y) = (-2^{1/2}+\xi, 0+\eta)$, then $L^* = -2^{3/2}/3-2^{-1/2}\xi^2+(2^{1/2}-1)\eta^2+\frac{1}{3}\xi^3+2^{1/2}p$. The quadratic form in L^* is nondegenerate; the constraint, linearized as above, gives $\xi \approx 2^{-1/2}p$, where $p \geq 0$. Substitution into L^* gives, neglecting higher-order terms, $L^* \approx -2^{3/2}/3+(2^{1/2}-1)\eta^2+2^{1/2}p(1-\frac{1}{2}p)$, hence a *minimum*.

Of course, as in these simple examples, tabulation of $f(\bar{x}, \bar{y})$ for each Kuhn–Tucker point $(\bar{x}, \bar{y})$ will find which are global maxima and minima. However, the Lagrangian methods described here will find the nature of a Kuhn–Tucker point, even if all the others have not been calculated, as may well be the case for a more complicated problem, where Kuhn–Tucker points have to be found by numerical approximation methods.

Suppose now that $\mathbf{c}$ is a Kuhn–Tucker point for (3.4.1). To simplify notation, omit the inactive (at $\mathbf{c}$) constraints from $\mathbf{g}$, and rewrite the Kuhn–Tucker conditions as $f'(\mathbf{c})+\sigma^{\mathrm{T}}\mathbf{k}'(\mathbf{c}) = \mathbf{0}$, where the rows of $\mathbf{k}$ consist of the rows of $\mathbf{h}$, and those rows of $\mathbf{g}$ which correspond to active constraints. The sign requirements on σ are then $\sigma_i \geq 0$ $(i = s+1, \ldots, s+r)$, and the constraints take the form $k_i(\mathbf{z}) = 0$ $(i = 1, 2, \ldots, s)$, $k_i(\mathbf{z}) \leq 0$ $(i = s+1, \ldots, s+r)$. As before, assume that $\mathbf{k}$ is continuously differentiable, and that the gradients $k_i'(\mathbf{c})$ are linearly independent.

Writing the constraints as $\mathbf{k}(\mathbf{z})+\mathbf{p} = \mathbf{0}$, where $p_i = 0$ $(i = 1, 2, \ldots, s)$, and $p_i \geq 0$ $(i = s+1, \ldots, s+r)$, the implicit function theorem gives a solution $\mathbf{z} = \mathbf{c}+\mathbf{u}$, thus $\mathbf{k}(\mathbf{c}+\mathbf{u})+\mathbf{p} = \mathbf{0}$, valid when $\|\mathbf{u}\|$ and $\|\mathbf{p}\|$ are small enough. By reordering columns, $\mathbf{k}'(\mathbf{c})$ may be partitioned as $[A \quad B]$, where A is an invertible submatrix, and correspondingly $\mathbf{u}^{\mathrm{T}} = [\mathbf{v}^{\mathrm{T}} \quad \mathbf{w}^{\mathrm{T}}]$. If higher-order terms are neglected, then $A\mathbf{v}+B\mathbf{w}+\mathbf{p} \approx \mathbf{0}$, hence $\mathbf{v} = -A^{-1}B\mathbf{w}-A^{-1}\mathbf{p}$. The implicit function theorem gives that $\mathbf{u} = M\mathbf{w}+N\mathbf{t}+o(\|\mathbf{w}\|+\|\mathbf{t}\|)$, where

$$M = \begin{bmatrix} -A^{-1}B \\ I \end{bmatrix}, \; \mathbf{t}^{\mathrm{T}} = [p_{s+1}, \ldots, p_{s+r}], \; N\mathbf{t} = \begin{bmatrix} -A^{-1} \\ 0 \end{bmatrix}\mathbf{p}. \tag{3.5.4}$$

The *modified Lagrangian* is $L^*(\mathbf{z}; \sigma, \mathbf{t}) = f(\mathbf{z})+\sigma^{\mathrm{T}}\mathbf{k}(\mathbf{z})+\sigma^{\mathrm{T}}\mathbf{t}$. Since $f'(\mathbf{z})-f(\mathbf{c}) = L^*(\mathbf{z}; \sigma, \mathbf{t})-L^*(\mathbf{c}; \sigma, \mathbf{t})$ when $\mathbf{k}(\mathbf{z})+\mathbf{p} = \mathbf{0}$, the nature of the critical point $\mathbf{c}$ depends on the behaviour of $L^*(\mathbf{z}; \sigma, \mathbf{t})$ for small $\|\mathbf{z}-\mathbf{c}\|$.

Suppose now that f and $\mathbf{k}$ are twice differentiable, and that the quadratic part of L^* is nondegenerate, say with matrix $\frac{1}{2}H$. Then

$$\begin{aligned} L^*(\mathbf{c}+\mathbf{u}; \sigma, \mathbf{t})-L^*(\mathbf{c}; \sigma, \mathbf{t}) &= \tfrac{1}{2}(M\mathbf{w}+N\mathbf{t})^{\mathrm{T}}H(M\mathbf{w}+N\mathbf{t})+\sigma^{\mathrm{T}}t \\ &\quad +\text{higher-order terms} \\ &= \tfrac{1}{2}\mathbf{w}^{\mathrm{T}}(M^{\mathrm{T}}HM)\mathbf{w}+\mathbf{t}^{\mathrm{T}}(\sigma^{\mathrm{T}}+N^{\mathrm{T}}HM\mathbf{w}+\tfrac{1}{2}N^{\mathrm{T}}HN\mathbf{t}) \\ &\quad +\text{higher-order terms}. \end{aligned} \tag{3.5.5}$$

If both negative and positive σ_i occur, then Equation (3.5.5) shows that $\mathbf{c}$ is a saddlepoint, noting that all $t_i \geq 0$. Suppose now that all

$\sigma_i \geq 0$; denote $I = \{i : \sigma_i = 0\}$. If $i \notin I$, then $\sigma_i > 0$, so the coefficient of t_i in (3.5.5) is positive, when $\|\mathbf{w}\|$ and $\|\mathbf{t}\|$ are small enough. If the terms in t_i for $i \notin I$ are deleted from Equation (3.5.5), what remains is a quadratic form, say $\mathbf{y}^{\mathrm{T}}p\mathbf{y}$, where $\mathbf{y}$ consists of $\mathbf{w}$, with the vector $\mathbf{q}$ of t_i $(i \in I)$ adjoined. Consequently, $\mathbf{c}$ is a *minimum* of Problem (3.4.1) if all $t_i \geq 0$, and if also the minimum value α of $\mathbf{y}^{\mathrm{T}}P\mathbf{y}$, subject to $\mathbf{y}^{\mathrm{T}}\mathbf{y} = 1$ and $\mathbf{q} \geq \mathbf{0}$, is positive. (Denote also by β the maximum value of this problem.) A necessary Lagrangian condition for this minimum to occur at $\mathbf{y} = \bar{\mathbf{y}}$ is $\bar{\mathbf{y}}^{\mathrm{T}}P = \rho\bar{\mathbf{y}}^{\mathrm{T}} + \pi^{\mathrm{T}}$, where the Lagrange multipliers π_i satisfy $\pi_i \geq 0$ for each i, and $\pi_i = 0$ for each inactive constraint. Denote $J = \{i : \pi_i > 0\}$; denote by J' the set of remaining indices i. Since $\pi_i > 0$ implies $\bar{y}_i = 0$, the Lagrangian condition gives

$$\textstyle\sum_{j \in J'} P_{ij}y_j - \rho y_j = 0 \text{ for each } i \in J'; \tag{3.5.6}$$

$$\textstyle\sum_{j \in J'} P_{ij}y_j = \pi_i > 0 \text{ for each } i \in J. \tag{3.5.7}$$

The following criterion is thus obtained, assuming that $\mathbf{g}'(\mathbf{c})$ has full rank, inactive constraints are omitted, and the Lagrangian has nondegenerate quadratic form:

If all $\sigma_i \geq 0$, all $\pi_i \geq 0$, and $\alpha > 0$, then $\mathbf{c}$ is a minimum for (3.4.1).
If all $\sigma_i \leq 0$, all $\pi_i \leq 0$, and $\beta < 0$, then $\mathbf{c}$ is a maximum.
If there are both positive and negative σ_i; or if $\alpha < 0 < \beta$; or if there are both positive and negative π_i, then $\mathbf{c}$ is a saddlepoint.

Observe that ρ is the minimum eigenvalue of a submatrix of P, described by Equation (3.5.6); and the corresponding eigenvector must satisfy the positivity condition (3.5.7). The latter determines J. In actual computation, a number of submatrices would have to be examined. If L^* has degenerate quadratic form, or if $\alpha = 0$ or $\beta = 0$, the above criterion fails, and higher-order terms would have to be examined.

The Kuhn–Tucker conditions have been obtained on the hypothesis that the gradients of the active constraints (at the critical point) are linearly independent. It is well known that this hypothesis can be replaced by some weaker assumptions; but it cannot be omitted altogether, as the following example shows.

Example

$$\underset{x \in \mathbb{R}}{\text{Minimize}}\ f(x) = -x \text{ subject to } g(x) \leq 0, \tag{3.5.8}$$

where (as in example (b) of Section 3.4) $g(x) = x^2$ for $x \geq 0$, $g(x) = 0$ when $x = 0$. Since $g(x) \leq 0$ if and only if $x \leq 0$, the minimum is attained at $x = 0$. Suppose, if possible, that $f'(0) + \lambda g'(0) = 0$ holds for some λ; then $-1+\lambda \cdot 0 = 0$, a contradiction. So the Kuhn–Tucker conditions do *not* hold for (3.5.8). Here there is only one active constraint, $g(x) \leq 0$; but since $g'(0) = 0$, the linear independence is not fulfilled (thus $\beta g'(0) = 0$ does not imply that $\beta = 0$.)

Exercise 3.5.1 Use the methods of Section 3.5 to discuss the nature of the critical points of the problem in Exercise 3.4.2.

FURTHER READING

Bazaraa, M.S. and Shetty, C.M. (1976), *Foundations of Optimization*, Springer-Verlag, Berlin. (Vol. 122 of *Lecture Notes in Economics and Mathematical Systems*). [For more general versions of the Kuhn–Tucker theorem.]

Ben-Israel, A., Ben-Tal, A. and Zlobec, S. (1976), Optimality conditions in convex programming, *IX International Symposium on Mathematical Programming* (Budapest, 1976), A. Prekopa (ed.), North-Holland, Amsterdam (1979), pp. 177–92. [For the last example in Section 3.5.]

Craven, B.D. (1978), *Mathematical Programming and Control Theory*, Chapman and Hall, London. [For more general constrained minimization theory, no longer restricted to finite dimensions.]

Craven, B.D. (1979), On constrained maxima and minima, *Austral. Math. Soc. Gazette*, **6** (2), 46–50. [For the discrimination of constrained stationary points.]

Hancock, H. (1917), *Theory of Maxima and Minima* (reprinted in 1960 by Dover, New York). [A classic account.]

Kuhn, H.W. and Tucker, A.W. (1951), Nonlinear programming, in *Proceedings of the Second Berkeley Symposium on Mathematical Statistics and Probability*, J. Neyman (ed.), University of California Press, Berkeley, pp. 481–92. [For the original version of the Kuhn–Tucker theorem.]

4. Integrating functions of several variables

4.1 BASIC IDEAS OF INTEGRATION

Consider first an integral, $\int_a^b f(x)\,\mathrm{d}x$, of a real function f over an interval in the real line. The definition and properties of this familiar integral will later be extended to integrals over areas, volumes, curves, and surfaces. An *interval* $\langle\alpha, \beta\rangle$ in $\mathbb{R}$ consists of the points x with $\alpha < x < \beta$, together with none, one, or both of the endpoints α, β. A *step-function* is a real function which takes only finitely many values, each on an interval. Consider the step-function h, defined on a closed interval $I = [a, b]$ (where $a < b$), taking value c_i on interval I_i $(i = 1, 2, \ldots, r)$, where the intervals I_i are non-overlapping, and their union is I. Then

$$\int_a^b h(x)\,\mathrm{d}x \equiv \int_I h(x)\,\mathrm{d}x = \sum_{i=1}^{r} c_i p(I_i), \tag{4.1.1}$$

where $p(I_i)$ denotes the length of I_i; if $I_i = \langle\alpha_i, \beta_i\rangle$, with $\alpha_i < \beta_i$, then $p(I_i) = \beta_i - \alpha_i$.

We now modify this customary definition, supposing now that the interval $[a, b]$ is traversed in a definite direction, either from a to b (in which case the integral has the value already given), or instead from b to a (when each $p(I_i)$ is given a negative sign). We thus define an *oriented integral* by Equation (4.1.1), defining (oriented) *length* $p(I_i)$ of $I_i = \langle \alpha_i, \beta_i \rangle$ (where $\alpha_i < \beta_i$) as either $\beta_i - \alpha_i$ (when traversing from a to b), or as $\alpha_i - \beta_i$ (when traversing from b to a. In either case, length is an *additive* function of intervals – if interval J is the union of two nonoverlapping intervals J' and J'', then

$$p(J) = p(J') + p(J''). \tag{4.1.2}$$

If, instead, J' and J'' are two intervals with a positive distance between them, it is convenient to define $p(J' \cup J'')$ as $p(J') + p(J'')$, so that Equation (4.1.2) extends to this case. Observe also, that since a, b is traversed in one definite direction, that either all $p(I_i) \leq 0$, or all $p(I_i) \geq 0$. Hence also

$$\sum |p(I_i)| = |p(I)| \tag{4.1.3}$$

when I is the union of the non-overlapping intervals I_i.

Now write, for brevity, $\int_I h$ for $\int_I h(x)\,dx$. From the definition (4.1.1), and (4.1.2), the integral (for a step-function) has the following properties:

Additivity

$$\int_{I \cup J} h = \int_I h + \int_J h \tag{4.1.4}$$

if I and J are non-overlapping intervals.

Linearity If h and k are step-functions, and λ and μ are constants, then

$$\int_I (\lambda h + \mu k) = \lambda \int_I h + \mu \int_I k. \tag{4.1.5}$$

There also holds

$$\left|\int_I h\right| \leq \sup_{x \in I} |h(x)| \cdot |p(I)|. \tag{4.1.6}$$

Now let f be a bounded continuous function on the interval I. A theorem of analysis states that f can be uniformly approximated on I by step-functions (see Fig. 4.1). Thus, if $\varepsilon > 0$, there is a step-function h for which $|f(x) - h(x)| < \varepsilon$ for all $x \in I$. Set $\varepsilon = 1, \frac{1}{2}, \frac{1}{3}, \ldots, \frac{1}{n}, \ldots$ to generate a corresponding sequence $h_1, h_2, \ldots, h_n, \ldots$ of step-functions. If $n < q$ then

$$\left|\int_I h_n - \int_I h_q\right| = \left|\int_I (h_n - h_q)\right| \leq \sup_{x \in I} |h_n(x) - h_q(x)| \cdot |p(I)|$$

$$< 2n^{-1}|p(I)| \to 0 \text{ as } n \to \infty, \tag{4.1.7}$$

using Equations (4.1.3), (4.1.5), (4.1.6). Since $\mathbb{R}$ is complete, there exists $\lim_{n\to\infty}\int_I h_n$, and this is taken to define $\int_I f$. The limit does not depend on the choice of sequence, since if $k_1, k_2, \ldots$ is another such sequence, then the same limit is obtained, as in (4.1.7), for the interlaced sequence $h_1, k_1, h_2, k_2, \ldots, h_n, k_n, \ldots$. Also, by taking limits of step-functions, the properties (4.1.4), (4.1.5) and 4.1.6) remain valid when the step-functions h and k are replaced by bounded continuous functions.

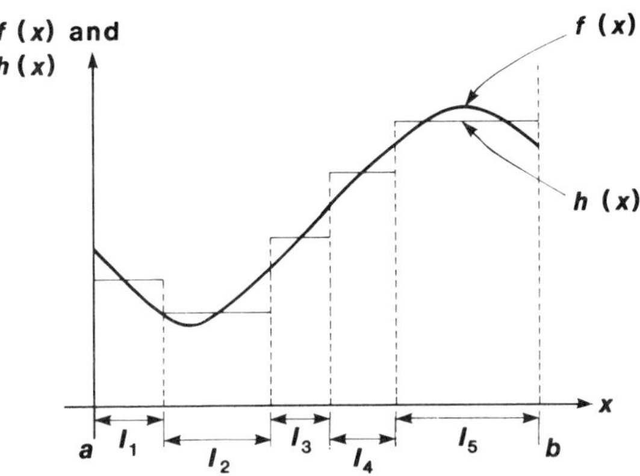

Figure 4.1 Approximation of a continuous function by a step-function

(The corresponding *nonoriented* integral (with $p(\cdot) \geq 0$ always) will occasionally be denoted by $\int_I f(x)|dx|$.)

Example

Let $\varphi : [a, b] \to \mathbb{R}$ be a strictly increasing $(x < x' \Rightarrow \varphi(x) < \varphi(x'))$ function, having a continuous derivative. Choose $\varepsilon > 0$. By a theorem of analysis, there is $\delta(\varepsilon) > 0$ such that $\varphi'(x)$ varies by less than ε, when x runs over any interval of length less than $\delta(\varepsilon)$. Approximate $\varphi'(\cdot)$ on $I = [a, b]$ by a step-function, having each $I_i = \langle x_i, x_{i+1}\rangle$ with length less than $\delta(\varepsilon)$, and $c_i = \varphi'(\xi_i)$ where, by the mean-value theorem, $\varphi(x_{i+1}) - \varphi(x_i) = \varphi'(\xi_i)(x_{i+1} - x_i)$ for some ξ_i in (x_i, x_{i+1}). Then the integral of this step-function equals

$$\sum_i \varphi'(\xi_i)(x_{i+1} - x_i) = \sum_i [\varphi(x_{i+1}) - \varphi(x_i)] = \varphi(b) - \varphi(a).$$

Hence

$$\int_a^b \varphi'(x)\,dx = \varphi(b) - \varphi(a). \tag{4.1.8}$$

Consider now a change of variable, given by $x = \varphi(y)$. Assume that the function φ is continuously differentiable and one-to-one; this means that, as x runs through interval I (in its chosen direction), y runs through an interval J (thus defining a direction for J). Here $I = \varphi(J) \equiv \{\varphi(y) : y \in J\}$; note that φ or $-\varphi$ must be strictly increasing. Let f be a bounded continuous function on I. Then $f(\varphi(\cdot))$ is bounded continuous on J; let $\tilde{h}$ be a step-function approximation to $f(\varphi(\cdot))$, which takes constant value c_i on interval J_i. Then

$$\begin{aligned}\int_J \tilde{h}(y)\varphi'(y)\,\mathrm{d}y &= \sum_i \int_{J_i} c_i\varphi'(y)\,\mathrm{d}y \qquad \text{since the integral is additive}\\ &= \sum_i c_i\varphi(J_i) \qquad \text{by Equation (4.1.8).}\\ &= \int_I h(x)\,\mathrm{d}x \end{aligned} \tag{4.1.9}$$

where h is the step-function on I, taking constant value c_i on interval $\varphi(J_i)$. Now h may be chosen to make $\int_I h(x)\,\mathrm{d}x$ arbitrarily close to $\int_I f(x)\,\mathrm{d}x$, and also $|\tilde{h}(y) - f(\varphi(y))| < \varepsilon$ for all $y \in J$, whence, from Equation (4.1.5),

$$\int_J \tilde{h}(y)\varphi'(y)\,\mathrm{d}y - \int_J f(\varphi(y))\varphi'(y)\,\mathrm{d}y| \leq \varepsilon \cdot \sup_{y \in J} |\varphi'(y)| \cdot |p(J)|.$$

This, with Equation (4.1.9), gives the change-of-variable formula

$$\int_{\varphi(J)} f(x)\,\mathrm{d}x = \int_J f(\varphi(y))\varphi'(y)\,\mathrm{d}y. \tag{4.1.10}$$

Observe that Equation (4.1.10) is valid for *oriented* integrals.

Example

$$\int_5^{10} x^2\,\mathrm{d}x = \int_2^3 (1+y^2)^2\, 2y\,\mathrm{d}y$$

by the change of variable $x = \varphi(y) \equiv 1+y^2$.

Example

Using the change of variable $x = \varphi(y) \equiv y^{-1}$,

$$\int_2^3 x^{-2}\,\mathrm{d}x = \int_{1/2}^{1/3} y^2(-y^{-2})\,\mathrm{d}y = -\int_{1/3}^{1/2} (-1)\,\mathrm{d}y,$$

the last step following because the integral is oriented. The integrals on left and right each evaluate to $\frac{1}{2} - \frac{1}{3} = \frac{1}{6}$.

Exercise 4.1.1 Let the interval I be the union of the non-overlapping intervals $I_1, I_2, \ldots, I_n$ (for example, $I_1 = [0, 1]$, $I_2 = (1, 2]$, $I_3 = (2, 3], \ldots, I_n = (n-1, n]$; thus $I = [0, n]$). Let f be a continuous function on I. Show that

$$\int_I f = \sum_{j=1}^{n} \int_{I_j} f.$$

Exercise 4.1.2 Use the change of variable $x = \sin\theta$ to evaluate

$$\int_0^{1/2} (1-x^2)^{-1/2}\, dx.$$

Exercise 4.1.3 What is wrong with the argument:

$$\int_{-1}^{1} (1+x^2)^{-1}\, dx = \int_{-1}^{1} (1+y^{-2})^{-1}(-y^{-2})\, dy \qquad \text{substituting } x = 1/y$$

$$= -\int_{-1}^{1} (1+y^2)^{-1}\, dy?$$

Exercise 4.1.4 For a continuous function f, show that

$$\int_x^{x+h} f = f(x)h + o(h) \text{ as } h \to 0.$$

(*Hint*: Consider $\int_x^{x+h} [f(t) - f(x)]\, dt$. Now denote $F(x) = \int_a^x f(t)\, dt$. Deduce that the derivative $F'(x) = f(x)$. Note that this assumes f is continuous.)

4.2 DOUBLE INTEGRALS

Consider now the integral of a continuous function $f : \mathbb{R}^2 \to \mathbb{R}$, of two real variables, over a region G in $\mathbb{R}^2$. The previous definitions extend, as follows, to this case. An *interval* in $\mathbb{R}^2$ shall mean any set

$$\{(x, y) \in \mathbb{R}^2 : x \in \langle\alpha, \beta\rangle,\ y \in \langle\gamma, \delta\rangle\}, \tag{4.2.1}$$

thus any product of intervals in $\mathbb{R}$. A step-function $h : \mathbb{R}^2 \to \mathbb{R}$ is a function which takes finitely many values, each on an interval. Suppose that h takes value c_i on interval I_i, for $i = 1, 2, \ldots, n$. Let G be a bounded open set in $\mathbb{R}^2$. The integral of h over G is now defined as

$$\int\int_G h(x, y)\, dx\, dy = \sum_{i=1}^{n} c_i p(I_i \cap G), \tag{4.2.2}$$

where p now denotes *area* in $\mathbb{R}^2$. Assume, for the present, that area is defined, and additive, for the sets $I_i \cap G$; this will require some restriction on the boundary of G (which must not be too complicated). Assuming this, properties (4.1.3), (4.1.4) and (4.1.5) follow, as for integrals on $\mathbb{R}$. Now G, being bounded, may be enclosed in a square region A (see Fig. 4.2); and f, being bounded and continuous on A, may be approximated, uniformly within r^{-1} on A, by a step-function h_r. Then define

$$\int\int_G f(x, y)\,dx\,dy = \lim_{r \to \infty} \int\int_G h_r(x, y)\,dx\,dy. \qquad (4.2.3)$$

The existence and uniqueness of (4.2.3) are proved, similarly to the proof of (4.1.6) for a function of one variable, as follows also the additive and linear properties of the integral (4.2.3).

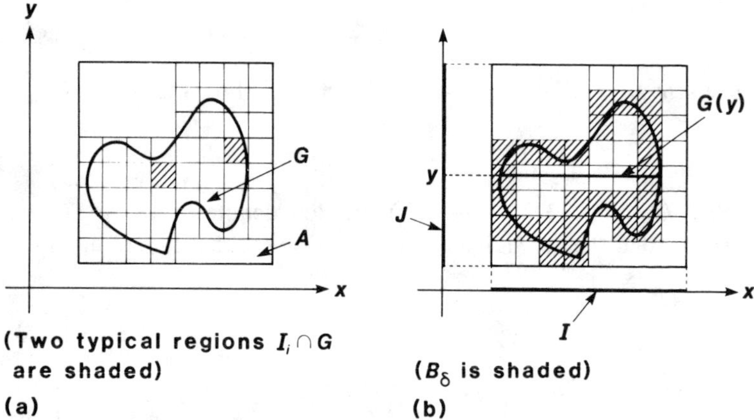

Figure 4.2 Integrating over a plane region

The boundary, ∂G, of G will be called *regular* if, for each $\delta > 0$, ∂G can be covered by a set B_δ of at most c/δ squares, each of side δ (and with sides parallel to the axes); the constant c depends on ∂G, but not on δ. It can be shown that ∂G is regular exactly when ∂G has finite length. Note also that ∂G can have corners (as in Fig. 4.2). Assume that the area of an interval in $\mathbb{R}^2$ is the product of its length and width. Let $H_\delta = G \backslash B_\delta$ (G with all points of B_δ deleted); and define *area* (H_δ) as the sum of the areas of the intervals comprising H_δ. Since *area* $(H_\delta) \leq$ *area* (Q), and *area*(H_δ) increases as $\delta \downarrow 0$, *area* (G) may be defined uniquely as $\lim_{\delta \downarrow 0}$ *area*(H_δ).

To prove that this area is *additive*, suppose $G = U \cup V$ where U and V have regular boundaries and do not overlap. Then all the boundaries of G, U, V may be covered by a union S_δ of squares, with total *area* $\leq (k/\delta)\delta^2$, where k is constant. Then $|area\ (G\backslash S_\delta) - area\ (U\backslash S_\delta) - area\ (V\backslash S_\delta)| \leq k\delta$. Letting $\delta \downarrow 0$, $area\ (G) - area\ (U) - area\ (V) = 0$, which proves the additivity.

Now denote by $G(y)$ the intersection of G with a line, parallel to the x-axis, at ordinate y. Assume that $Q = I \times J$.

Theorem 4.1 (Fubini theorem for continuous integrand)
Let G be a bounded open set in $\mathbb{R}^2$, having regular boundary; let $f: \mathbb{R}^2 \to \mathbb{R}$ be continuous. Then

$$\int\int_G f(x, y)\,\mathrm{d}x\,\mathrm{d}y = \int_J\left(\int_{G(y)} f(x, y)\,\mathrm{d}x\right)\mathrm{d}y. \tag{4.2.4}$$

Remark An integral with respect to area ('double integral') is thus equated to a 'repeated integral' (in which each integration is with respect to one variable).

Proof Choose $\varepsilon > 0$. There is a step-function h which approximates f, uniformly on A, within ε. For sufficiently small δ, h can be arranged to be constant on the interior of each square (with sides parallel to the axes) of side δ, subdividing $A \cap G$. Denote M = maximum $|h(x, y)|$, and $H \equiv H_\delta = G\backslash B_\delta$. Then

$$\int\int_H h(x, y)\,\mathrm{d}x\,\mathrm{d}y = \int_J\left(\int_{H(y)} h(x, y)\,\mathrm{d}x\right)\mathrm{d}y, \tag{4.2.5}$$

since each side of Equation (4.2.5) is the sum, over the finitely many squares I_i comprising H, of terms $h_i\delta^2$, where h_i is the value of h on I_i. From Equation (4.1.6),

$$\left|\int\int_G h(x, y)\,\mathrm{d}x\,\mathrm{d}y - \int\int_H h(x, y)\,\mathrm{d}x\,\mathrm{d}y\right| \leq M|p(B)| \leq M(c/\delta)\delta^2 = Mc\delta.$$

Also

$$\begin{aligned}
&\left|\int_J\left(\int_{G(y)} h(x, y)\,\mathrm{d}x\right)\mathrm{d}y - \int_J\left(\int_{H(y)} h(x, y)\,\mathrm{d}x\right)\mathrm{d}y\right| \\
&\quad = \left|\int_J\left(\int_{G(y)\backslash H(y)} h(x, y)\,\mathrm{d}x\right)\mathrm{d}y\right| \\
&\quad \leq \int_J\left(\int_{G(y)\backslash H(y)} |h(x, y)||\mathrm{d}x|\right)|\mathrm{d}y| \leq \int_J\left(\int_{B_\delta(y)} M|\mathrm{d}x|\right)|\mathrm{d}y| \\
&\quad = \int\int_{B_\delta(y)} M|\mathrm{d}x||\mathrm{d}y| \qquad \text{by Equation (4.2.5)} \\
&\quad \leq Mc\delta \qquad \text{as in Equation (4.1.6).}
\end{aligned}$$

Hence, letting $\delta \to 0$, Equation (4.2.4) holds, with h replacing f. But the integrals with f and with h differ arbitrarily little, by choosing ε sufficiently small. Hence Equation (4.2.4) holds with integrand f. □

Define $F(x, y) = f(x, y)$ when $(x, y) \in G$; $F(x, y) = 0$ when $(x, y) \notin G$. Then (4.2.4) may be rewritten as

$$\int\int_Q F(x, y)\,\mathrm{d}x\,\mathrm{d}y = \int_J\left(\int_I F(x, y)\,\mathrm{d}x\right)\mathrm{d}y. \tag{4.2.6}$$

In order to obtain a change-of-variable theorem for a double integral, consider a continuously differentiable mapping $\begin{bmatrix} x \\ y \end{bmatrix} = \varphi\left(\begin{bmatrix} v \\ u \end{bmatrix}\right)$, defined by $x = \rho(u, v)$, $y = \sigma(u, v)$. Assume that σ_v does not vanish; then the implicit function theorem solves $y = \sigma(u, v)$ for $v = \tau(y, u)$. Applying the chain rule to the identity $y = \sigma(u, \tau(y, u))$ gives $0 = \sigma_u + \sigma_v \tau_u$, from which $\tau_u = -\sigma_v^{-1}\sigma_u$. Substituting $v = \tau(y, u)$ into $\rho(u, v)$ gives $x = \theta(u, y) \equiv \sigma(u, \tau(y, u))$. From the chain rule, $\theta_u = \rho_u + \rho_v \tau_u = \rho_u - \rho_v \sigma_v^{-1}\sigma_u$. The mapping φ thus decomposes into two successive mappings: (a) $x = \theta(u, y)$, and (b) $y = \sigma(u, v)$, in each of which only one of the variables is transformed. Now the Fréchet derivative of φ is

$$\varphi'\left(\begin{bmatrix} x \\ y \end{bmatrix}\right) = \begin{bmatrix} \rho_u & \rho_v \\ \sigma_u & \sigma_v \end{bmatrix} \tag{4.2.7}$$

and this matrix has determinant

$$\Delta = \rho_u \sigma_v - \sigma_u \rho_v = \sigma_v[\rho_u - \rho_v \sigma_v^{-1} \rho_u]. \tag{4.2.8}$$

Theorem 4.2 (Change of variable in a double integral)
Let $f : \mathbb{R}^2 \to \mathbb{R}$ be continuous; let $U \subset \mathbb{R}^2$ be a bounded open set, with regular boundary; let $\varphi : U \to \mathbb{R}^2$ be a continuously differentiable mapping, which maps U one-to-one onto a bounded open set G, having regular boundary. Then

$$\int\int_G f(x, y)\,\mathrm{d}x\,\mathrm{d}y = \int\int_U (f \circ \varphi)(u, v)\,\det \varphi'(u, v)\,\mathrm{d}u\,\mathrm{d}v, \tag{4.2.9}$$

where $\varphi'(u, v)$ denotes the Fréchet derivative of φ, det means determinant, and the integrals are oriented.

Remark For conventional (non-oriented) integrals, replace det $\varphi'(u, v)$ by its absolute value. The formula (4.2.9) remains true, without the assumptions about boundaries; but it then needs a more complicated definition of integral. We shall prove the theorem under the additional assumption that σ_v does not vanish on U (or that ρ_u does not vanish). Observe that if both vanish on some ball, then $\Delta = 0$, and hence ρ and σ are functionally dependent (by Section 2.6), thus φ is not one-to-one. However, φ may vanish at isolated points.

Proof Assume that σ_v does not vanish on U; then the equation $y = \sigma(u, v)$ can be solved locally for $v = \tau(y, u)$. For simplicity, assume that this solution holds globally (over the whole region U); if not, divide U into smaller regions, to which the implicit function theorem applies, and add the corresponding integrals. Define $f(x, y) = 0$ for $(x, y) \notin G$. Then

$$\int\int_G f(x, y)\,\mathrm{d}x\,\mathrm{d}y = \int\int_{\mathbb{R}^2} f(x, y)\,\mathrm{d}x\,\mathrm{d}y = \int_{\mathbb{R}}\left(\int_{\mathbb{R}} f(x, y)\,\mathrm{d}x\right)\mathrm{d}y$$

by Fubini's theorem

$$= \int_{\mathbb{R}}\left(\int_{\mathbb{R}} f(\theta(u, y), y)\theta_u(u, y)\,\mathrm{d}u\right)\mathrm{d}y$$

by the change of variable $x = \theta(u, y)$ in the inner integral

$$= \int_{\mathbb{R}}\left(\int_{\mathbb{R}} f(\theta(u, y)\theta_u(u, y)\,\mathrm{d}y\right)\mathrm{d}u$$

by two applications of Fubini's theorem, to interchange the order of integration

$$= \int_{\mathbb{R}}\left(\int_{\mathbb{R}} (f \circ \varphi)(u, v)\theta_u(u, \sigma(u, v))\sigma_v(u, v)\,\mathrm{d}v\right)\mathrm{d}u$$

by the change of variable $y = \sigma(u, v)$ in the inner integral

$$= \int\int_U (f \circ \varphi)(u, v) \det \varphi'(u, v)\,\mathrm{d}u\,\mathrm{d}v$$

by Equation (4.2.8). □

Example
The change of variable φ given by $x = u \cos v, y = u \sin v$, has Fréchet derivative

$$\begin{bmatrix} \cos v, & \sin v \\ -u \sin v, & u \cos v \end{bmatrix},$$

whose determinant is u. Hence

$$\int\int_{\varphi(U)} f(x, y)\,\mathrm{d}x\,\mathrm{d}y = \int\int_U f(u \cos v, u \sin v)u\,\mathrm{d}u\,\mathrm{d}v. \quad (4.2.10)$$

Integrals with respect to *volume* may be similarly constructed. This leads to *triple*, instead of double integrals, however with a similar theory. The order of integration can be permuted, assuming a continuous integrand, and a regular boundary. Here, $G \subset \mathbb{R}^3$, and its boundary ∂G is *regular* if, for each $\delta > 0$, ∂G can be covered by at most c/δ^2 cubes, each of side δ (and with sides parallel to the axes). This property corresponds to ∂G having finite surface area (with a suitable definition).

Example
Denote by G the 'quarter ellipse' region (see Fig. 4.3):

$$G = \left\{(x, y) \in \mathbb{R}^2 : \frac{x^2}{4} + \frac{y^2}{9} \leq 1, x \geq 0, y \geq 0\right\}$$

Let f be a continuous function on G. Then

$$\iint_G f(x, y)\, dx\, dy = \int_0^3 \left(\int_0^{h(y)} f(x, y)\, dx \right) dy$$

where $h(y) = 2(1 - y^2/9)^{1/2}$.

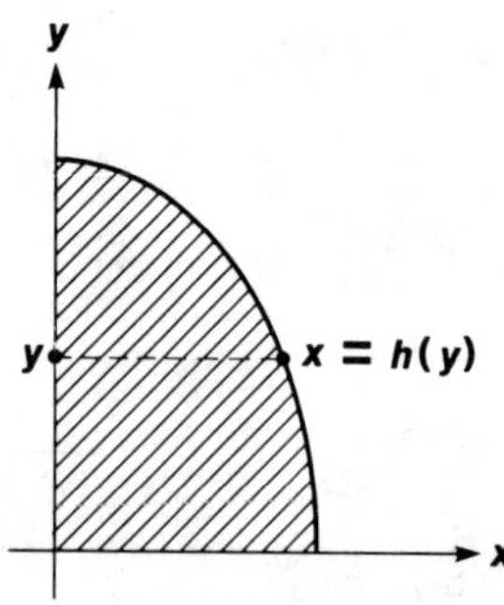

Figure 4.3 Region for a repeated integral

Example (Differentiation 'under integral sign')
For $-c < y < c$, define $F(y) = \int_a^b f(x, y)\, dx$ (note that y is a parameter in this integral). Assume that the partial derivative $f_y(x, y)$ is

a continuous functions of (x, y). For $|t| < c$, the Fubini theorem then gives

$$\int_0^t \left(\int_a^b f_y(x, y)\, dx\right) dy = \int_a^b \left(\int_0^t f_y(x, y)\, dy\right) dx$$

$$= \int_a^b [f(x, t) - f(x, 0)]\, dx = F(t) - F(0).$$

Hence (see Exercise 4.1.4) differentiating with respect to t, then setting $t = y$,

$$F'(y) = \int_a^b f_y(x, y)\, dx.$$

(Thus the order of the operations d/dy and $\int_a^b \ldots dx$ can here be interchanged.)

Exercise 4.2.1 Evaluate the repeated integral

$$\int_0^1 dy \int_0^{h(y)} xy\, dx \equiv \int_0^1 \left(\int_0^{h(y)} xy\, dx\right) dy$$

where $h(y) = \min\{1, \log 1/y\}$. Express it as an equivalent double integral $\int\int_G xy\, dx\, dy$, specifying the region $G \subset \mathbb{R}^2$.

Exercise 4.2.2 Let $g : \mathbb{R} \to \mathbb{R}$ and $h : \mathbb{R} \to \mathbb{R}$ satisfy $g(x) \leq h(x)$ for $a \leq x \leq b$. The area of the region G enclosed by the curves $y = g(x)$ and $y = h(x)$, for $a \leq x \leq b$, then equals $\int_a^b [h(x) - g(x)]\, dx$. This area is also given by the double integral $\int\int_G dx\, dy$. Show that these two expressions for area give the same answer, when $G = \{(x, y) \in \mathbb{R}^2 : x^2 \leq y \leq x+3\}$.

Exercise 4.2.3 By changing to polar coordinates (thus $x = u \cos v$, $y = u \sin v$, where more conventionally r is written for u, and θ for v) evaluate the double integral

$$\int\int_G e^{-x^2-y^2}\, dx\, dy$$

where G is the region $\{(x, y) \in \mathbb{R}^2 : x \geq 0, y \geq 0, x^2+y^2 \leq c^2\}$. (*Remark*: As $c \to \infty$, G tends to the whole of the first quadrant; using Fubini's theorem, the integral evaluated tends to $[\lim_{c \to \infty} \int_0^c e^{-x^2}\, dx]^2$.

This leads to the formula

$$\lim_{c \to \infty} \int_0^c e^{-x^2} \, dx = \tfrac{1}{2}\pi^{1/2}.)$$

Exercise 4.2.4 Evaluate the integral

$$\int\int (1+x^2+y^2)^{-2} \, dx \, dy$$

over the area enclosed by one loop of the *lemniscate* curve

$$(x^2+y^2)^2-(x^2-y^2) = 0.$$

Exercise 4.2.5 Evaluate the triple integral $\int\int\int xyz \, dx \, dy \, dz$, taken over the ellipsoid $(x^2/a^2)+(y^2/b^2)+(z^2/c^2) \leq 1$. (*Note*: Here, *ellipsoid* means the volume, not the boundary surface. Using Fubini's theorem, this integral is evaluated as a repeated integral $\int(\int(\int \ldots dx) \, dy) \, dz$.)

Exercise 4.2.6 Consider the double integral of Exercise 4.2.3, but use instead the change of variable $x = u \sin v$, $y = u \cos v$. Show that (for *oriented* integrals)

$$\int\int_G e^{-x^2-y^2} \, dx \, dy = \int\int_H e^{-u^2}(-u) \, du \, dv,$$

where H is the region $\{(u, v) : 0 \leq u \leq c, 0 \leq v \leq \tfrac{1}{2}\pi$. Evaluate the integral on the right (as a repeated integral), and discuss why a minus sign occurs. (*Hint*: does v run from 0 to $\tfrac{1}{2}\pi$, or from $\tfrac{1}{2}\pi$ to 0?)

Exercise 4.2.7 Let $f : \mathbb{R} \to \mathbb{R}$ satisfy $f(x) > 0$ when $a \leq x \leq b$. If the graph of the curve $y = f(x)$, $a \leq x \leq b$ is rotated about the x-axis, this generates in $\mathbb{R}^3$ the *surface of revolution* $\{(x, y, z) \in \mathbb{R}^3 : (y^2+z^2)^{1/2} = f(x), a \leq x \leq b\}$. The solid region enclosed by this surface is the *solid of revolution*

$$\{(x, y, z) \in \mathbb{R}^3 : (y^2+z^2)^{1/2} \leq f(x), a \leq x \leq b\}.$$

The volume of this solid of revolution is given by $\int_a^b \pi[f(x)]^2 \, dx$, and its surface area (see Section 4.3) by $\int_a^b 2\pi f(x)[1+(f'(x))^2]^{1/2} \, dx$. Evaluate these quantities for the hemisphere obtained by rotating the curve $y = f(x) = (c^2-x^2)^{1/2}$, $0 \leq x \leq c$, and compare with the usual formulas for volume and area of a hemisphere. For the volume, calculate it also as a triple integral of the function 1 over the volume. (Note that if a function misbehaves at $x = c$, then an integral $\int_0^c$ may be considered as a limit, $\lim_{a \to c} \int_0^c$.)

Exercise 4.2.8 By the change of variable $p = x^2+y^2$, $q = x^2-y^2$, calculate the integral $\int\int_G f(x, y)\,dx\,dy$, where $G = \{(x, y) : 0 \leq x^2+y^2 \leq 3,\ x^2-y^2 \leq 1\}$, and $f(x, y) = x^2$. (*Hint*: Integrate over the first quadrant, and multiply by 4.)

Exercise 4.2.9 Calculate the volume cut off from the region bounded by the paraboloid

$$\frac{x^2}{a^2}+\frac{y^2}{b^2} = z$$

by the plane $z = h$.

4.3 LENGTH, AREA AND VOLUME

The area of a flat region, thus of $G \subset \mathbb{R}^2$, has already been defined, and satisfies the *additive* property provided that the boundaries are regular. In order to define area of a curved surface, we shall consider a small portion of the surface as approximated by its tangent plane, and shall consider the area of the surface as approximated by the sum of areas of suitable portions of tangent planes. Consider first a linear mapping of $\mathbb{R}^2$ into $\mathbb{R}^3$, given by $\mathbf{w} = A\mathbf{q}$ where $\mathbf{q} \in \mathbb{R}^2$, $\mathbf{w} \in \mathbb{R}^3$, and A is a 3×2 matrix. The two columns of A define two vectors, $\mathbf{a}$ and $\mathbf{b}$ say. The unit square $\{(q_1, q_2) : 0 \leq q_1 \leq 1, 0 \leq q_2 \leq 1\}$ is mapped by A to a parallelogram, with $\mathbf{a}$ and $\mathbf{b}$ as two adjacent sides, and therefore whose area equals $\|\mathbf{a}\|\,\|\mathbf{b}\|\,|\sin\theta|$, where θ is the angle between $\mathbf{a}$ and $\mathbf{b}$. Now the inner product $\langle \mathbf{a}, \mathbf{b}\rangle = \|\mathbf{a}\|\,\|\mathbf{b}\|\cos\theta$, and the identity

$$\begin{aligned}(\|\mathbf{a}\|\,\|\mathbf{b}\|\sin\theta)^2 &= \|\mathbf{a}\|^2\|\mathbf{b}\|^2-\langle \mathbf{a}, \mathbf{b}\rangle^2 \qquad (4.3.1)\\ &= (a_1^2+a_2^2+a_3^2)(b_1^2+b_2^2+b_3^2)-(a_1b_1+a_2b_2+a_3b_3)^2\end{aligned}$$

is immediate. Now the determinant

$$\det(A^{\mathrm{T}}A) = \det\left(\begin{bmatrix} a_1 & a_2 & a_3 \\ b_1 & b_2 & b_3 \end{bmatrix}\begin{bmatrix} a_1 & b_1 \\ a_2 & b_2 \\ a_3 & b_3 \end{bmatrix}\right) = \begin{vmatrix} \|\mathbf{a}\|^2 & \langle \mathbf{a}, \mathbf{b}\rangle \\ \langle \mathbf{a}, \mathbf{b}\rangle & \|\mathbf{b}\|^2 \end{vmatrix}. \qquad (4.3.2)$$

Hence the area of the parallelogram equals $[\det(A^{\mathrm{T}}A)]^{1/2}$.

Consider now a mapping of $\mathbb{R}^3$ into $\mathbb{R}^3$ given by $\mathbf{w} = B\mathbf{q}$, where B is a 3×3 matrix. The unit cube $(q_1, q_2, q_3) : 0 \leq q_i \leq 1$ $(i = 1, 2, 3)$ is mapped into a parallelepiped, defined by three adjacent edges $\mathbf{a}$, $\mathbf{b}$, $\mathbf{c}$, where $\mathbf{a}$, $\mathbf{b}$, $\mathbf{c}$ are the columns of B. The face of this parallelepiped, defined by the edges $\mathbf{a}$ and $\mathbf{b}$, has area given by Equation (4.3.2). Let $\mathbf{d}$ denote a vector, perpendicular to the plane defined by $\mathbf{a}$ and $\mathbf{b}$, and whose length equals this area. Then the volume of the parallelepiped equals $\|\mathbf{d}\|\,\|\mathbf{c}\|\cos\varphi$, where φ is the angle between $\mathbf{c}$ and $\mathbf{d}$, since $\|\mathbf{d}\|\cos\varphi$ is the height of the parallelepiped, measured from the plane of $\mathbf{a}$ and $\mathbf{b}$ (see Fig. 4.4). Hence the volume equals $\langle\mathbf{c}, \mathbf{d}\rangle$, apart from a $\pm$ sign.

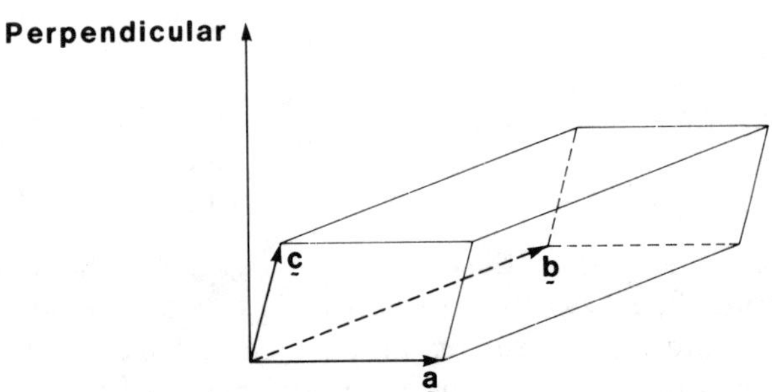

Figure 4.4 Volume of parallelepiped

Now the vector $\mathbf{d}$ equals the *vector product* $\mathbf{a}\times\mathbf{b}$, whose components are

$$(a_2b_3 - a_3b_2,\ a_3b_1 - a_1b_3,\ a_1b_2 - a_2b_1) = \left(\begin{vmatrix} a_2 & b_2 \\ a_3 & b_3 \end{vmatrix}, \begin{vmatrix} a_3 & b_3 \\ a_1 & b_1 \end{vmatrix}, \begin{vmatrix} a_1 & b_1 \\ a_2 & b_2 \end{vmatrix} \right), \tag{4.3.3}$$

in terms of 2×2 determinants. It can be readily calculated that $\langle\mathbf{d}, \mathbf{a}\rangle = 0$ and $\langle\mathbf{d}, \mathbf{b}\rangle = 0$, so that $\mathbf{d}$ is, as claimed, perpendicular to the plane of $\mathbf{a}$ and $\mathbf{b}$, and also that $\|\mathbf{d}\|^2$ equals the expression (4.3.1). Then $\langle\mathbf{c}, \mathbf{d}\rangle$ equals the determinant

$$\begin{vmatrix} a_1 & b_1 & c_1 \\ a_2 & b_2 & c_2 \\ a_3 & b_3 & c_3 \end{vmatrix},$$

by the formula for expanding a determinant by the elements c_1, c_2, c_3 of one column. Hence the volume of the parallelepiped equals $\det B$.

But also, by determinants, $\det(B^{\mathrm{T}}B) = \det(B^{\mathrm{T}})\det(B) = [\det(B)]^2$, so it also follows that the volume equals $[\det(B^{\mathrm{T}}B)]^{1/2}$.

Consider the line in $\mathbb{R}^3$, given by $\mathbf{w} = \mathbf{c}q$ where $q \in \mathbb{R}$. The unit interval $\{q : 0 \leq q \leq 1\}$ is mapped onto a segment whose length is $\|\mathbf{c}\| = (\mathbf{c}^{\mathrm{T}}\mathbf{c})^{1/2}$.

Now let $\mathbf{w} = K^{\mathrm{T}}\mathbf{q}$ define a linear mapping from a *parameter space* of vectors $\mathbf{q}$ into $\mathbb{R}^3$. The unit interval, square or cube in $\mathbf{q}$-space is thus mapped to a region in $\mathbf{w}$-space whose appropriate measure (length, area, or volume) is given, from the above calculations, as $[\det(KK^{\mathrm{T}})]^{1/2}$, apart from any $\pm$ sign which orientation may demand.

Consider now a mapping φ from a parameter space Q in $\mathbb{R}$, $\mathbb{R}^2$, or $\mathbb{R}^3$ into $\mathbb{R}^3$ (or $\mathbb{R}^2$); write $\mathbf{w} = \varphi(\mathbf{q})$, and let $M = \varphi(Q) \equiv \{\varphi(q) : q \in Q\}$. In order to define an appropriate measure (arc length or area of curved surface or volume) for M, consider small intervals I_i in Q, and attach to each a measure of $\varphi(I_i)$, given (when I_i is small) by

$$\hat{p}(q)|I_i| = [\det(\varphi'(q)^{\mathrm{T}}\varphi'(q))]^{1/2}|I_i|. \tag{4.3.4}$$

Here $|I_i|$ denotes the length, area, or volume of the flat region I_i, and the expression $[\det(KK^{\mathrm{T}})]^{1/2}$ is applied to the *linear part* of $\varphi(q)$, for some q in I_i; this replaces K by $(\varphi'(q))^{\mathrm{T}}$. Then, similarly to the definition of a double integral, Equation (4.3.4) leads (for $E \subset Q$) to the integral

$$\int_E \hat{p}(q)\,\mathrm{d}q = \int_E [\det(\varphi'(q)^{\mathrm{T}}\varphi'(q))]^{1/2}\,\mathrm{d}q, \tag{4.3.5}$$

for the measure of E.

Here $\mathrm{d}q$ means $\mathrm{d}q_1$ or $\mathrm{d}q_1\,\mathrm{d}q_2$ or $\mathrm{d}q_1\,\mathrm{d}q_2\,\mathrm{d}q_3$ according as Q has dimension 1, 2, or 3; for brevity, only one integral sign is written, instead of several; and this area, etc., is not oriented. (Orientation is discussed in Section 4.4.)

Example

Specify a semicircle by

$$\begin{bmatrix} x \\ y \end{bmatrix} = \varphi(q) = \begin{bmatrix} -a\cos q \\ a\sin q \end{bmatrix}, \text{ where } q \in Q = [-\pi, \pi], \text{ and } a > 0.$$

Then

$$\varphi'(q)^{\mathrm{T}}\varphi'(q) = [a\sin q,\ a\cos q]\begin{bmatrix} a\sin q \\ a\cos q \end{bmatrix} = a^2.$$

In this case, $p(q) = \det(a^2)^{1/2} = a$.

Example
Specify a surface by $z = f(x, y)$, where $(x, y) \in G \subset \mathbb{R}^2$. (Note that this sort of specification restricts the surface, since each (x, y) corresponds to only one point of the surface. Other choices of parameters, such as in Exercise 4.3.5, can specify less restricted surfaces.) Then

$$\begin{bmatrix} x \\ y \\ z \end{bmatrix} = \varphi(q) \equiv \varphi\left(\begin{bmatrix} x \\ y \end{bmatrix}\right) = \begin{bmatrix} x \\ y \\ f(x, y) \end{bmatrix}; \; \varphi'(q) = \begin{bmatrix} 1 & 0 \\ 0 & 1 \\ f_x & f_y \end{bmatrix}.$$

Hence

$$[\det(\varphi'(q)^{\mathrm{T}}\varphi'(q))]^{1/2} = \begin{vmatrix} 1+f_x^2 & f_x f_y \\ f_x f_y & 1+f_y^2 \end{vmatrix}^{1/2}$$

$$= [1+f_x^2+f_y^2]^{1/2} = \hat{p}(q).$$

Exercise 4.3.1 Show that

$$\|\mathbf{a}\|^2\|\mathbf{b}\|^2 - \langle \mathbf{a}, \mathbf{b}\rangle^2 = \|\mathbf{a} \times \mathbf{b}\|^2.$$

(The inner product $\langle \mathbf{a}, \mathbf{b}\rangle$ is often written as $\mathbf{a} \cdot \mathbf{b}$).

Exercise 4.3.2 Show that $\langle \mathbf{a}, \mathbf{a} \times \mathbf{b}\rangle = 0$; so that, geometrically the vector $\mathbf{a} \times \mathbf{b}$ is perpendicular to the vector $\mathbf{a}$ (and also to $\mathbf{b}$, similarly).

Exercise 4.3.3 A plane curve is described by $x = X(t)$, $y = Y(t)$, $a \le t \le b$. From the theory given, show that the arc length of this curve equals

$$\int_a^b \{[X'(t)]^2 + [Y'(t)]^2\}^{1/2}\, dt.$$

Suppose that a polygon P is inscribed in the curve, by joining the points $(X(t_i), \; Y(t_i))$ by line segments, where $a = t_0 < t_1 < \ldots < t_n = b$. Write down an expression for the arc length of P, and observe that this arc length tends to the arc length of the curve as the maximum $|t_i - t_{i-1}|$ tends to 0 (assuming that X and Y are continuously differentiable functions).
(*Remark*: This polygon method is the classical definition of arc length. We don't follow it in the theory, because an analogous approach does not work for surfaces. It is, regrettably, possible to construct a surface S, made of triangles, with all their vertices lying

on a cylinder C, and with every point of S arbitrarily near to C, and still have the area of S as large as one chooses. Obviously, the areas of such surfaces S do *not* tend to the area of C. This is why we define the area of a surface in terms of areas of small pieces of tangent planes – which is what the *linear parts* in the definition represent geometrically.)

Exercise 4.3.4 If a plane curve is specified, instead, by $y = f(x)$, $a \leq x \leq b$, show that the arc length equals $\int_a^b\{1+[f'(x)]^2\}^{1/2}\,dx$.

Exercise 4.3.5 Consider the half-ellipsoid

$$z = c\left(1-\frac{x^2}{a^2}-\frac{y^2}{b^2}\right)^{1/2} \equiv f(x, y)$$

where a, b, c are positive constants. For this surface, (x, y) runs over the elliptical region $H = \{(x, y) : (x^2/a^2)+(y^2/b^2) \leq 1\}$. One way to parametrize H is to set $x = au\cos v$, $y = bu\sin v$, where $0 \leq u \leq 1$ and $0 \leq v \leq 2\pi$. (Observe that $v = 0$ and $v = 2\pi$ describe the same points, but this 'doubling' of the boundary does not hurt.) Hence the surface can be parametrized by

$$\begin{bmatrix} x \\ y \\ z \end{bmatrix} = \varphi(q) \equiv \varphi\left(\begin{bmatrix} u \\ v \end{bmatrix}\right) = \begin{bmatrix} au\cos v \\ bu\sin v \\ c(1-u^2)^{1/2} \end{bmatrix}$$

where $q = (u, v) \in G = \{(u, v) : 0 \leq u \leq 1,\ 0 \leq v \leq 2\pi\}$. Calculate $\hat{p}(q)$, from Equation (4.3.5), for this surface. What happens in the special case of a hemisphere (when $a = b = c$)? For this special case, relate the result obtained to $(1+f_x^2+f_y^2)^{1/2}$.

Exercise 4.3.6 Prove the formula given in Exercise 4.2.7 for the surface area of a surface of revolution.

Exercise 4.3.7 Let Γ be a plane curve, of finite length L. Enclose in a square A of side L, with sides parallel to the axes. By horizontal and vertical lines, subdivide A into small squares, each of side δ. Show that the number of these squares, of side δ, necessary to cover Γ is less than $4(L/\delta)+4$; and hence that Γ is *regular* (as defined in Section 4.2). (*Hint*: Divide Γ into arcs, each of length $\leq \delta$. Show that each such arc can have points in common with at most four of the squares.)

Exercise 4.3.8 A surface is defined by the equation $y = x\tan(z/h)$. Calculate the area of the part of this surface, specified by $a \leq x^2+y^2 \leq b$, $|x| \leq \frac{1}{2}\pi h$.

4.4 INTEGRALS OVER CURVES AND SURFACES

Define a *curve* in $\mathbb{R}^3$ by an equation

$$\mathbf{w} = \varphi(u), \text{ where } \varphi : I \to \mathbb{R}^3 \text{ is continuously differentiable, } I = [a, b] \subset \mathbb{R}. \tag{4.4.1}$$

Define a *surface* in $\mathbb{R}^3$ by an equation

$$\mathbf{w} = \varphi(u, v), \text{ where } \varphi : \bar{G} \to \mathbb{R}^3 \text{ is differentiable, and } \bar{G} \subset \mathbb{R}^2; \tag{4.4.2}$$

take $\bar{G}$ as the union of a bounded open set and its boundary, assumed regular. These definitions are called *parametric* definitions of curve and surface; the variables u or (u, v) are the *parameters*. For both curve and surface, we may consider also several parametric curves or surfaces, joined together continuously at the boundaries.

Examples

The curve described by $x = a\cos u$, $y = a\sin u$, $z = cu$ (with constants a, b, c) is a *helix*.

The surface described by $x = a\sin u\cos v$, $y = b\sin u\sin v$, $z = c\cos u$ (with a, b, c positive constants, and $0 \leq u \leq \pi$ and $0 \leq v \leq 2\pi$) is an *ellipsoid*, otherwise described by the equation $(x/a)^2+(y/b)^2+(z/c)^2 = 1$. Observe that $v = 0$ and $v = 2\pi$ describe the same points on this surface.

The surface of a cube may be described by six parametric surfaces, one for each face, joined continuously at their boundaries.

The circle $x^2+y^2 = 1$ may be described by two parametric curves, $y = +(1-x^2)^{1/2}(-1 \leq x \leq 1)$, and $y = -(1-x^2)^{1/2}(-1 \leq x \leq 1)$.

Observe that the mapping from parameter space ($[a, b]$ or $\bar{G}$) to surface is *not* generally one-to-one. For the present purpose, this does not matter, since only certain boundaries are affected. An alternative kind of description of a surface covers the surface by several overlapping *patches*, each being a parametrized surface of the form $\mathbf{w} = \varphi(u, v)$ where $(u, v) \in G$, an open (instead of closed) region in $\mathbb{R}^2$.

Example

Let $U = \{(u, v) : u^2+v^2 < 2\}$. Define $\varphi : U \to \mathbb{R}^3$ by $\varphi(u, v) = (x, y, z)$, where

$$x = 2u/(1+\theta),\ y = 2v/(1+\theta),\ z = (1-\theta)/(1+\theta), \text{ where } \theta \equiv u^2+v^2. \tag{4.4.3}$$

Then φ maps U one-to-one onto that part of the sphere $x^2+y^2+z^2 = 1$ for which $z > -\frac{1}{3}$. This mapping is obtained by mapping $(u, v, 0) \in \mathbb{R}^3$ to the point (x, y, z) on the sphere which lies on the line joining $(0, 0, -1)$ to $(u, v, 0)$. Note that the whole sphere cannot be thus represented, since no (u, v) can correspond to $(0, 0, -1)$. Another patch, overlapping this one, could be obtained using, instead, the point $(0, 0, 1)$.

Both the curve (4.4.1) and the surface (4.4.2) are represented as $\mathbf{w} = \varphi(q)$ where $\varphi : Q \to \mathbb{R}^3$ is continuously differentiable, and Q is the *parameter space* (I or $\bar{G}$). (A curve in the plane is similarly represented, with $\varphi : Q \to \mathbb{R}^2$.) We consider now integrals with respect to a *measure* p (arc length or surface area) on a curve or surface. These contrast with the ordinary integral (Section 4.1) or double integral (Section 4.2), which are integrals with respect to ordinary length (on a straight line) or area (on a flat surface). What is now required is arc length (along a curve), or area (on a curved surface). The integrals are called *line integrals* (on a curve; *curve integral* would be a better name, but it is not in use), and *surface integrals* (over a surface).

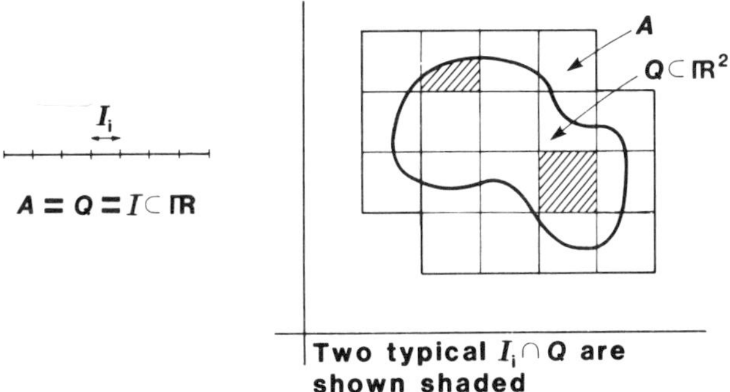

Figure 4.5 Length and area

Let $f : M \to \mathbb{R}^3$ be a continuous function on the curve, or surface, $M = \varphi(Q) \subset \mathbb{R}^3$. Let $\varepsilon > 0$. Assume that $f \circ \varphi$ extends to a continuous function on a closed interval (or union of finitely many closed intervals) $A \subset Q$. (In $\mathbb{R}$, $A = I$; in $\mathbb{R}^2$, such an $A \supset Q$ can always be found – we omit the proof.) Then there is a step-function $h : A \to \mathbb{R}^3$, for which $|(f \circ \varphi)(q) - h(q)| < \varepsilon$ for each $q \in A$. Subdivide Q into smaller intervals I_i (thus intervals in $\mathbb{R}$ of length $< \delta$, or squares in $\mathbb{R}^2$ of side $< \delta$), with δ chosen small enough that h is constant in the interior of each I_i (see Fig. 4.5). From Section 4.3, the measure p is represented by

$$p(M_i) = \int_{Q \cap I_i} \hat{p}(q)\, \mathrm{d}q \text{ where } M_i = \varphi(Q \cap I_i). \qquad (4.4.4)$$

Thus $p(M_i)$ is the measure (length or area) of the portion of M parametrized by $I_i \cap Q$; $\mathrm{d}q$ means $\mathrm{d}u$ or $\mathrm{d}u\,\mathrm{d}v$ (in $\mathbb{R}$ or $\mathbb{R}^2$); and $\hat{p}$ depends on derivatives of φ (see Section 4.3).

Let h take constant value c_i on the interior of I_i. Define

$$\int_Q h\hat{p} = \sum_i c_i p(M_i). \qquad (4.4.5)$$

Let step-function h_r correspond to $\varepsilon = 1/r$. For $r < s$,

$$\left| \int_Q h_r\hat{p} - \int_Q h_s\hat{p} \right| = \left| \int_Q [h_r(q) - h_s(q)]\hat{p}(q)\, \mathrm{d}q \right|$$

$$\leq \sup_{q \in Q} |h_r(q) - h_s(q)| \cdot \sup_{q \in Q} |p(q)| \cdot \left|\int_Q \mathrm{d}q\right|$$

by (4.1.6)

$$\leq (2/r) \sup_{q \in Q} |p(q)| \cdot \left|\int_Q \mathrm{d}q\right|$$

$$\to 0 \text{ as } r \to \infty.$$

Hence $\int_Q h_r\hat{p}$ tends to a limit, as $r \to \infty$, and this limit is unique (by the same proof as for Equation (4.1.7)). Define therefore the *line*, or *surface, integral*

$$\int_M f\, \mathrm{d}p = \lim_{r \to \infty} \int_Q h\hat{p}. \qquad (4.4.6)$$

Observe that the linear and additive properties are retained by this integral (4.4.6); and inequality (4.1.6) is modified to

$$\left|\int_M f\,\mathrm{d}p\right| \leq \sup_{m \in M} |f(m)| \cdot |p(M)|. \tag{4.4.7}$$

Here $|p(M)|$ is required, since $p(M)$ may have either sign.

From Equation (4.4.6), noting that $h_r \to f$ as $r \to \infty$,

$$\int_M f\,\mathrm{d}p = \int_Q (f \circ \varphi)(q)\,\hat{p}(q)\,\mathrm{d}q, \tag{4.4.8}$$

where the integral on the right is an ordinary integral (as in Sections 4.1 or 4.2). Some books *define* the line or surface integral by the corresponding integral over Q. However, the conceptual meaning is given by Equation (4.4.5); the integral is a limit of approximative sums, like Equation (4.1.1), except that p now denotes the relevant arc length or surface area. Now $M = \varphi(Q) \equiv \{\varphi(q) : q \in Q\}$. We may consider $\lambda \equiv f\,\mathrm{d}p$ as a *differential form*, and $(f \circ \varphi)(q)\,\hat{p}(q)\,\mathrm{d}q$ as another differential form, which may also be written as $\varphi^*\lambda$, to denote its dependence on φ and λ. Then Equation (4.4.8) becomes

$$\int_M \lambda = \int_Q \varphi^*\lambda, \tag{4.4.9}$$

in these symbols. A general formula for calculating $\varphi^*\lambda$ is given later (Equation (4.5.12)).

Example (line integral)

Let Γ denote the curve (4.4.1); let $\mathbf{g} : \Gamma \to \mathbb{R}^3$ be a vector function defined on Γ. The vector $\varphi'(u)$ is tangent to Γ at the point $\varphi(u)$. Denote $\hat{\mathbf{t}}(u) = \|\varphi'(u)\|^{-1}\varphi'(u)$, the unit vector tangent to Γ at $\varphi(u)$. The inner product of $\mathbf{g} = \mathbf{g}(u)$ and $\mathbf{t} = \mathbf{t}(u)$ is

$$\mathbf{g}\cdot\mathbf{t} = \langle \mathbf{g}, \mathbf{t}\rangle = g_1t_1 + g_2t_2 + g_3t_3. \tag{4.4.10}$$

Define the line integral

$$\int_\Gamma (g_1\,\mathrm{d}w_1 + g_2\,\mathrm{d}w_2 + g_3\,\mathrm{d}w_3) = \int_\Gamma \mathbf{g}\cdot\hat{\mathbf{t}}\,\mathrm{d}s \tag{4.4.11}$$

by Equation (4.4.6) with $f = \mathbf{g}\cdot\hat{\mathbf{t}}$, $p = s =$ arc length, and $\mathrm{d}w_i = t_i\,\mathrm{d}s$ $(i = 1, 2, 3)$.

In order to validate the symbolism $\mathrm{d}w_i$, assume that, in (4.4.11), the w_i are cartesian coordinates in $\mathbb{R}^3$. From Equation (4.3.5), arc length is described by

$$\hat{p}(u) = \left[\left(\frac{d\varphi_1}{du}\right)^2 + \left(\frac{d\varphi_2}{du}\right)^2 + \left(\frac{d\varphi_3}{du}\right)^2\right]^{1/2}. \qquad (4.4.12)$$

Also $\hat{\mathbf{t}}_i = \varphi_i'(u)/p(u)$, for $i = 1, 2, 3$. Hence, from Equation (4.4.8),

$$\int_\Gamma \left(\sum_{i=1}^{3} g_i \hat{t}_i\right) ds = \int_I \left(\sum_{i=1}^{3} g_i \varphi_i'(u)/\hat{p}(u)\right) \hat{p}(u)\, du, \qquad (4.4.13)$$

wherein $dw_i = \varphi_i'(u)\, du$. This is motivated by the following approximation. For $i = 1, 2, 3$, denote by δw_i a small increment in the cartesian coordinate w_i; then the corresponding change in arc length is approximately

$$\delta s = [(\delta w_1)^2 + (\delta w_2)^2 + (\delta w_3)^2]^{1/2},$$

by Pythagoras theorem. Then $\hat{t}_i \approx (\delta w_i)/(\delta s)$, so that $\delta w_i \approx \hat{t}_i(\delta s)$. An alternative symbolism for Equation (4.4.10) is $\int_\Gamma (P\, dx + Q\, dy + R\, dz)$, using coordinates x, y, z and components P, Q, R of g.

Example

Consider the semicircle Γ, given by $y = (1-x^2)^{1/2}$, traversed from $x = -1$ to $x = 1$. Here x is the parameter; however, $\varphi(x) = (x, (1-x^2)^{1/2})$ is not differentiable at the endpoints $x = \pm 1$. Another parametrization is $(x, y) = \varphi(q) \equiv (-\cos q, \sin q)$, where q runs from 0 to π. Since

$$\varphi'(q)^{\mathrm{T}}\varphi'(q) = [\sin q, \cos q]\begin{bmatrix}\sin q \\ \cos q\end{bmatrix} = 1,$$

$\hat{p}(q) = 1$ here. Define $f(x, y) = 2x + y$, and $g(x, y) = (x, -y)$. Then

$$\int_\Gamma f\, ds = \int_{-\pi}^{\pi} (f \circ \varphi)(q)\hat{p}(q)\, dq = \int_{-\pi}^{\pi} (-2\cos q + \sin q)1\, dq = 2,$$

where s denotes arc length along Γ. If, instead, we use x as parameter, then (see Exercise 4.3.4) $\hat{p}(x) = (1 + \theta'(x)^2)^{1/2}$ where $\theta(x) = (1-x^2)^{1/2}$, so that $\hat{p}(x) = (1-x^2)^{-1/2}$. Hence (formally)

$$\int_\Gamma f\, ds = \int_{-1}^{1} (2x + (1-x^2)^{1/2})(1-x^2)^{-1/2}\, dx.$$

But this integrand becomes infinite at the endpoints, $x = \pm 1$, so that $\int_{-1}^{1}$ must be interpreted here as an *improper integral*, $\lim_{\varepsilon \downarrow 0} \int_{-1+\varepsilon}^{1-\varepsilon}$. This integral evaluates to $[-(1-x^2)^{1/2}+x]_{-1}^{1} = 2$. (The value of the line integral is independent of the choice of parametrization.) The unit tangent vector $\hat{\mathbf{t}}$ has the direction of $\varphi'(q)$; here $\varphi'(q)$ happens to have unit length, so that $\hat{\mathbf{t}} = \varphi'(q)^{\mathrm{T}} = (\sin q, \cos q)^{\mathrm{T}}$, and $\mathbf{g}\cdot\hat{\mathbf{t}} = (-\cos q, -\sin q)(\sin q, \cos q)^{\mathrm{T}} = -2 \sin q \cos q$. Hence

$$\int_{\Gamma} \mathbf{g}\cdot\hat{\mathbf{t}}\, \mathrm{d}s = \int_0^{\pi}(-2 \sin q \cos q)1\, \mathrm{d}q = 0.$$

If we consider only half the curve, from (0, 1) to (1, 0), then the integral becomes $\int_{\pi/2}^{\pi} \ldots \mathrm{d}q = 1$. For this latter case, the parametrization with x gives

$$\int_0^1[x \quad -(1-x^2)^{1/2}]\begin{bmatrix}(1-x^2)^{1/2}\\ -x\end{bmatrix}(1-x^2)^{-1/2}\, \mathrm{d}x = \int_0^1 2x\, \mathrm{d}x = 1.$$

Note that $\int \mathbf{g}\cdot\hat{\mathbf{t}}\, \mathrm{d}s$ may also be written as $\int(x\, \mathrm{d}x - y\, \mathrm{d}y)$.

Consider now the line integral $\int_{\Gamma}[P(x, y)\, \mathrm{d}x + Q(x, y)\, \mathrm{d}y]$, taken along a plane curve Γ, commencing at (0, 0) and ending at (ξ, η). In general, the value of this line integral depends, not only on (ξ, η), but also on the curve Γ from (0, 0) to (ξ, η). It is sometimes the case that the integral is *independent of the path*; this means that

$$F(\xi, \eta) = \int_{\Gamma} [P\, \mathrm{d}x + Q\, \mathrm{d}y], \tag{4.4.14}$$

with $F(\xi, \eta)$ taking the same value, regardless of the curve Γ from (0, 0) to (ξ, η). To discuss when this happens, assume that P and Q are continuously differentiable in a rectangle $\{(x, y) : -c \leq x \leq c, -c \leq y \leq c\}$. (This region has no holes in it; this fact turns out to be important.)

Theorem 4.3

Let P and Q be continuously differentiable in a rectangle containing (0, 0). Then $\int_{\Gamma}(P(x, y)\, \mathrm{d}x + Q(x, y)\, \mathrm{d}y)$ is independent of the path (for curves Γ in the rectangle) if and only if $P_y(x, y) = Q_x(x, y)$ (for each (x, y) in the rectangle).

Proof Assume the integral is independent of the path; thus that (4.4.14) is independent of the curve Γ from (0, 0) to (ξ, η). Consider a curve Γ from (0, 0) to (ξ, η), followed by a straight segment from (ξ, η) to $(\xi+\beta, \eta)$. For this combined curve, since the integral is independent of the path,

$$F(\xi+\beta, \eta) = F(\xi, \eta) + \int_{\xi}^{\xi+\beta} P(x, \eta)\, \mathrm{d}x, \tag{4.4.15}$$

since also $dy/dq = 0$ on the straight segment. It follows that the partial derivative $F_\xi(\xi, \eta) = P(\xi, \eta)$. Similarly, $F_\eta(\xi, \eta) = Q(\xi, \eta)$. Therefore

$$P_y(x, y) = F_{xy}(\xi, \eta) \text{ and } Q_x(x, y) = F_{yx}(x, y),$$

(writing now x, y for ξ, η); by Theorem 2.8, $F_{xy} = F_{yx}$, since these functions are continuous. Hence $P_y = Q_x$ for each (x, y).

Conversely, assume $P_y(x, y) = Q_x(x, y)$ for each (x, y) in the rectangle. Define

$$\hat{F}(\xi, \eta) = \int_0^\xi P(x, 0)\,dx + \int_0^\eta Q(\xi, y)\,dy. \tag{4.4.16}$$

Noting that P and Q are continuous functions, it follows that $\hat{F}_\eta(\xi, \eta) = Q(\xi, \eta)$, and (differentiating under the integral sign)

$$\begin{aligned}\hat{F}_\xi(\xi, \eta) &= P(\xi, 0) + \int_0^\eta Q_x(\xi, y)\,dy \\ &= P(\xi, 0) + \int_0^\eta P_y(\xi, y)\,dy \qquad (\text{since } Q_x = P_y) \\ &= P(\xi, 0) + [P(\xi, \eta) - P(\xi, 0)] = P(\xi, \eta).\end{aligned}$$

Hence, by the chain rule,

$$P(x(q), y(q))x'(q) + Q(x(q), y(q))y'(q) = \frac{d}{dq}\hat{F}(x(q), y(q)).$$

Therefore the line integral (4.4.14), with Γ from $(0, 0)$ to (ξ, η), now equals $\hat{F}(\xi, \eta) - \hat{F}(0,0)$, and is thus independent of path. (Also $\hat{F}(\xi, \eta) = F(\xi, \eta)$.) □

Example

The line integral

$$\oint_\Gamma (x^2+y^2)^{-1}(x\,dy - y\,dx)$$

has value zero along any closed curve Γ which does not enclose the origin. (The symbol $\oint$ denotes a line integral around a *closed* curve.) Suppose first that Γ can be enclosed in a rectangle, which does not include the origin. On such a region, $P_y(x, y) = Q_x(x, y) = -2xy(x^2+y^2)^{-1}$, and so Theorem 4.3 applies. However, P_y and Q_x do not exist at the origin. If Γ' denotes the circle $x^2+y^2 = 1$, taken anticlockwise, then (setting $x = \cos q$, $y = \sin q$),

$$\begin{aligned}&\oint_{\Gamma'} (x^2+y^2)^{-1}(x\,dy - y\,dx) \\ &= \int_0^{2\pi} (\cos^2 q + \sin^2 q)^{-1}[\cos q(\cos q) - \sin q(-\sin q)]\,dq = 2\pi.\end{aligned}$$

(So Theorem 4.3 does *not* apply to a *punctured* region (with one exceptional point).) To show that $\oint_\Gamma = 0$ for a general (differentiable) curve which does not enclose the origin, consider (as in Fig. 4.6) $\oint_\Gamma$ as equal to the sum of several integrals , $\oint_{\Gamma_i}$ arranged so that each Γ_i lies in a rectangle which does not enclose the origin.

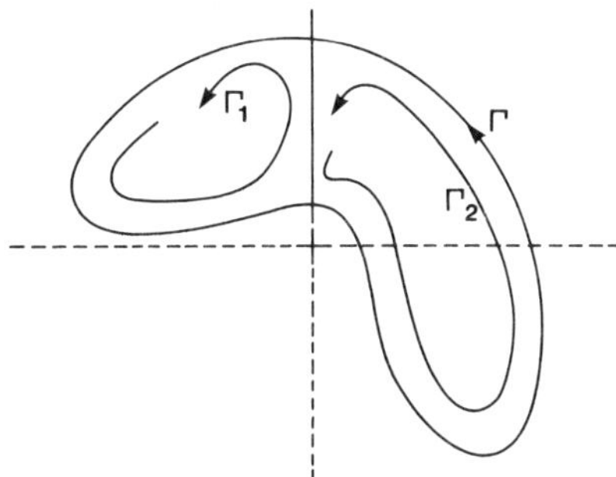

Figure 4.6 Line integral

Theorem 4.3 has the following extension to line integrals in $\mathbb{R}^3$.

Theorem 4.4
Let J be an interval in $\mathbb{R}^3$; let P, Q, and R be continuously differentiable functions on J. Then $\int_\Gamma(P\,\mathrm{d}x+Q\,\mathrm{d}y+R\,\mathrm{d}z)$ is independent of the path (for curves Γ in J) if and only if $P_y = Q_x$, $Q_z = R_y$, and $R_x = P_z$.

The proof is essentially the same as that of Theorem 4.3, but replacing Equation (4.4.16) by

$$\hat{F}(\xi, \eta, \zeta) = \int_0^\xi P(x, 0, 0)\,\mathrm{d}x + \int_0^\eta Q(\xi, y, 0)\,\mathrm{d}y + \int_0^\zeta R(\xi, \eta, z)\,\mathrm{d}z. \tag{4.4.17}$$

The detailed proof is omitted here, since the result follows from a later theorem.

Example (surface integral)
Let Λ denote the surface (4.4.2); let $g : \Lambda \to \mathbb{R}^3$ be a vector function on Λ. At the point (u, v) of Λ, let $\hat{\mathbf{n}}$ denote the unit vector *normal* to

the surface (that is, perpendicular to the tangent plane to the surface at the point). Define then the *surface integral*

$$\int_{\Lambda} (g_1 \, \mathrm{d}w_2 \, \mathrm{d}w_3 + g_2 \, \mathrm{d}w_2 \, \mathrm{d}w_3 + g_3 \, \mathrm{d}w_3 \, \mathrm{d}w_1) = \int_{\Lambda} \mathbf{g} \cdot \hat{\mathbf{n}} \, \mathrm{d}A, \tag{4.4.18}$$

using (4.4.6) or (4.4.8) with $f = \mathbf{g} \cdot \hat{\mathbf{n}}$, and $p = A =$ surface area. Here $\mathrm{d}w_2 \, \mathrm{d}w_3$ is written for $n_1 \, \mathrm{d}A$, and other similar expressions. These are validated as follows.

The curves $\mathbf{w} = \varphi(\cdot, v_0)$ and $\mathbf{w} = \varphi(u_0, \cdot)$ are tangent to the surface at the point (u_0, v_0). These two curves have gradients $\mathbf{a}$ and $\mathbf{b}$, where $a_i = \partial\varphi_i/\partial u$ and $b_i = \partial\varphi_i/\partial v$ (for $i = 1, 2, 3$). Denote

$$K = \begin{bmatrix} a_1 & a_2 & a_3 \\ b_1 & b_2 & b_3 \end{bmatrix}; \; n_1 = \begin{vmatrix} a_2 & a_3 \\ b_2 & b_3 \end{vmatrix};$$

$$n_2 = \begin{vmatrix} a_3 & a_1 \\ b_3 & b_1 \end{vmatrix}; \; n_3 = \begin{vmatrix} a_1 & a_2 \\ b_1 & b_2 \end{vmatrix}. \tag{4.4.19}$$

Then $\mathbf{n} = (n_1^2, n_2^2, n_3^2)$ is normal to the surface, and, from (4.3.3) and (4.3.5), $\hat{p}(u, v) = [n_1^2 + n_2^2 + n_3^2]^{1/2}$ for surface area. Therefore

$$\int_{\Lambda} g_1 \hat{n}_1 \, \mathrm{d}A = \int_{Q} g_1 (n_1/\hat{p}(u, v)) \hat{p}(u, v) \, \mathrm{d}u \, \mathrm{d}v, \tag{4.4.20}$$

and similarly for the two other terms in (4.4.14). Now $g_1 \, \mathrm{d}w_2 \, \mathrm{d}w_3$

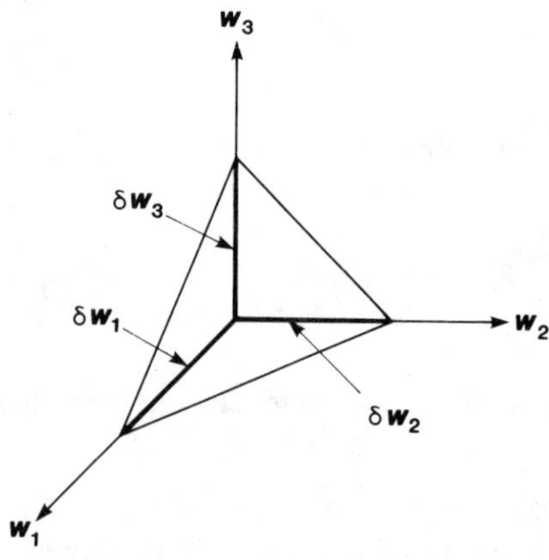

Figure 4.7 Element of surface area

may be considered (using $w_i = \varphi_i(u, v)$) as

$$g_1(a_1\,du+b_1\,dv)(a_2\,du+b_2\,dv) = g_1 n_1\,du\,dv, \qquad (4.4.21)$$

in agreement with (4.4.20), provided that $(du)^2 = 0$ and $(du)(dv) = -(dv)(du)$. The latter items are explained in Section 4.5, in terms of differential forms.

Geometrically, let δw_i denote a small increment in w_i, for $i = 1, 2, 3$. The increment, δA_i, of surface area is then approximated by a flat region, half of which is the slanting face of the tetrahedron shown in Fig. 4.7. Here **n** is normal to δA, and $\hat{n}_1 \delta A \approx \delta w_2 \delta w_3$.

Example

Consider the surface integral

$$\int\int_\Lambda (x^2+y^2+z^2)^{-3/2}(x\,dy\,dz+y\,dz\,dx+z\,dx\,dz), \qquad (4.4.22)$$

where the surface Λ is a part of the unit sphere, parametrized by $x = \sin u \cos v$, $y = \sin u \cos v$, $z = \cos u$. In this example,

$$K = \begin{bmatrix} \cos u \cos v & \cos u \sin v & -\sin u \\ -\sin u \sin v & \sin u \cos v & 0 \end{bmatrix};$$

$$(n_1, n_2, n_3) = (\sin^2 u \cos v, \sin^2 u \sin v, \cos u \sin u);$$
$$g_1 n_1 + g_2 n_2 + g_3 n_3 = \sin u; \hat{\mathbf{n}} = \|\mathbf{n}\|^{-1}\mathbf{n} \text{ where } \|\mathbf{n}\| = \sin u.$$

So the surface integral equals $\int\int \sin u\,du\,dv$, taken over the appropriate region of (u, v). Since $\|\mathbf{n}\| = \sin u$, this integral represents the *area* of the surface Λ. (A surface integral is sometimes written $\int\int$, and sometimes $\int$.)

Exercise 4.4.1 Let the curve Γ be the helix $x = a \cos u$, $y = a \sin u$, $z = cu$. Let the vector function $\mathbf{g}(x, y, z)$ have components (x, y, kz) where k is constant. Use Equation (4.4.13) to evaluate the line integral

$$\int \mathbf{g}\cdot\mathbf{t}\,ds = \int (x\,dx+y\,dy+kz\,dz)$$

along Γ from $((a, 0, 0)$ to $(a \cos \theta, a \sin \theta, c\theta)$, and show that it equals $h(\theta)-h(0)$, where $h(\theta) = \frac{1}{2}(a \cos \theta)^2+\frac{1}{2}(a \sin \theta)^2+\frac{1}{2}k(c\theta)^2$.

Exercise 4.4.2 Evaluate $\int(y^k\,dx+x^k\,dy)$, for $k = 4$ and for $k = 5$, along the ellipse $(x^2/a^2)+(y^2/b^2) = 1$, from $(a, 0)$ to $(-a, 0)$ via $(0, b)$, and also from $(0, -b)$ to $(0, b)$ via $(a, 0)$.

Exercise 4.4.3 Evaluate $\oint_\Gamma (a^2+xy)^{-1}(y\,dx+x\,dy)$ around the closed curve Γ, given by the equation $|x|+|y| = a$. (Break this curve into four pieces. Traverse the curve anticlockwise. What difference does it make if the curve is traversed clockwise?)

Exercise 4.4.4 Let Γ be a plane curve, starting at (x_1, y_1) and ending at (x_2, y_2). For what such curves is it true that

$$\int (x^2+y^2)^{-1}(-y\,dx+x\,dy) = F(x_2, y_2)-F(x_1, y_1),$$

where $F(x, y) = \arctan(y/x)$? How does your answer relate to the fact that this line integral is *not*, in general, independent of the path?

Exercise 4.4.5 Evaluate the line integral $\oint (x^2-ay)\,dx+(y^2-ax)\,dy$ around the closed curve $x^{2/3}+y^{2/3} = a^{2/3}$. Then show that this integral must equal zero, both by the test of Theorem 4.3, and also by finding the function F (as in the proof of Theorem 4.3).

Exercise 4.4.6 Show that the line integral

$$\int_\Gamma \frac{\sin y\,dx-\sinh x\,dy}{\cosh x-\cos y} = 0$$

along any closed curve Γ not crossing the y-axis.

Exercise 4.4.7 An electric current flows along a wire directed along the z-axis. At a point in the (x, y)-plane, the magnetic field intensity has components $P(x, y) = -cy(x^2+y^2)^{-1}$, $Q(x, y) = cx(x^2+y^2)^{-1}$, where c is proportional to the electric current. The work done against the field in carrying a unit magnetic pole around a closed curve Γ in the (x, y)-plane is $W = \oint_\Gamma (P\,dx+Q\,dy)$. Show that $W = 2\pi c$ when Γ is the ellipse $(x/a)^2+(y/b)^2 = 1$. What is W when Γ is $((x-2a)/a)^2+(y/b)^2 = 1$? Why?

Exercise 4.4.8 Using Equation (4.4.13), prove the statement (made above without proof) that, for surface area,

$$\hat{p}(u, v) = \|\mathbf{n}\| \equiv (n_1^2+n_2^2+n_3^2)^{1/2}.$$

Exercise 4.4.9 Obtain an integral expression for the surface area of an ellipsoid. (See Exercise 4.3.5.)

Exercise 4.4.10 Let the functions P and Q be continuously differentiable on a rectangle $J \subset \mathbb{R}^2$. Show that $\int_\Gamma (P\, dx + Q\, dy)$ is *independent of the path* (for each curve $\Gamma \subset J$) if and only if $\oint_\Gamma (P\, dx + Q\, dy) = 0$ for each *closed* curve $\Gamma \subset J$.

4.5 DIFFERENTIAL FORMS

The expressions integrated in Equations (4.4.11) and (4.4.12), namely $g_1\, dw_1 + g_2\, dw_2 + g_3\, dw_3$ and $g_1\, dw_2\, dw_3 + g_2\, dw_3\, dw_1 + g_3\, dw_1\, dw_2$, are examples of *differential forms*. In general, define a *differential form* of degree r in $\mathbb{R}^n$ as a sum of expressions of the form

$$f(\mathbf{w})\, dw_{i_1} \wedge dw_{i_2} \wedge \ldots \wedge dw_{i_r}. \tag{4.5.1}$$

Here f is a real function of $\mathbf{w} \in \mathbb{R}^n$, and $i_1, i_2, \ldots, i_r$ are integers from $1, 2, \ldots, n$. The symbol $\wedge$ is called *wedge*; it serves as a reminder that the *order* of the symbols dw_{i_j} now carries meaning; this is required, so that the calculus of differential forms shall apply to oriented integrals. From the change-of-variable formula for double integrals (Equation (4.2.9)), we have (in the present notation) that

$$dx \wedge dy = [\det \varphi'(u, v)]\, du \wedge dv. \tag{4.5.2}$$

Since the interchange of two columns of a determinant multiplies the determinant by -1, we must assume, for consistency with Equation (4.5.2), that

$$dw_i \wedge dw_j = -\, dw_j \wedge dw_i. \tag{4.5.3}$$

Since a determinant with two identical columns is zero, we assume also that

$$dw_i \wedge dw_i = 0. \tag{4.5.4}$$

It will be shown that much of the preceding theory of (oriented) line, surface, double and triple integrals, including change-of-variable formulas, can be presented systematically in terms of differential forms.

The operations of multiplication (called *exterior product*), differentiation, and change of variable will now be defined for differential forms. The product is defined by

$$[f(\mathbf{w})\, dw_{i_1} \wedge dw_{i_2} \wedge \ldots \wedge dw_{i_r}] \wedge [g(\mathbf{w}) \wedge dw_{j_1} \wedge \ldots \wedge dw_{j_s}]$$
$$= f(\mathbf{w})g(\mathbf{w})\, dw_{i_1} \wedge dw_{i_2} \wedge \ldots \wedge dw_{i_r} \wedge dw_{j_1} \wedge \ldots \wedge dw_{j_s}, \tag{4.5.5}$$

together with distributivity over addition, namely

$$\left(\sum_i \lambda_i\right) \wedge \left(\sum_j \mu_j\right) = \sum_i \sum_j \lambda_i \wedge \mu_j, \tag{4.5.6}$$

in which λ_i and μ_j denote any differential forms on $\mathbb{R}^n$. Thus, for example, in $\mathbb{R}^3$,

$$\begin{aligned}&[f(x, y, z)\, dx \wedge dy] \wedge [g(x, y, z)\, dz] \\ &\qquad = f(x, y, z)g(x, y, z)\, dx \wedge dy \wedge dz;\end{aligned}$$

and

$$\begin{aligned}&[f(x, y, z)\, dx \wedge dy] \wedge [g(x, y, z)\, dx] \\ &\qquad = f(x, y, z)g(x, y, z)\, dx \wedge dy \wedge dx \\ &\qquad = 0 \text{ because } dx \wedge dx = 0.\end{aligned}$$

Observe that if λ is an r-form (meaning a form of degree r), and if μ is an s-form, then

$$\mu \wedge \lambda = (-1)^{rs}\lambda \wedge \mu. \tag{4.5.7}$$

The reason for the multiplier $(-1)^{rs}$ is that it takes rs interchanges of pairs of terms to put $\mu \wedge \lambda$ into the form $\lambda \wedge \mu$, and Equation (4.5.3) is applied. Note also that Equation (4.5.6) allows grouping of terms; thus for example,

$$\begin{aligned}&(P_1\, dw_1 + P_2\, dw_2 + P_3\, dw_3) \wedge (Q_1\, dw_1 + Q_2\, dw_2 + Q_3\, dw_3) \\ &\quad = (P_2Q_3 - P_3Q_2)\, dw_2 \wedge dw_3 + (P_3Q_1 - P_1Q_3)\, dw_3 \wedge dw_1 \\ &\quad + (P_1Q_2 - P_2Q_1)\, dw_1 \wedge dw_2.\end{aligned} \tag{4.5.8}$$

Here P_i and Q_i are functions of $\mathbf{w} \in \mathbb{R}^3$, and Equation (4.5.3) has again been used.

Consider now the differential forms (on $\mathbb{R}^n$):

$$\lambda = f(\mathbf{w})\, dm \text{ where } dm = dw_{i_1} \wedge dw_{i_2} \wedge \ldots \wedge dw_{i_r}; \tag{4.5.9}$$

$$\mu = g(\mathbf{w})\, dr \text{ where } dr = dw_{j_1} \wedge dw_{j_2} \wedge \ldots \wedge dw_{j_s}; \tag{4.5.10}$$

and also the change of variable $\mathbf{w} = \varphi(\mathbf{z})$, where $\varphi : \mathbb{R}^m \to \mathbb{R}^n$, and also the real functions f and g, are twice continuously differentiable. (In fact, we require continuous differentiability, up to the order of derivatives which appear in the formulas. Some books specify C^∞, but we don't need it.) Define now a *differentiation* d, which maps each r-form to an $(r+1)$-form, and a *change-of-variable operation* φ^*, which maps a form on $\mathbb{R}^n$ to a form on $\mathbb{R}^m$. (Note that φ^* will later turn out to agree with Equation (4.4.9)). Define, then,

$$\mathrm{d}\lambda = \mathrm{d}f(w) \wedge \mathrm{d}m \text{ where } \mathrm{d}f(w) = f'(w)\,\mathrm{d}w, \tag{4.5.11}$$

where $f'(w)$ is the Fréchet derivative of f, and

$$\varphi^*\lambda = (f \circ \varphi_1)(z)[\varphi'_{i_1}(z)\,\mathrm{d}z] \wedge [\varphi'_{i_2}(z)\,\mathrm{d}z] \wedge \ldots \wedge [\varphi'_{i_r}(z)\,\mathrm{d}z], \tag{4.5.12}$$

where $\varphi'_{i_j}(z)$ is the Fréchet derivative of component i_j of $\varphi(\cdot)$. Also d and φ^* are made into *linear* mappings by requiring that

$$\mathrm{d}(\alpha\lambda+\beta\mu) = \alpha\,\mathrm{d}\lambda+\beta\,\mathrm{d}\mu;\ \varphi^*(\alpha\lambda+\beta\mu) = \alpha\varphi^*\lambda+\beta\varphi^*\mu; \tag{4.5.13}$$

for any real constants α and β.

Theorem 4.5

The mappings d and φ^* have the following properties:

(i) $\varphi^*(\lambda \wedge \mu) = (\varphi^*\lambda) \wedge (\varphi^*\mu)$. (4.5.14)

(ii) $\mathrm{d}(\mathrm{d}\lambda) = 0$. (4.5.15)

(iii) $\mathrm{d}(\lambda \wedge \mu) = (\mathrm{d}\,\lambda) \wedge \mu+(-1)^r\lambda \wedge (\mathrm{d}\mu)$, where λ has degree r. (4.5.16)

(iv) $\varphi^*(\mathrm{d}f(w)) = \mathrm{d}((f\circ\varphi)(z))$. (4.5.17)

(v) $\varphi^*(\mathrm{d}\lambda) = \mathrm{d}(\varphi^*\lambda)$. (4.5.18)

Proof (i)

$$\begin{aligned}\varphi^*(\lambda \wedge \mu) &= \varphi^*(f(w)g(w)\,\mathrm{d}m \wedge \mathrm{d}r)\\ &= (f\circ\varphi)(z)(g\circ\varphi)(z)\varphi^*(\mathrm{d}m) \wedge \varphi^*(\mathrm{d}r)\\ &\quad \text{by (4.5.12)}\\ &= (\varphi^*\lambda) \wedge (\varphi^*\mu).\end{aligned}$$

(ii) $$\mathrm{d}(\mathrm{d}\lambda) = \mathrm{d}\left(\sum_i \frac{\partial f(w)}{\partial w_i}\,\mathrm{d}w_i\right) \wedge \mathrm{d}m = \sum_{j,\,i} \frac{\partial^2 f(w)}{\partial w_j \partial w_i}\,\mathrm{d}w_j \wedge \mathrm{d}w_i \wedge \mathrm{d}m.$$

For $i = j$, $\mathrm{d}w_i \wedge \mathrm{d}w_i = 0$. For $i \neq j$, $\mathrm{d}w_j \wedge \mathrm{d}w_i = -\,\mathrm{d}w_i \wedge \mathrm{d}w_j$ and $\dfrac{\partial^2 f(w)}{\partial w_j \partial w_i} = \dfrac{\partial^2 f(w)}{\partial w_i \partial w_j}$ by Theorem 2.8. So the sum vanishes.

(iii) $\mathrm{d}(\lambda \wedge \mu) = \mathrm{d}(f(w)g(w)\,\mathrm{d}m \wedge \mathrm{d}r)$
$= \mathrm{d}f(w) \wedge g(w)\,\mathrm{d}m \wedge \mathrm{d}r + f(w)\,\mathrm{d}g(w) \wedge \mathrm{d}m \wedge \mathrm{d}r$
$= (\mathrm{d}\lambda) \wedge \mu + (-1)^r f(w)\,\mathrm{d}m \wedge \mathrm{d}g(w) \wedge \mathrm{d}r$
after r interchanges of pairs of terms, using Equation (4.5.3)
$= (\mathrm{d}\lambda) \wedge \mu + (-1)^r \lambda \wedge (\mathrm{d}\mu)$.

(iv) $\varphi^*(\mathrm{d}f(w)) = f'(\varphi(z))\varphi'(z)\,\mathrm{d}z = (f \circ \varphi)'(z)\,\mathrm{d}z$ by the chain rule
$= \mathrm{d}((f \circ \varphi)(z))$.

(v) This holds, by (iv), when λ has degree $r = 0$. Suppose Equation (4.5.18) holds when λ has degree r. Then
$\varphi^*\mathrm{d}(\lambda \wedge w_k) = \varphi^*(\mathrm{d}\lambda \wedge \mathrm{d}w_k)$ by (4.5.11)
$= [\varphi^*(\mathrm{d}\lambda)] \wedge [\varphi^*(\mathrm{d}w_k)]$ by (4.5.14)
$= (\mathrm{d}\varphi^*\lambda) \wedge (\varphi^*(\mathrm{d}w_k))$ by assumption
$= \mathrm{d}[(\varphi^*\lambda) \wedge (\varphi^*(\mathrm{d}w_k))] - (-1)^r(\varphi^*\lambda) \wedge \mathrm{d}(\varphi^*\,\mathrm{d}w_k)$
by (4.5.16)
$= \mathrm{d}\varphi^*(\lambda \wedge w_k) - 0$ using (4.5.14), and $\mathrm{d}(\varphi^*\,\mathrm{d}w_k) = 0$
(which follows from (4.5.4)). Hence (4.5.18) holds for $(r+1)$-forms, and hence, by induction, for all forms. □

Example
Let $\lambda = g_1\,\mathrm{d}w_1 + g_2\,\mathrm{d}w_2 + g_3\,\mathrm{d}w_3$ in $\mathbb{R}^3$, where $g_i = g_i(\mathbf{w})$. Then

$$\mathrm{d}(g_1\,\mathrm{d}w_1) = \sum_i \frac{\partial g_i}{\partial w_i}\,\mathrm{d}w_i \wedge \mathrm{d}w_1 = \frac{\partial g_1}{\partial w_2}\,\mathrm{d}w_2 \wedge \mathrm{d}w_1 + \frac{\partial g_1}{\partial w_3}\,\mathrm{d}w_3 \wedge \mathrm{d}w_1.$$

Combining three such expressions gives

$$\mathrm{d}(g_1\,\mathrm{d}w_1 + g_2\,\mathrm{d}w_2 + g_3\,\mathrm{d}w_3) = \left(\frac{\partial g_3}{\partial w_2} - \frac{\partial g_2}{\partial w_3}\right)\mathrm{d}w_2 \wedge \mathrm{d}w_3$$
$$+\left(\frac{\partial g_1}{\partial w_3} - \frac{\partial g_3}{\partial w_1}\right)\mathrm{d}w_3 \wedge \mathrm{d}w_1 + \left(\frac{\partial g_2}{\partial w_1} - \frac{\partial g_1}{\partial w_2}\right)\mathrm{d}w_1 \wedge \mathrm{d}w_2. \tag{4.5.19}$$

The right side of Equation (4.5.19) may be written, with the surface integral (4.4.14) in mind, as $P_1\,\mathrm{d}w_2 \wedge \mathrm{d}w_3 + P_2\,\mathrm{d}w_3 \wedge \mathrm{d}w_1 + P_3\,\mathrm{d}w_1 \wedge \mathrm{d}w_2$, where P_1, P_2, P_3 are the components of a vector, denoted by curl $\mathbf{g}$.

Example

Let $f : \mathbb{R}^3 \to \mathbb{R}$ be differentiable. Then

$$\mathrm{d}f(\mathbf{w}) = (\text{grad } f)\cdot \mathrm{d}\mathbf{w} \tag{4.5.20}$$

where grad f denotes the vector whose components are $\partial f/\partial w_i$ ($i = 1, 2, 3$), and $\mathrm{d}\mathbf{w}$ denotes the vector with components $\mathrm{d}w_i$ ($i = 1, 2, 3$). Often, grad f is denoted by ∇f.

Example

$$\text{Let } \mu = F_1\, \mathrm{d}w_2 \wedge \mathrm{d}w_3 + F_2\, \mathrm{d}w_3 \wedge \mathrm{d}w_1 + F_3\, \mathrm{d}w_1 \wedge \mathrm{d}w_2, \tag{4.5.21}$$

where $(F_1, F_2, F_3) = \mathbf{F} \equiv \mathbf{F}(\mathbf{w})$ is a vector function in $\mathbb{R}^3$. Then

$$\mathrm{d}\mu = (\text{div } \mathbf{F})\, \mathrm{d}w_1 \wedge \mathrm{d}w_2 \wedge \mathrm{d}w_3, \tag{4.5.22}$$

where the *divergence* of $\mathbf{F}$ is defined as

$$\text{div } \mathbf{F} = \frac{\partial F_1}{\partial w_1} + \frac{\partial F_2}{\partial w_2} + \frac{\partial F_3}{\partial w_3}. \tag{4.5.23}$$

A differential form λ (in a region E) is called *closed* if $\mathrm{d}\lambda = 0$; it is called *exact* if $\lambda = \mathrm{d}\theta$ for some differential form θ (in E). For example, if $\theta = P(x, y)\, \mathrm{d}x + Q(x, y)\, \mathrm{d}y$ (in $E \subset \mathbb{R}^2$), then $\lambda = \mathrm{d}\theta = (Q_x - P_y)\, \mathrm{d}x \wedge \mathrm{d}y$ is exact in E. An exact form is always closed (since $\mathrm{d}(\mathrm{d}\theta) = 0$ by Theorem 4.5(ii)). (See Exercises 4.5.7 and 4.5.8, and Section 4.6, for further discussion.)

(The word *closed* has many uses: a *closed curve* – final point equals initial point; a *closed set* – including its boundary points; a *closed surface* – with no boundary curves, as e.g. a sphere; and a *closed differential form*; are all different.)

Exercise 4.5.1 Calculate the exterior product of the two differential forms

$\lambda = (x^2 + y^2 + z^2)\, \mathrm{d}x$ and $\mu = x\, \mathrm{d}y \wedge \mathrm{d}z + y\, \mathrm{d}z \wedge \mathrm{d}x$ (in $\mathbb{R}^3$).

Exercise 4.5.2 Express, in its simplest form, the exterior product

$(A(x, y)\, \mathrm{d}x + B(x, y)\, \mathrm{d}y) \wedge (C(x, y)\, \mathrm{d}x + D(x, y)\, \mathrm{d}y)$ (in $\mathbb{R}^2$).

Exercise 4.5.3 Calculate $\mathrm{d}\lambda$ when:

(i) $\lambda = xy^2\, \mathrm{d}x - x^2y\, \mathrm{d}y$ (in $\mathbb{R}^2$);

(ii) $\lambda = x\, \mathrm{d}y \wedge \mathrm{d}z - y\, \mathrm{d}z \wedge \mathrm{d}x$ (in $\mathbb{R}^3$);

(iii) $\lambda = \sin(x^2+y^2)\, \mathrm{d}x \wedge \mathrm{d}z \qquad (\text{in } \mathbb{R}^3)$.
(Note that $\mathrm{d}\lambda$ is often called the *exterior differential* of λ.)

Exercise 4.5.4 A differential form λ is defined in $\mathbb{R}^3\backslash\{0\}$ by

$$\lambda = r^{-3}(x\, \mathrm{d}y \wedge \mathrm{d}z + y\, \mathrm{d}z \wedge \mathrm{d}x + z\, \mathrm{d}x \wedge \mathrm{d}y),$$
$$\text{where } r = (x^2+y^2+z^2)^{1/2}.$$

Show that $d\lambda = 0$ in $\mathbb{R}^3\backslash\{0\}$. Explain why the point 0 must here be removed from $\mathbb{R}^3$.

Exercise 4.5.5 Verify $\mathrm{d}(\mathrm{d}\lambda) = 0$ when λ is the form of Exercise 4.5.2.

Exercise 4.5.6 Let $\varphi : \mathbb{R}^2 \to \mathbb{R}^2$ be the linear mapping, given by the matrix M. If λ is the differential form of Exercise 4.5.2, calculate $\varphi^*\lambda$, from its definition, and also using the result of Theorem 4.5(i). Also verify the result of Theorem 4.5(v) in this instance.

Exercise 4.5.7 Show that the differential form $\lambda = P(x, y)\, \mathrm{d}x + Q(x, y)\, \mathrm{d}y$ (in $\mathbb{R}^2$) is *closed* if and only if $P_y(x, y) = Q_x(x, y)$ for each point $(x, y) \in \mathbb{R}^2$. Conversely, assuming that $P_y = Q_x$, show that $\lambda = \mathrm{d}\hat{F}(x, y)$ where $\hat{F}$ is given by Equation (4.4.16), and deduce that λ is *exact*. Observe that, if λ is an exact form and Γ is a closed curve, then $\oint_\Gamma \lambda = 0$. Why does this *not* always hold when the *exact* property only holds for $(x, y) \in \mathbb{R}^2\backslash\{0\}$? (Consider, for example, functions P and Q which do not have finite values at (0, 0). What goes wrong with the argument, following from Equation (4.4.16), if there is such an exceptional point, removed from the rectangle?)

Exercise 4.5.8 Show that $P\, \mathrm{d}x + Q\, \mathrm{d}y + R\, \mathrm{d}z$ (where P, Q and R are continuously differentiable on $\mathbb{R}^3$) is *exact* if and only if $P_y = Q_x$, $Q_z = R_y$, $R_x = P_z$ hold for *all* $(x, y, z) \in \mathbb{R}^3$. (Use Theorem 4.4.)

Exercise 4.5.9 For $\mathbf{w} \in \mathbb{R}^3$, define $\mathbf{f}(\mathbf{w}) = \mathbf{w}$. Show that div $\mathbf{f} = 3$ and curl $\mathbf{f} = \mathbf{0}$. If $\mathbf{g}(\mathbf{w}) = \|\mathbf{w}\|^n\mathbf{w}$, show that div $\mathbf{g}(\mathbf{w}) = (n+3)\|\mathbf{w}\|^n$. (Note that a traditional notation writes $\mathbf{r}$, meaning radius vector, for both $\mathbf{w}$ and $\mathbf{f}(\mathbf{w})$, and thus, for example, obtains div $\mathbf{r} = 3$. But the use of the same notation for function and function value can confuse.)

Exercise 4.5.10 Let $\mathbf{f} : \mathbb{R}^3 \to \mathbb{R}^3$ and $\mathbf{g} : \mathbb{R}^3 \to \mathbb{R}^3$ be given differentiable functions; let $\mathbf{a} \in \mathbb{R}^3$. Denote inner product of $\mathbf{a}$ with

$\mathbf{f}(\mathbf{w})$ by $\mathbf{a}\cdot\mathbf{f}(\mathbf{w})$. If $\mathbf{p}, \mathbf{q} \in \mathbb{R}^3$, then $\mathbf{p}\times\mathbf{q}$ is the vector with components $(p_2q_3-p_3q_2,\ p_3q_1-p_1q_3,\ p_2q_1-p_1q_2)$. Note that, if ∇ denotes the 'vector' $(\partial/\partial w_1,\ \partial/\partial w_2,\ \partial/\partial w_3)$, then Equations (4.5.19) and (4.5.23) show that, formally,

$$\operatorname{curl} \mathbf{f}(\mathbf{w}) = \nabla \times \mathbf{f}(\mathbf{w}) \qquad \text{and} \qquad \operatorname{div} \mathbf{f}(\mathbf{w}) = \nabla \cdot \mathbf{f}(\mathbf{w}).$$

Now show that:

(i) $\operatorname{grad}(\mathbf{a}\cdot\mathbf{f}(\mathbf{w})) = \mathbf{a}\cdot\operatorname{grad}\mathbf{f}(\mathbf{w})+\mathbf{a}\times\operatorname{curl}\mathbf{f}(\mathbf{w})$.

(ii) $\operatorname{div}(\mathbf{a}\times\mathbf{f}(\mathbf{w})) = -\mathbf{a}\cdot\operatorname{curl}\mathbf{f}(\mathbf{w})$.

(iii) $\operatorname{curl}(\mathbf{a}\times\mathbf{f}(\mathbf{w})) = \mathbf{a}\operatorname{div}\mathbf{f}(\mathbf{w})-\mathbf{a}\cdot\nabla\mathbf{f}(\mathbf{w})$, noting that $\mathbf{a}\cdot\nabla\mathbf{f}(\mathbf{w})$ equals the directional derivatives $\mathbf{f}'(\mathbf{w})\mathbf{a}$.

(iv) $\operatorname{div}(\mathbf{f}(\mathbf{w})\times\mathbf{g}(\mathbf{w})) = \mathbf{g}(\mathbf{w})\cdot\operatorname{curl}\mathbf{f}(\mathbf{w})-\mathbf{f}(\mathbf{w})\cdot\operatorname{curl}\mathbf{g}(\mathbf{w})$.

(v) $\operatorname{curl}(\mathbf{f}(\mathbf{w})\times\mathbf{g}(\mathbf{w})) = \mathbf{g}(\mathbf{w})\cdot\nabla\mathbf{f}(\mathbf{w})-\mathbf{f}(\mathbf{w})\cdot\nabla\mathbf{g}(\mathbf{w})+\mathbf{f}(\mathbf{w})\operatorname{div}\mathbf{g}(\mathbf{w})-\mathbf{g}(\mathbf{w})\operatorname{div}\mathbf{f}(\mathbf{w})$ in which $\mathbf{g}(\mathbf{w})\cdot\nabla\mathbf{f}(\mathbf{w})$ means the directional derivative $\mathbf{f}'(\mathbf{w})\mathbf{g}(\mathbf{w})$.

(vi) $\operatorname{div}(h(\mathbf{w})\mathbf{f}(\mathbf{w})) = (\operatorname{grad} h(\mathbf{w}))\cdot\mathbf{f}(\mathbf{w})+h(\mathbf{w})\operatorname{div}\mathbf{f}(\mathbf{w})$, where $h : \mathbb{R}^3 \to \mathbb{R}$ is a real differentiable function.

4.6 STOKES'S THEOREM

Let M denote a curve, surface, or volume, specified as $M = \varphi(Q)$, where φ is continuously differentiable, and Q is an *interval* in $\mathbb{R}^m$. For convenience in proving a theorem, assume that the coordinates are scaled to make Q a *cube* of side 1 (thus $Q = [0, 1]^m$ – see Fig. 4.8). (This restriction to a cube will not be needed in applications.)

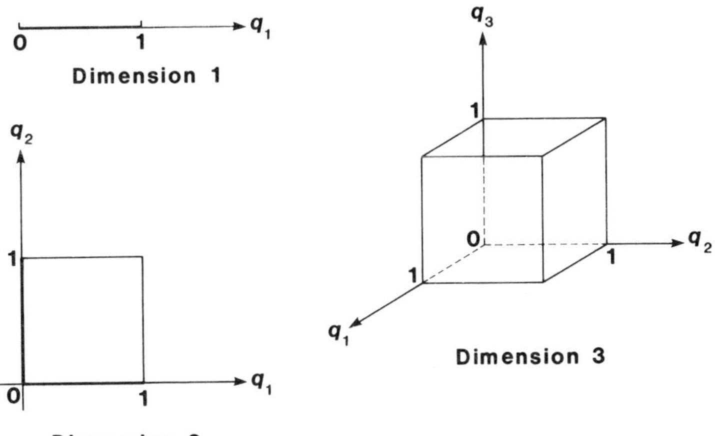

Figure 4.8 Intervals and boundaries

The *boundary* ∂Q of Q consists of 2^m faces, specified respectively by

$$q_1 = 0, q_1 = 1, q_2 = 0, q_2 = 1, \text{etc.}$$

To the face specified by $q_k = 0$, attach a sign $(-1)^k$; to the face specified by $q_k = 1$, attach a sign $(-1)^{k+1}$. Let θ denote a differential form

$$\theta = f(q)\,dq_1 \wedge dq_2 \wedge \ldots \wedge \widehat{dq_k} \wedge \ldots \wedge dq_m; \qquad (4.6.1)$$

here the coordinates occur in numerical order, and $\widehat{dq_k}$ indicates that dq_k is *omitted.* The integral $\int_{\partial Q}\theta$ is now considered as the sum of integrals of θ over the faces comprising Q, with the sign $(-1)^k$ or $(-1)^{k+1}$ attached to each face.

In particular, consider $m = 3$, and $\theta = f(q)\,dq_1 \wedge dq_2$. The Fubini theorem (Theorem 4.1) permits a double integral to be evaluated as a repeated integral. Using this, and the above sign convention for faces,

$$\begin{aligned}\int_{\partial Q}\theta &= \int_{\partial Q} f(q)\,dq_1 \wedge dq_2 \\ &= \int\int\int_Q [f(q_1, q_2, 1) - f(q_1, q_2, 0)]\,dq_1\,dq_2\,dq_3, \quad (4.6.2)\end{aligned}$$

where now we omit the wedges, for brevity. From Equations (4.5.11) and (4.5.4),

$$d\theta = \sum_{i=1}^{3}\left(\frac{\partial f}{\partial q_i}dq_i\right)dq_1\,dq_2 = \frac{\partial f}{\partial q_3}dq_3\,dq_1\,dq_2$$

Hence, using Fubini's theorem again,

$$\begin{aligned}\int_Q d\theta &= \int\int_A\left(\int_0^1\frac{\partial f}{\partial q_3}dq_3\right)dq_1\,dq_2 \\ &= \int\int\int_Q [f(q_1, q_2, 1) - f(q_1, q_2, 0)]\,dq_1\,dq_2\,dq_3, (4.6.3)\end{aligned}$$

where A is the square $[0, 1]^2$, and we note that $\int_0^1 \ldots dq_3$ has no effect when the integrand does not depend on q_3. Comparison of Equations (4.6.2) and (4.6.3) shows that

$$\int_{\partial Q}\theta = \int_Q d\theta. \qquad (4.6.4)$$

A similar proof proves (4.6.4) for any $(m-1)$-form, with Q a cube in $\mathbb{R}^m$, if the sign convention is assumed for faces of ∂Q.

Consider now integrals over M which satisfy Equation (4.4.9), namely

$$\int_M \lambda \equiv \int_{\varphi(Q)} \lambda = \int_Q \varphi^* \lambda. \tag{4.6.5}$$

For such integrals, assuming that Q is a cube, with faces following the sign convention, the following theorem holds (note that $\partial M = \varphi(\partial Q)$).

Theorem 4.6 (Stokes's theorem)
Let λ be an $(m-1)$-form in $\mathbb{R}^n$; let $M = \varphi(Q)$ where $\varphi : \mathbb{R}^m \to \mathbb{R}^n$ is continuously differentiable, and Q is an interval of dimension m in $\mathbb{R}^m$ (the product of m intervals in $\mathbb{R}$). Then

$$\int_M \mathrm{d}\lambda = \int_{\partial M} \lambda. \tag{4.6.6}$$

Proof Using Equation (4.6.5) twice, and (4.5.18),

$$\int_{\partial M} \lambda = \int_{\partial Q} \varphi^* \lambda \text{ and } \int_M \mathrm{d}\lambda = \int_Q \varphi^*(\mathrm{d}\lambda) = \int_Q \mathrm{d}(\varphi^* \lambda). \tag{4.6.7}$$

Then (4.6.6) follows from (4.6.7), and (4.6.4) with $\theta = \varphi^* \lambda$. □

Example
Let Λ denote a surface (in $\mathbb{R}^3$), with $\Lambda = \varphi(Q)$ where Q is an interval in $\mathbb{R}^2$. Then the boundary $\partial\Lambda$ is a closed curve; intuitively, the surface 'has no holes in it'. Let $\mathbf{g} : \Lambda \to \mathbb{R}^3$ be a continuously differentiable vector function. Then, from Equation (4.6.6) with $\lambda = g_1\, \mathrm{d}w_1 + g_2\, \mathrm{d}w_2 + g_3\, \mathrm{d}w_3$,

$$\int_{\partial\Lambda} (g_1\, \mathrm{d}w_1 + g_2\, \mathrm{d}w_2 + g_3\, \mathrm{d}w_3) \equiv \int_{\partial\Lambda} \mathbf{g} \cdot \hat{\mathbf{t}}\, \mathrm{d}s = \int_\Lambda (\mathrm{curl})\, \mathbf{g} \cdot \hat{\mathbf{n}}\, \mathrm{d}A \tag{4.6.8}$$

using (4.5.19) for $\mathrm{d}\lambda$. Result (4.6.8) is the historic theorem proved by Stokes, of which (4.6.7) is a generalization.

Example
Let Q be a cube in $\mathbb{R}^3$; let $\varphi : \mathbb{R}^3 \to \mathbb{R}^3$ define a volume $V = \varphi(Q)$ in $\mathbb{R}^3$. Observe that the boundary ∂V may be pictured as a

deformed sphere (deformed like a rubber sheet, allowing any amount of stretching, but no cutting or joining). Then, using Equations (4.5.22) and (4.5.23), we obtain Gauss's *divergence theorem*:

$$\int_V \operatorname{div} \mathbf{F} \, dv = \int_{\partial V} \mathbf{F} \cdot \hat{\mathbf{n}} \, dA. \qquad (4.6.9)$$

Here $\mathbf{F} : \mathbb{R}^3 \to \mathbb{R}^3$ is a continuously differentiable vector function, $\hat{\mathbf{n}}$ is the outward-pointing normal to V at a point of ∂V, and $\int \ldots dv$ and $\int \ldots dA$ denote respectively integrals with respect to volume and surface area (of ∂V).

Example Consider now a surface $\Lambda \subset \mathbb{R}^3$, but now with a 'hole' in it. Then the boundary $\partial\Lambda$ consists of (at least) two parts. Assume here that $\partial\Lambda$ consists of an outer boundary Γ and an inner boundary Π, each of them being a 'rubber sheet deformation' of a circle. Since the

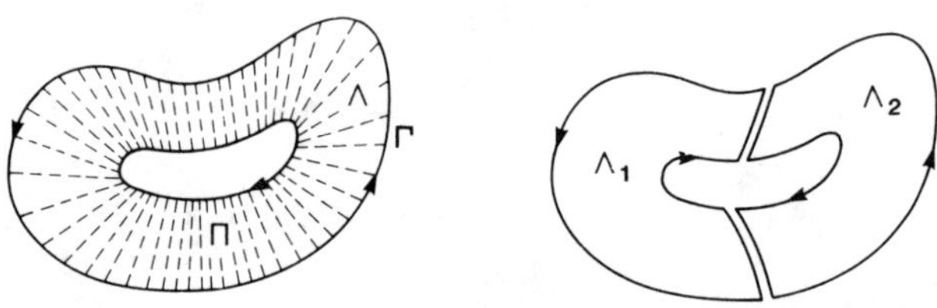

Figure 4.9 Integrating over a surface

historic Stokes's theorem cannot be applied to Λ as it stands, we make two transversal cuts (as shown in Fig. 4.9) to divide Λ into two surfaces Λ_1 and Λ_2, to each of which Stokes's theorem can be applied. (We shall assume here, without discussion, that each of Λ_1 and Λ_2 can be suitably parametrized.) Given a continuously differentiable function $\mathbf{g} : \Lambda \to \mathbb{R}^3$, we now apply Equation (4.6.8) to Λ_1 and to Λ_2 separately, then add the results. The line integrals along the transversal cuts cancel out, since their directions are opposite for $\partial\Lambda_1$ and $\partial\Lambda_2$. The result is:

$$\int_{\partial\Lambda} (\operatorname{curl} \mathbf{g}) \cdot \hat{\mathbf{n}} \, dA = \int_\Gamma \mathbf{g} \cdot \hat{\mathbf{t}} \, ds + \int_\Pi \mathbf{g} \cdot \hat{\mathbf{t}} \, ds = \int_{\partial\Lambda} \mathbf{g} \cdot \hat{\mathbf{t}} \, ds, \quad (4.6.10)$$

provided that Γ and Π are given (as shown) opposite orientations (anticlockwise and clockwise respectively), to agree with the orientations of $\partial\Lambda_1$ and $\partial\Lambda_2$. On $\Pi \subset \partial\Lambda$, the normal $\hat{\mathbf{n}}$ points out of Λ, and thus into the 'hole'.

Consider now two regions (curves, surfaces or volumes) M and N, related to the parameter interval Q as shown in Fig. 4.10.

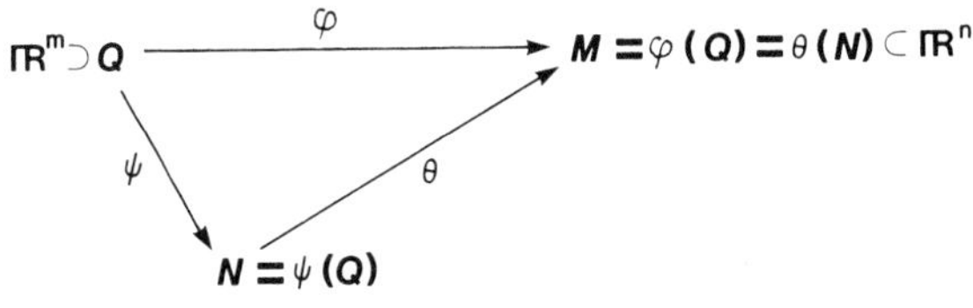

Figure 4.10

The mappings φ, ψ and θ are assumed continuously differentiable. The change-of-variable formula for integration of a differential form is given by the following theorem.

Theorem 4.7
Let λ be a differential form in $\mathbb{R}^n$; let Q be an interval in $\mathbb{R}^m$; let φ, ψ and θ be continuously differentiable mappings for which $M = \varphi(Q)$, $N = \psi(Q)$, $M = \theta(N)$. Then

$$\int_M \lambda = \int_N \theta^* \lambda. \tag{4.6.11}$$

Proof From Equation (4.6.5),

$$\int_M \lambda = \int_Q \varphi^* \lambda = \int_Q \psi^*(\theta^* \lambda) = \int_{\psi(Q)} \theta^* \lambda = \int_N \theta^* \lambda.$$

This has assumed that $(\theta \circ \psi)^* = \psi^* \circ \theta^*$, which follows readily from Equation (4.5.12) and the chain rule. □

Remark Consider $\lambda = f(w)\, dw_1 \wedge \ldots \wedge dw_r$ in $\mathbb{R}^n$. From Equations (4.5.12) and (4.5.7),

$$\varphi^* \lambda = (f \circ \varphi)(z) \cdot \left[\sum_{j_1, j_2, \ldots, j_r = 1}^{m} \varepsilon_{j_1 j_2 \ldots j_r} \frac{\partial \varphi_{i_1}}{\partial z_{j_1}} \frac{\partial \varphi_{i_2}}{\partial z_{j_2}} \cdots \frac{\partial \varphi_{i_r}}{\partial z_{j_r}} \right] dz_{j_1} \wedge \ldots \wedge dz_{j_r}, \tag{4.6.12}$$

in which $\varepsilon_{j_1 j_2 \ldots j_r}$ denotes the number of transpositions (interchanges of pairs of elements) to change the sequence $\{j_1, j_2, \ldots, j_r\}$

of integers into $\{1, 2, \ldots, r\}$. In particular, if $m = r$, then the expression in [ ] equals the determinant of the matrix whose i, j element is $\partial\varphi_i/\partial z_j$; thus [ ] then equals $\det \varphi'(z)$. Hence, in this case, Equation (4.6.11) reduces to the earlier change-of-variable theorem (Theorem 4.2 – see Equation 4.2.9).

Remark This discussion of differential forms has assumed *cartesian coordinates*; thus, in particular, the expressions (4.5.19) for curl $\mathbf{g}$ and (4.5.23) for div $\mathbf{F}$ are only valid when w_1, w_2, w_3 are cartesian coordinates in $\mathbb{R}^3$. However, Theorems 4.6 and 4.7 remain valid for some more general coordinate systems. We show by examples how this works.

Let w_1, w_2, w_3 be cartesian coordinates in $\mathbb{R}^3$; let p_1, p_2, p_3 be cylindrical polar coordinates, defined by

$$w = \theta(\mathbf{p}) \Leftrightarrow \{w_1 = p_1 \cos p_2,\ w_2 = p_1 \sin p_2,\ w_3 = p_3\}, \tag{4.6.13}$$

where $p_1 \in \mathbb{R}_+ \equiv [0, \infty)$, $0 \leq p_2 \leq \pi$, $p_3 \in \mathbb{R}$. (Conventionally, r, φ, z are written for these p_1, p_2, p_3.) Calculate

$$\theta'(\mathbf{p}) = \begin{bmatrix} \cos p_2 & -p_1 \sin p_2 & 0 \\ \sin p_2 & p_1 \cos p_2 & 0 \\ 0 & 0 & 1 \end{bmatrix} \tag{4.6.14}$$

Let $\mathbf{F} = (F_1, F_2, F_3) : \mathbb{R}^3 \to \mathbb{R}^3$ be a continuously differentiable vector function. Denote $\bar{F}_i = F_i \circ \theta$, for $i = 1, 2, 3$. At each point of $\mathbb{R}^3$, the three columns of $\theta'(\mathbf{p})$ define three directions, given by the unit vectors

$$\begin{bmatrix} \cos p_2 \\ \sin p_2 \\ 0 \end{bmatrix}, \begin{bmatrix} -\sin p_2 \\ \cos p_2 \\ 0 \end{bmatrix}, \begin{bmatrix} 0 \\ 0 \\ 1 \end{bmatrix}. \tag{4.6.15}$$

(Note that the columns of $\theta'(\mathbf{p})$ have been thus divided by the *scale factors* $1, p_1, 1$). We now express $\mathbf{F}(\mathbf{p})$ in terms of new components, in the directions given by (4.6.15), namely components

$$\begin{aligned} \hat{F}_1(\mathbf{p}) &= \bar{F}_1(\mathbf{p}) \cos p_2 + \bar{F}_2(\mathbf{p}) \sin p_2, \\ \hat{F}_2(\mathbf{p}) &= -\bar{F}_1(\mathbf{p}) \sin p_2 + \bar{F}_2(\mathbf{p}) \cos p_2,\ \hat{F}_3(\mathbf{p}) = \bar{F}_3(\mathbf{p}). \end{aligned} \tag{4.6.16}$$

Observe that (4.6.16) is valid because the vectors (4.6.15) are mutually perpendicular; a coordinate system (p_1, p_2, p_3) for which this happens is called a system of *orthogonal curvilinear coordinates.*

Define now the differential forms

$$\mu = F_1(w)\,\mathrm{d}w_2 \wedge \mathrm{d}w_3 + F_2(w)\,\mathrm{d}w_3 \wedge \mathrm{d}w_1 + F_3(w)\,\mathrm{d}w_1 \wedge \mathrm{d}w_3; \tag{4.6.17}$$

$$\lambda = F_1(w)\,\mathrm{d}w_1 + F_2(w)\,\mathrm{d}w_2 + F_3(w)\,\mathrm{d}w_3. \tag{4.6.18}$$

We calculate, using Equations (4.5.11) and (4.5.3), that

$$\begin{aligned}\theta^*\mu &= \bar{F}_1(\mathbf{p})((\sin p_2)\,\mathrm{d}p_1 + (p_1 \cos p_2)\,\mathrm{d}p_2) \wedge \mathrm{d}p_3 \\ &\quad + \bar{F}_2(\mathbf{p})\,\mathrm{d}p_3 \wedge ((\cos p_2)\,\mathrm{d}p_1 + (-p_1 \sin p_2)\,\mathrm{d}p_2) \\ &\quad + \bar{F}_3(\mathbf{p})((\cos p_2)\,\mathrm{d}p_1 + (-p_1 \sin p_2)\,\mathrm{d}p_2) \wedge ((\sin p_2)\,\mathrm{d}p_1 \\ &\quad + (p_1 \cos p_2)\,\mathrm{d}p_2) \\ &= p_1(\bar{F}_1(\mathbf{p}) \cos p_2 + \bar{F}_2(\mathbf{p}) \sin p_2)\,\mathrm{d}p_2 \wedge \mathrm{d}p_3 \\ &\quad + (-\bar{F}_1(\mathbf{p}) \sin p_2 + \bar{F}_2(\mathbf{p}) \cos p_2)\,\mathrm{d}p_3 \wedge \mathrm{d}p_1 + \bar{F}_3(\mathbf{p}) p_1\,\mathrm{d}p_1 \wedge \mathrm{d}p_2 \\ &= \bar{F}_3(\mathbf{p}) p_1\,\mathrm{d}p_1 \wedge \mathrm{d}p_2 + p_1 \hat{F}_1(\mathbf{p})\,\mathrm{d}p_2 \wedge \mathrm{d}p_3 + \hat{F}_2(\mathbf{p})\,\mathrm{d}p_3 \wedge \mathrm{d}p_1.\end{aligned} \tag{4.6.19}$$

A similar calculation shows that

$$\theta^*\lambda = \hat{F}_1(\mathbf{p})\,\mathrm{d}p_1 + p_1 \hat{F}_2(\mathbf{p})\,\mathrm{d}p_2 + \hat{F}_3(\mathbf{p})\,\mathrm{d}p_3. \tag{4.6.20}$$

Then, using Equation (4.5.12), we calculate

$$\mathrm{d}(\theta^*\mu) = \left[\frac{\partial}{\partial p_3}(p_1 \hat{F}_3(\mathbf{p})) + \frac{\partial}{\partial p_1}(p_1 \hat{F}_1(\mathbf{p})) + \frac{\partial}{\partial p_2}\hat{F}_2(\mathbf{p})\right] \mathrm{d}p_1 \wedge \mathrm{d}p_2 \wedge \mathrm{d}p_3. \tag{4.6.21}$$

In cartesian coordinates, $\mathrm{d}w_1\,\mathrm{d}w_2\,\mathrm{d}w_3$ represents an element of volume (which may be pictured as the volume of a small parallelepiped). In the coordinates p_1, p_2, p_3, the volume element is, instead,

$$(1\,\mathrm{d}p_1) \wedge (p_1\,\mathrm{d}p_2) \wedge (1\,\mathrm{d}p_3) = p_1\,\mathrm{d}p_1 \wedge \mathrm{d}p_2 \wedge \mathrm{d}p_3, \tag{4.6.22}$$

using the above scale factors, and the orthogonality of the coordinates (so that volume = length × width × height). Otherwise, the factor p_1 in (4.6.22) may be obtained as det $\theta'(\mathbf{p})$, using Theorem 4.2. Hence (4.6.21) may be rewritten, noting (4.5.23), as

$$\mathrm{d}(\theta^*\mu) = \theta^*(\mathrm{d}\mu) = (\operatorname{div} \mathbf{F})\, p_1\,\mathrm{d}p_1 \wedge \mathrm{d}p_2 \wedge \mathrm{d}p_3, \tag{4.6.23}$$

where

$$\operatorname{div} \mathbf{F} = p_1^{-1}\frac{\partial}{\partial p_1}(p_1 \hat{F}_1(\mathbf{p})) + p_1^{-1}\frac{\partial}{\partial p_2}\hat{F}_2(\mathbf{p}) + \frac{\partial}{\partial p_3}\hat{F}_3(\mathbf{p}). \tag{4.6.24}$$

Note that (from Theorem 4.7) Theorem 4.6 remains valid in the **p** coordinates:

$$\int_N \theta^*(\mathrm{d}\mu) = \int_N \mathrm{d}(\theta^*\mu) = \int_{\partial N} \theta^*\mu, \tag{4.6.25}$$

where $M = \theta(N)$.

Similarly, from Equation (4.6.20),

$$\begin{aligned}\mathrm{d}(\theta^*\lambda) = &\left[p_1^{-1}\frac{\partial}{\partial p_2}\hat{F}_3(\mathbf{p}) - \frac{\partial}{\partial p_3}\hat{F}_1(\mathbf{p})\right] p_1\,\mathrm{d}p_2 \wedge \mathrm{d}p_3 \\ &+ \left[\frac{\partial}{\partial p_3}\hat{F}_1(\mathbf{p}) - \frac{\partial}{\partial p_1}\hat{F}_3(\mathbf{p})\right] \mathrm{d}p_3 \wedge \mathrm{d}p_1 \\ &+ \left[p_1^{-1}\left(\frac{\partial}{\partial p_1}(p_1\hat{F}_2(\mathbf{p})) - \frac{\partial}{\partial p_2}\hat{F}_1(\mathbf{p})\right)\right] p_1\,\mathrm{d}p_1 \wedge \mathrm{d}p_2.\end{aligned} \tag{4.6.26}$$

Here the expressions $(p_1\,\mathrm{d}p_2) \wedge \mathrm{d}p_3$, $\mathrm{d}p_3 \wedge \mathrm{d}p_1$, and $\mathrm{d}p_1 \wedge (p_1\,\mathrm{d}p_2)$ represent elements of area. Note that the scale factors 1, p_1, 1 also enter here, since they are required in the terms n_1, n_2, n_3 of Equations (4.4.19) and (4.4.20). Consequently, from Equation (4.5.19), curl **F** has components (in the **p** coordinates) given by the three [ ] expressions in Equation (4.6.26).

A similar discussion may be given for spherical polar coordinates, defined by

$$w_1 = p_1 \sin p_2 \cos p_3,\ w_2 = p_1 \sin p_2 \sin p_3,\ w_3 = p_1 \cos p_2, \tag{4.6.27}$$

where $p_1 \in \mathbb{R}_+$, $p_2 \in [0, \pi]$, $p_3 \in [0, 2\pi]$.

Exercise 4.6.1 Use Equation (4.6.8) and Theorem 4.6 to prove Theorem 4.4 (Note that the line integral is *independent of the path* if and only if the line integral equals zero for every *closed* curve in the region). Thus show that:

Exercise 4.6.2 Let $f : \mathbb{R}^3 \to \mathbb{R}$ be a continuously differentiable function. Use Equation (4.6.9) to show that (when $\hat{\mathbf{n}}$ is the unit outward normal)

$$\int_V \operatorname{grad} f\,\mathrm{d}v = \int_{\partial V} f\hat{\mathbf{n}}\,\mathrm{d}A. \tag{4.6.28}$$

(*Hint*: Define $\mathbf{F} : \mathbb{R}^3 \to \mathbb{R}^3$ by $\mathbf{F}(\mathbf{w}) = (f(\mathbf{w}), 0, 0)$.)

Exercise 4.6.3 In Equation (4.6.9), set $\mathbf{g} = \mathbf{G}\times\mathbf{c}$ where $\mathbf{G}$ is a vector function, $\mathbf{c}$ is a fixed vector. (The 'cross product' is defined in Exercise 4.5.10.) Deduce that

$$\int_V \text{curl}\, \mathbf{G}\, \mathrm{d}v = \int_{\partial V} \hat{\mathbf{n}}\times\mathbf{G}\, \mathrm{d}A. \tag{4.6.29}$$

Exercise 4.6.4 Fill in the details of the following deduction from the divergence theorem (Equation (4.6.9)). From div $(f \text{ grad } g) = (\text{grad } f)\cdot(\text{grad } g) + f\nabla^2 g$ (where $\nabla^2 g \equiv \text{div (grad } g) \equiv \nabla\cdot(\nabla g)$), show that (integrating over suitable volume and surface)

$$\int f(\text{grad } g)\cdot\hat{\mathbf{n}}\, \mathrm{d}A = \int((\text{grad } f)\cdot(\text{grad } g) + f\nabla^2 g)\, \mathrm{d}v.$$

Transposing a term, and using a similar result got by exchanging f and g,

$$\int(\text{grad } f)\cdot(\text{grad } g)\, \mathrm{d}v = \int f\hat{\mathbf{n}}\cdot\text{grad } g\, \mathrm{d}A - \int f\nabla^2 g\, \mathrm{d}v.$$

Hence

$$\begin{aligned}\int(f\nabla^2 g - g\nabla^2 f)\, \mathrm{d}v &= \int(f \text{ grad } g - g \text{ grad } f)\cdot\hat{\mathbf{n}}\, \mathrm{d}A \\ &\equiv \int\left(f\frac{\partial g}{\partial n} - g\frac{\partial f}{\partial n}\right) \mathrm{d}A. \end{aligned} \tag{4.6.30}$$

These various results are often called *Green's theorem*. (They are not his only theorem.)

Exercise 4.6.5 From Equation (4.6.8), deduce *Green's theorem in the plane*:

$$\int_{\partial E}[P(x, y)\, \mathrm{d}x + Q(x, y)]\, \mathrm{d}y = \int\int_E[Q_y(x, y) - P_x(x, y)]\, \mathrm{d}x\, \mathrm{d}y, \tag{4.6.31}$$

where E is a (suitably specified) region in the plane.

Exercise 4.6.6 Define $f : \mathbb{R}^3 \to \mathbb{R}^3$ by $\mathbf{f}(\mathbf{w}) = \mathbf{w}$. Show that (under any suitable conditions) $\frac{1}{2}\int_{\partial\Lambda}\mathbf{f}\times\hat{\mathbf{t}}\, \mathrm{d}s$ measure the area of a surface Λ, and $\frac{1}{2}\int_{\partial V}\mathbf{f}\cdot\hat{\mathbf{n}}\, \mathrm{d}A$ measures the volume of V.

Exercise 4.6.7 Use spherical polar coordinates to calculate the surface area of the cylinder specified by $x^2+y^2 = a^2$, $0 \le z \le b$. (Thus confirm the expressions used for 'elements of area' in Equation (4.6.26).)

Exercise 4.6.8 Define a differential form λ in $\mathbb{R}^4$ by $\lambda = (E_1\,\mathrm{d}w_1 + E_2\,\mathrm{d}w_2 + E_3\,\mathrm{d}w_3) \wedge \mathrm{d}w_4 + B_1\,\mathrm{d}w_2 \wedge \mathrm{d}w_3 + B_2\,\mathrm{d}w_3 \wedge \mathrm{d}w_1 + B_3\,\mathrm{d}w_1 \wedge \mathrm{d}w_2$, in which $\mathbf{E} = (E_1, E_2, E_3)$ and $\mathbf{B} = (B_1, B_2, B_3)$ are vector functions on $\mathbb{R}^3$. Show that $\mathrm{d}\lambda = 0$ if and only if $\left[\text{curl }\mathbf{E} + \frac{\partial \mathbf{B}}{\partial \mathbf{w}_4} = \mathbf{0},\ \text{div }\mathbf{B} = 0\right]$. (The latter system is half of Maxwell's equations of electrodynamics. The other half can also be put in terms of differential forms.)

Exercise 4.6.9 From (4.6.8), show that (for differentiable $f : \mathbb{R}^3 \to \mathbb{R}$):

(i) $\int_\Lambda \hat{\mathbf{n}} \cdot (\text{curl grad } f)\,\mathrm{d}A = \oint_{\partial\Lambda} (\text{grad } f) \cdot \hat{\mathbf{t}}\,\mathrm{d}s = 0$ (and deduce that curl grad $f = 0$ always);

(ii) $\int_\Lambda (\hat{\mathbf{n}} \cdot \text{grad } f)\,\mathrm{d}A = \oint_{\partial\Lambda} f\,\hat{\mathbf{t}}\,\mathrm{d}s$.

Exercise 4.6.10 Let $f : \mathbb{R}^3 \to \mathbb{R}$ and $\rho : \mathbb{R}^3 \to \mathbb{R}$ satisfy *Poisson's equation*: $\nabla^2 f = -4\pi\rho$. Deduce that, for all suitable volumes V,

$$\int_{\partial V} (\text{grad } f) \cdot \hat{\mathbf{n}}\,\mathrm{d}A = -4\pi \int_V \rho\,\mathrm{d}v.$$

Exercise 4.6.11 Let $w = \theta(\mathbf{p})$ where (p_1, p_2, p_3) are spherical polar coordinates (see Equation (4.6.27)) in $\mathbb{R}^3$. Define λ and μ by Equations (4.6.17) and (4.6.18). Show that:

(i) $\theta^*\mu = \hat{F}_1(\mathbf{p})\, p_1^2 \sin p_2\, \mathrm{d}p_2 \wedge \mathrm{d}p_3 + \hat{F}_2(\mathbf{p})\, p_1 \sin p_2\, \mathrm{d}p_3 \wedge \mathrm{d}p_1 + \hat{F}_3(\mathbf{p}) p_1\, \mathrm{d}p_1 \wedge \mathrm{d}p_2$;

(ii) $\mathrm{d}(\theta^*\mu) = (\text{div }\mathbf{F})(p_1^2 \sin p_2)\, \mathrm{d}p_1 \wedge \mathrm{d}p_2 \wedge \mathrm{d}p_3$ where $\text{div }\mathbf{F} = p_1^{-2} \frac{\partial}{\partial p_1}(p_1^2 \hat{F}_1(\mathbf{p})) + (p_1 \sin p_2)^{-1} \frac{\partial}{\partial p_2}(\hat{F}_2(\mathbf{p}) \sin p_2) + (p_1 \sin p_2)^{-1} \frac{\partial}{\partial p_3}(\hat{F}_3(\mathbf{p}))$;

(iii) $\det \theta'(\mathbf{p}) = p_1^2 \sin p_2$;

(iv) (by considering $d(\theta^*\lambda)$) curl **F** has spherical polar components

$$(p_1 \sin p_2)^{-1}\left\{\frac{\partial}{\partial p_2}(\hat{F}_3(\mathbf{p}) \sin p_2) - \frac{\partial}{\partial p_3}\hat{F}_2(\mathbf{p})\right\},$$

$$p_1^{-1}\left\{(\sin p_2)^{-1}\frac{\partial}{\partial p_3}\hat{F}_1(\mathbf{p}) - \frac{\partial}{\partial p_1}(p_1\hat{F}_3(\mathbf{p}))\right\},$$

$$p_1^{-1}\left\{\frac{\partial}{\partial p_1}(p_1\hat{F}_2(\mathbf{p})) - \frac{\partial}{\partial p_2}\hat{F}_1(\mathbf{p}))\right\}.$$

Exercise 4.6.12 In cylindrical polar coordinates (now denoted r, φ, z), show that grad f has components $(\partial f/\partial r, r^{-1}\partial f/\partial\varphi, \partial f/\partial z)$, and consequently that $\nabla^2 f \equiv$ div grad f has expression

$$r^{-1}\frac{\partial}{\partial r}\left(r\frac{\partial f}{\partial r}\right) + r^{-2}\frac{\partial^2 f}{\partial r^2} + \frac{\partial^2 f}{\partial z^2}.$$

Show also that, in spherical polar coordinates (now denoted r, θ, φ), grad f has components $(\partial f/\partial r, r^{-1}\partial f/\partial\theta, (r \sin \theta)^{-1}\partial f/\partial\varphi)$.

FURTHER READING

Craven, B.D. (1964), A note on Green's theorem, *Journal of the Australian Mathematical Society*, **4,** 289–92. [For an alternative, simple, approach to Green's theorem in the plane.]

Craven, B.D. (1968), On the Gauss–Green theorem, *Journal of the Australian Mathematical Society*, **8,** 385–96. [For proof that a boundary curve is regular if and only if it has finite length – see Lemma 2, p. 387.]

Flanders, H. (1967), Differential forms, in *Studies in Global Geometry and Analysis*, (ed. S.S. Chern), Math. Assoc. of America/Prentice-Hall, pp. 57–95. [A very lucid introduction.]

Rudin, W. (1976), *Principles of Mathematical Analysis* (3rd edn) McGraw-Hill Kogakusha Ltd [Chapter 9].

Spivak, M. (1965), *Calculus on Manifolds*, Benjamin, New York.

Weatherburn, C.E. (1924, reprinted 1947), *Advanced Vector Analysis*, Bell, London. [For those applicable aspects of vector calculus, especially to physics, which many modern books omit, in favour of more theory.]

Appendices

A. BACKGROUND REQUIRED IN LINEAR ALGEBRA AND ELEMENTARY CALCULUS

A *matrix* is a rectangular array of numbers, together with rules for algebraic operations (additions, multiplication, etc.) on such arrays. An $m \times n$ matrix means a matrix with m rows and n columns; as special cases, we have $m \times 1$ matrices (*column vectors*) and $1 \times n$ matrices (*row vectors*). We shall only consider matrices whose elements are real numbers. The rules for addition and multiplication are indicated by the following typical examples.

$$\begin{bmatrix} a_{11} & a_{12} & a_{13} \\ a_{21} & a_{22} & a_{23} \end{bmatrix} + \begin{bmatrix} b_{11} & b_{12} & b_{13} \\ b_{21} & b_{22} & b_{23} \end{bmatrix}$$

$$= \begin{bmatrix} a_{11}+b_{11} & a_{12}+b_{12} & a_{13}+b_{13} \\ a_{21}+b_{21} & a_{22}+b_{22} & a_{23}+b_{23} \end{bmatrix}.$$

$$\begin{bmatrix} a_{11} & a_{12} & a_{13} \\ a_{21} & a_{22} & a_{23} \end{bmatrix} \begin{bmatrix} b_{11} & b_{21} & b_{13} & b_{14} \\ b_{21} & b_{22} & b_{23} & b_{24} \\ b_{31} & b_{32} & b_{33} & b_{34} \end{bmatrix} = \begin{bmatrix} c_{11} & c_{12} & c_{13} & c_{14} \\ c_{21} & c_{22} & c_{23} & c_{24} \end{bmatrix},$$

where $c_{ij} = \sum_{k=1}^{3} a_{ik}b_{kj}$. Observe that matrices of the same size and shape can be added (and then corresponding matrix elements are added). We can multiply an $m \times n$ matrix by an $n \times p$ matrix, getting a product which is an $m \times p$ matrix. In these operations, each matrix is treated as a single entity (a sort of 'super number'). However, not all properties of numbers extend to matrices; observe that AB is not usually equal to BA, and that $AB = 0$ and $A \neq 0$ do not imply $B = 0$. (For example,

$$\begin{bmatrix} 1 & 0 \\ 0 & 0 \end{bmatrix} \begin{bmatrix} 0 & 0 \\ 0 & 1 \end{bmatrix} = \begin{bmatrix} 0 & 0 \\ 0 & 0 \end{bmatrix}.)$$

If A is the matrix with elements a_{ij}, and λ is a real number, then λA is the matrix with elements λa_{ij}.

Matrix operations satisfy distributive laws: $A(B+C) = AB+AC$ and $(P+Q)R = PR+QR$, provided that all the matrix expressions make sense.

The *transpose* of the $m \times n$ matrix A is obtained from A by interchanging rows and columns. If A has element a_{ij} in row i and column j, then the transpose matrix, A^{T}, has a_{ij} in row j and column i; thus A^{T} is a $n \times m$ matrix. The alternative notation A' for transpose is not used in this book, to avoid confusion with derivative.

$$\begin{bmatrix} a_{11} & a_{12} & a_{13} \\ a_{21} & a_{22} & a_{23} \end{bmatrix}^{\mathrm{T}} = \begin{bmatrix} a_{11} & a_{21} \\ a_{12} & a_{22} \\ a_{13} & a_{23} \end{bmatrix}.$$

In the above matrix multiplication formula, the matrix elements a_{ij} and b_{ij} may themselves be smaller matrices (called *submatrices*); then matrix multiplication is still valid, provided that all matrix products and sums involved in calculating the c_{ij} make sense. For example, we may partition

$$A = \left[\begin{array}{ccc} a_{11} & a_{12} & a_{13} \\ \hline a_{21} & a_{22} & a_{23} \end{array}\right], \quad B = \begin{bmatrix} b_{11} & b_{12} & b_{13} & b_{14} \\ b_{21} & b_{22} & b_{23} & b_{24} \\ b_{31} & b_{32} & b_{33} & b_{34} \end{bmatrix}$$

each into four submatrices, as shown; the result of partitioned multiplication then must agree with the ordinary matrix product AB.

Note that the columns of A and the rows of B must be partitioned in the same way.

Denote by I_n, or sometimes by I, the $n \times n$ *unit matrix*

$$I_n = \begin{bmatrix} 1 & 0 & 0 & \ldots & 0 \\ 0 & 1 & 0 & \ldots & 0 \\ 0 & 0 & 1 & \ldots & 0 \\ \cdot & \cdot & \cdot & \ldots & \cdot \\ 0 & 0 & 0 & \ldots & 1 \end{bmatrix}.$$

Let A be a square $(n \times n)$ matrix. The *inverse* of A, if it exists, is an $n \times n$ matrix B, satisfying $AB = BA = I_n$. Then denote B by A^{-1}. A theorem states that the following are equivalent:

(i) A is *invertible* (or *nonsingular*; meaning that A has an inverse);
(ii) the rows of A are linearly independent;
(iii) the columns of A are linearly independent;
(iv) the determinant of A is nonzero.

Here, a set of vectors $\{v_1, v_2, \ldots, v_r\}$ is *linearly independent* if the only numbers $\alpha_1, \alpha_2, \ldots, \alpha_r$ satisfying $\alpha_1 v_1 + \alpha_2 v_2 + \ldots + \alpha_r v_r = 0$ are $\alpha_1 = \alpha_2 = \ldots = \alpha_r = 0$. For present purposes, the *determinant* det A may be defined by the following calculation. If

$$A = \begin{bmatrix} a_{11} & a_{12} & a_{13} \\ a_{21} & a_{22} & a_{23} \\ a_{31} & a_{32} & a_{33} \end{bmatrix}, \text{ then}$$

$$\det A = a_{11} \begin{vmatrix} a_{22} & a_{23} \\ a_{32} & a_{33} \end{vmatrix} - a_{21} \begin{vmatrix} a_{12} & a_{13} \\ a_{32} & a_{33} \end{vmatrix} + a_{31} \begin{vmatrix} a_{12} & a_{13} \\ a_{22} & a_{23} \end{vmatrix}$$

where the submatrix $\begin{bmatrix} a_{22} & a_{23} \\ a_{32} & a_{33} \end{bmatrix}$ has determinant $\begin{vmatrix} a_{22} & a_{23} \\ a_{32} & a_{33} \end{vmatrix} =$

$a_{22}a_{33} - a_{32}a_{23}$, and similarly for the others. Observe the changes of sign $+ \; - \; +$ as we proceed down the column a_{11}, a_{21}, a_{22}. This expression for det$A$ can be extended analogously to larger square matrices (thus, if A is 4×4, then det A is expressed in terms of four 3×3 matrices).

The Euclidean space $\mathbb{R}^n$ consists of all column vectors of n (real) elements. If such a vector has elements $a_1, a_2, \ldots, a_n$, then this vector can be written as the *linear combination* $a_1\mathbf{e}_1+a_2\mathbf{e}_2+\ldots+a_n\mathbf{e}_n$, where the vectors

$$\mathbf{e}_2 = \begin{bmatrix}1\\0\\0\\\cdot\\\cdot\\0\end{bmatrix}, \mathbf{e}_1 = \begin{bmatrix}0\\1\\0\\\cdot\\\cdot\\0\end{bmatrix}, \ldots, \mathbf{e}_n = \begin{bmatrix}0\\0\\0\\\cdot\\\cdot\\1\end{bmatrix}$$

form a *basis* for $\mathbb{R}^n$. A *basis* means a linearly independent set of vectors, with every vector in the space expressible as a linear combination of them.

The *rank* of a $m \times n$ matrix A is the largest number of linearly independent rows of A (or columns of A). The matrix A has *full rank* if A has the largest rank allowed by m and n, namely the smaller of m and n.

Consider now the eigenvalue equation

$$A\mathbf{w} = \lambda\mathbf{w}, \ \mathbf{w} \neq \mathbf{0},$$

for the $n \times n$ matrix A. The numbers λ which satisfy this equation are called *eigenvalues* of A, and the corresponding column vectors $\mathbf{w}$ are the *eigenvectors* of A. Note that λ is an eigenvalue of A if and only if the matrix $A-\lambda I_n$ has no inverse, and thus if and only if the polynomial equation (of degree n) $\det(A-\lambda I_n) = 0$. When A is (real) symmetric (thus when $A^{\mathrm{T}} = A$), the eigenvalues of A are the n real roots (with perhaps some roots coinciding) of this equation.

Let A be a symmetric $n \times n$ matrix. Consider the *quadratic form* $q = \mathbf{w}^{\mathrm{T}}A\mathbf{w}$. Thus, if A is the 2×2 matrix with elements a_{ij}, then
$q = a_{11}w_1{}^2+(a_{12}+a_{21})w_1w_2+a_{22}w_2{}^2 = a_{11}w_1{}^2+2a_{12}w_1w_2+a_{22}w_2{}^2$.
A theorem in linear algebra states then that, if $\lambda_{\min}$ and $\lambda_{\max}$ denote the least and greatest eigenvalues of A, then

$$\lambda_{\max}\mathbf{w}^{\mathrm{T}}\mathbf{w} \geq \mathbf{w}^{\mathrm{T}}A\mathbf{w} \geq \lambda_{\min}\mathbf{w}^{\mathrm{T}}\mathbf{w}$$

holds for every vector $\mathbf{w}$.

Some other aspects of linear algebra are described elsewhere in this book. These include the representation of a linear map by a matrix (Section 2.1). Note that a map (or function) M from $\mathbb{R}^n$ into $\mathbb{R}^m$ is *linear* if

$$M(\alpha\mathbf{v}+\beta\mathbf{w}) = \alpha M(\mathbf{v})+\beta M(\mathbf{w})$$

holds for all vectors $\mathbf{v},\mathbf{w}$ in $\mathbb{R}^n$ and all real numbers α, β. For more details on matrices, and proofs, the reader should refer to any book on matrix algebra (or linear algebra).

Concerning calculus, the reader is assumed to be familiar with the differentiation of real functions of one real variable. Suppose now that f is a real function of two real variables, x and y. The *partial derivative* of $f(x,y)$ with respect to x, denoted $\partial f(x,y)/\partial x$, is obtained by differentiating with respect to x, holding y fixed. Thus, for example, if $f(x,y) = x^2y^3$, then $\partial f/\partial x = 2xy^3$ and $\partial f/\partial y = 3x^2y^2$.

Suppose that f is a real function of a real variable x, and suppose that, for $0 \leqslant x \leqslant 1$, the derivatives $f'(x) = df/dx$, $f''(x) = df'(x)/dx, \ldots, f^{(n)}(x) = df^{(n-1)}(x)/dx$ all exist. Then we have the *Taylor expansion* (with remainder):

$$f(x) = f(0)+f'(0)x+f''(0)x^2/2! + \ldots + f^{(n-1)}(0)x^{(n-1)}/(n-1)! \\ +f^{(n)}(\theta)x^n/n!,$$

where $n! = 1\cdot2\cdot3\cdot \ldots \cdot(n-1)n$, and θ (which depends on x) lies in the interval $(0, x)$.

The usual function notation, such as $g : \mathbb{R}^n \to \mathbb{R}^m$, will be used; this means that g has domain $\mathbb{R}^n$, and takes its values in $\mathbb{R}^m$. The set notation $\{x\in A : B\}$ means the set of all elements x in the set A, which satisfy condition B. The notation $\{c_n\}$ is also used to denote a sequence $c_1, c_2, \ldots, c_n, \ldots$. If E denotes a set of real numbers, then its greatest lower bound is denoted by inf E, and its least upper bound is denoted by sup E.

Chapters 1,2,3 make occasional use of integrals of continuous functions (of one real variable). The more general notions of integration introduced in Section 4.1 start from the beginning, however.

Now let E be a *closed bounded* set in $\mathbb{R}^n$. (*Closed* means that if $\{w_r\}$ is a sequence in E, and $\{w_r\}$ converges to a limit $\bar{w}$, then also $\bar{w}$ is in E. This convergence means that $\|w_r-\bar{w}\| \to 0$ as $r \to \infty$, where $\|w_r-\bar{w}\|$ denotes the length of the vector $w_r-\bar{w}$. (For details on length, or *norm*, of vectors, see Section 2.1.) *Bounded* means that, for some finite constant k, every $\mathbf{w}$ in E satisfies $\|\mathbf{w}\| \leqslant k$.) Also let $f : E \to \mathbb{R}$ be a *continuous* real function on E. A theorem in analysis then states that f attains a finite *maximum* on E; this means that, for some $\hat{x} \in E$,

$$f(\hat{x}) = \sup_{x \in E} f(x) \text{ is finite.}$$

A similar statement applies to *minimum*. (Appendix B gives some more discussion – but it may be omitted on first reading the book.)

B. COMPACT SETS, CONTINUOUS FUNCTIONS AND PARTITIONS OF UNITY

Let E be a given subset of $\mathbb{R}^n$. An *open cover* of E is a family $\{U_\alpha\}$ of open sets, whose union contains E. The set E is called *compact* if, to every open cover $\{U_\alpha\}$ of E, there exist finitely many of these U_α whose union contains E. The *Heine–Borel theorem* states that $E \subset \mathbb{R}^n$ is *compact* if and only if E is *closed* (contains all its limit points) and *bounded* (for some finite constant k, $\|\mathbf{x}\| \leq k$ for every $\mathbf{x} \in E$).

Now let E be a *compact* subset of $\mathbb{R}^n$, and let $f : E \to \mathbb{R}$ be a *continuous* function. It then follows that f attains a finite maximum; this means that $\sup_{\mathbf{x} \in E} f(\mathbf{x})$ is finite, and, for some $\bar{\mathbf{x}} \in E$, $f(\bar{\mathbf{x}}) = \sup_{\mathbf{x} \in E} f(\mathbf{x})$. It also follows that, to each $\varepsilon > 0$, there exists a *step-function* $h : E \to \mathbb{R}$ such that, for all $\mathbf{x} \in E$, $|f(\mathbf{x}) - h(\mathbf{x})| < \varepsilon$. (Observe that the compactness is needed; if E is the noncompact interval $(0, 1)$ in $\mathbb{R}$, then $f(x) = 1/x$ defines a continuous function which neither attains a finite maximum, nor can be approximated, uniformly within ε, by a step-function.)

These theorems will be assumed without proof in this book. Proofs may be found in texts on analysis. (One such is G.F. Simmons (1963), *Introduction to Topology and Modern Analysis*, McGraw-Hill; see Ch. 4). For present purposes, we indicate, for dimension $n = 1$, the idea of the proofs only. Suppose that E is a bounded closed subset of $\mathbb{R}$. Shift the origin, and scale, to make $E \subset [0, 1]$. If E is not compact, then there is some open cover $\{U_\alpha\}$ of E, such that no finite subfamily of the U_α will cover E. If so, then either $E \cap [0, \frac{1}{2}]$, or $E \cap [\frac{1}{2}, 1]$, or both, requires infinitely many U_α to cover it. If $E \cap [\frac{1}{2}, 1]$ requires infinitely many U_α, then so also does at least one of $E \cap [\frac{1}{2}, \frac{3}{4}]$ and $E \cap [\frac{3}{4}, 1]$. Continuing thus by halving the length of intervals, we construct a sequence I_r of closed intervals, with length of $I_r \to 0$, such that each $E \cap I_r$ requires infinitely many U_α

to cover it. Denote by x_r the upper end of I_r; then the sequence $\{x_r\}$ converges to some real number $\bar{x}$, where $\bar{x}$, and hence also I_r for r large enough, is covered by some *one* of the U_α, contradicting the previous sentence. Hence E is compact. A similar proof for $\mathbb{R}^2$ works with squares instead in intervals. The theorem about uniform approximation by step-functions is deduced by taking $U_\alpha = \{x \in E : |f(x) - f(\alpha)| < \varepsilon\}$, for each $\alpha \in E$; then using compactness to show that E is covered by some *finite* subfamily of these U_α. The theorem that f attains its maximum on compact E is produced by showing that f maps E to some compact interval in $\mathbb{R}$.

Suppose now that $\{U_\alpha\}$ is an open cover of a subset $E \subset \mathbb{R}^n$. We shall first construct another open cover $\{V_i\}$ of E, consisting of a sequence of open sets $V_1, V_2, \ldots$, with the properties that each V_i lies in some U_α, and every $\mathbf{x} \in E$ has some open ball B, with centre $\mathbf{x}$, such that B meets only finitely many of the V_i, and the closure $\bar{V}_i$ of V_i is compact. If (as in many applications) the U_i are finitely many bounded open sets, then it suffices to set $V_i = U_i$. Otherwise, we may proceed as follows. Denote $B_j = \{x \in \mathbb{R}^n : \|x\| \leq j\}$, for $j = 1, 2, \ldots$; and denote difference of sets by the symbol $\backslash$. Then $\bar{B}_j \backslash B_{j-1}$ is a compact set, contained in $B_{j+1} \backslash \bar{B}_{j-2}$. For each $j \geq 3$, use compactness to choose finitely many of the open sets $U_\alpha \cap (B_{j+1} \backslash \bar{B}_{j-2})$ which form a cover of the compact set $\bar{B}_j \backslash B_{j-1}$, and choose finitely many $U_\alpha \cap B_3$ which cover $\bar{B}_2$. This countable family of open sets, just found, has the properties required of the V_i.

We now construct bounded open sets W_i such that $\bar{W}_i \subset V_i$ and $\cup W_i \supset E$. Suppose first that $E = \mathbb{R}^n$. Choose $W_1 = V_1$. Suppose that $W_1, \ldots, W_{k-1}$ have been chosen, so that these sets, together with $V_k, V_{k+1}, \ldots$, cover $\mathbb{R}^n$. Then $\mathbb{R}^n$ minus the union of $W_1, \ldots, W_{k-1}$ $V_{k+1}, \ldots$ is a *closed* set, F_k say, with F_k contained in the *open* set V_k. Then the distance, δ, from F_k to the boundary of V_k is positive. Define W_k as the set of points whose distance from some point of V_k is less than $\frac{1}{2}\delta$. Then W_k is open, with $\bar{W}_k \subset V_k$ as required, and $W_1, \ldots, W_k, V_{k+1}, \ldots$ covering $\mathbb{R}^n$. Thus all the W_k are found by induction. A similar proof applies when $E \neq \mathbb{R}^n$, discarding points outside E.

We now construct a C^∞ function $h_k : \mathbb{R}^n \to \mathbb{R}$ such that $h_k(x) > 0$ for $x \in \bar{W}_k$, $h_k(x) = 0$ for $x \notin V_k$, and $0 \leq h_k(x)$ for all x. Consider first the C^∞ function $\varphi : \mathbb{R} \to \mathbb{R}$ defined by

$$\varphi(t) = e^{-1/t^2} \text{ for } t > 0, \varphi(t) = 0 \text{ for } t \leq 0.$$

The proof that φ is a C^∞ function is similar to that for the function $f(t) = e^{-1/t^2}$ for $t \neq 0$, $f(0) = 0$, discussed in Section 2.2. Define the *distance* $d(x, W_k)$ of the point x from W_k by

$$d(x, W_k) = \inf_{y \in W_k} \|x - y\|.$$

Observe that $d(x, W_k)$ is a continuous, but not C^∞, function of x, with $d(x, W_k) = 0$ when $x \in W_k$. However, the function $\varphi(d(x, W_k))$ is C^∞, vanishes on W_k, and is positive outside W_k. Define then h_k by

$$h_k(x) = \varphi(1 - \varepsilon^{-1}\varphi(d(x, W_k))).$$

Then h_k is a C^∞ function, $h_k(x) > 0$ for $x \in W_k$, $h_k(x) > 0$ for all $x \notin W_k$ but near enough to W_k. By choice of positive ε sufficiently small, $h_k\ (x)$ vanishes outside V_k.

Since each $x \in E$ lies in some ball which meets only finitely many of the V_k, the infinite series

$$h(x) = \sum_{k=1}^{\infty} h_k(x)$$

reduces, for each x, to a finite sum. Define now $\theta_k(x) = h_k(x)/h(x)$.

The set of functions $\{\theta_k : k = 1, 2, \ldots\}$ is called a *partition of unity*, subordinate to the cover $\{U_\alpha\}$ of E, because it possesses the following properties:

Each $\theta_k : \mathbb{R}^n \to \mathbb{R}$ is a C^∞ function, with $0 \leq \theta_k(x) \leq 1$ for all x;

Each $\theta_k(x)$ vanishes for $x \notin V_k$ (and $V_k \subset U_\alpha$ for some α);

For each $x \in E$, $\sum_{k=1}^{\infty} \theta_k(x) = 1$ (and this sum reduces to a *finite* sum).

To see how *partitions of unity* are applied, suppose that a surface S is specified by several parametrizations $\mathbf{w} = \varphi_i(\mathbf{q})$ $(\mathbf{q} \in U_i)$, where the parameter domains U_i overlap; let E denote the union of all the U_i. For discussion, see Section 4.4. Note that we must assume consistency; φ_i and φ_j must agree on $U_i \cap U_j$. Let $f : S \to \mathbb{R}$ be a continuous function. We have already definitions of $\int_A f$ when A is contained in some U_i, but not yet for $\int_S f$. Assume that each U_i is an open subset of E. Construct, as above, a partition of unity $\{\theta_k\}$ subordinate to the cover $\{U_i\}$. Then $\int_S f$ may be defined as

$$\int_S f = \sum_i \int_{U_i} f\theta_i.$$

Observe that $\sum_i f(q)\theta_i(q)$ is, for each q, a finite sum. If f vanishes outside a particular U_k, then $\int_S f$ reduces, as it should, to

$$\int_{U_k}(\sum_i f\theta_i) = \int_{U_k} f.$$

The value of $\int_S f$ turns out not to depend on which partition of unity is chosen. The method of partitions of unity can be used to extend most results of Sections 4.5 and 4.6 to surfaces which require several parametrizations for their definition.

C. ANSWERS TO SELECTED EXERCISES

Chapter 1

Ex. 1.2.1 $-2(x-\frac{1}{4}\pi)-3(y-0)$.

Ex. 1.2.2 $\pi\cos(\frac{1}{4}\pi^2)\cdot(y-\frac{1}{2}\pi)$.

Ex. 1.2.3 (i) $f_x = h(y)g'(x)$, $f_y = g(x)h'(y)$.

(ii) $f_x = h(y)g(x)^{h(y)-1}h'(y)$, $f_y = g(x)h(y)[\log g(x)]h'(y)$, assuming $g(x) > 0$.

(iii) $f_x = g'(x)$, $f_y = 0$.

Ex. 1.4.1 $[-2, -3]\begin{bmatrix} l \\ m \end{bmatrix} = -2l-3m$. This agrees with

$$\frac{\mathrm{d}}{\mathrm{d}\alpha}\cos(2(\tfrac{1}{4}\pi+\alpha l)+3(0+\alpha m))$$

at $\alpha = 0$.

Ex. 1.4.2 $\pi\cos(\frac{1}{4}\pi^2)\cos\gamma$.

Ex. 1.5.2 Consider the half-hyperboloid $z = +c[-1+(x/a)^2+(y/b)^2]^{1/2}$. Calculate $z_x = (x/a^2)[\quad]^{-1/2} = (ca/\alpha^2)/(\gamma/c) = c^2\alpha/(a^2\gamma)$ at the point (α, β, γ). Similarly, at this point, $z_y = c^2\beta/(b^2\gamma)$. So the tangent plane has equation

$$z-\gamma = c^2\alpha(a^2\gamma)^{-1}(x-\alpha)+c^2\beta(b^2\gamma)^{-1}(y-\beta),$$

which simplifies, using $(\alpha/a)^2+(\beta/b)^2-(\gamma/c)^2 = 1$, to

$$\frac{\alpha x}{a^2}+\frac{\beta y}{b^2}-\frac{\gamma z}{c^2} = 1,$$

Ex. 1.6.1 $f'\left(\begin{bmatrix} x \\ y \end{bmatrix}\right) = \begin{bmatrix} 2x & -2y \\ y^2 & 2xy \end{bmatrix}$; $f'\left(\begin{bmatrix} 1 \\ 2 \end{bmatrix}\right) = \begin{bmatrix} 2 & -4 \\ 4 & 4 \end{bmatrix}$.

Ex. 1.7.1 From the chain rule,

$$(f\circ\varphi)'(t) = \begin{bmatrix} 2x & -2y \\ 2y & 2x \end{bmatrix}\begin{bmatrix} \sinh t \\ \cosh t \end{bmatrix} \text{ (in which } x = \cosh t,\ y = \sinh t)$$

$$= \begin{bmatrix} 0 \\ 2(\sinh^2 t + \cosh^2 t) \end{bmatrix} \text{ (after substituting and multiplying).}$$

Compare this with

$$(f\circ\varphi)(t) = \begin{bmatrix} \cosh^2 t - \sinh^2 t \\ 2\cosh t \sinh t \end{bmatrix} = \begin{bmatrix} 1 \\ 2\cosh t \sinh t \end{bmatrix};$$

$$(f\circ\varphi)'(t) = \begin{bmatrix} 0 \\ 2\cosh^2 t + 2\sinh^2 t \end{bmatrix}.$$

Ex. 1.7.2 $f'\left(\begin{bmatrix} x \\ y \end{bmatrix}\right) = [2x\cos(x^2+y^2),\ 2y\cos(x^2+y^2)]$.

$g'\left[\begin{pmatrix} x \\ y \end{pmatrix}\right] = (1+(x^2+xy+y^2)^2)^{-1}\,[2x+y,\ x+2y]$.

Ex. 1.7.4 Define $\varphi(\mathbf{w}) = f(\mathbf{w})+g(\mathbf{w})$, $\theta\left[\begin{pmatrix} u \\ v \end{pmatrix}\right] = u+v$, $h(\mathbf{w}) = \begin{bmatrix} f(\mathbf{w}) \\ g(\mathbf{w}) \end{bmatrix}$

Then $\varphi = \theta\circ h$. By the chain rule,

$$\varphi'(\mathbf{w}) = \theta'(h(\mathbf{w}))\circ h'(\mathbf{w}) = [1,\ 1]\begin{bmatrix} f'(\mathbf{w}) \\ g'(\mathbf{w}) \end{bmatrix} = f'(\mathbf{w})+g'(\mathbf{w}).$$

Ex. 1.7.5 $f = r\circ g$ where $r(z) = z^{-1}$ (when $z \neq 0$). By the chain rule, $f'(\mathbf{w}) = r'(g(\mathbf{w}))\circ g'(\mathbf{w}) = -(g(\mathbf{w}))^{-2}\,g'(\mathbf{w})$.

Chapter 2

Ex. 2.1.1 For (N3), $\|A+B\| = \sum_i \max_j |a_{ij}+b_{ij}|$

$$\leq \sum_i \max_j(|a_{ij}|+|b_{ij}|) \leq \sum_i(\max_j|a_{ij}|+\max_j|b_{ij}|)$$

$= \|A\|+\|B\|$, using the norm (2.1.9).

Also $\|Aw\|_1 = \sum_i |\sum_j a_{ij}w_j| \leq \sum_i \sum_j |a_{ij}| \cdot |w_j|$

$$\leq \sum_i \max_j |a_{ij}| \cdot \sum_j |w_j| = \|A\| \cdot \|w\|_1,$$

here defining $\|A\|$ by (2.1.9).

Ex. 2.1.2 For (N3), $(A+B)\mathbf{w} = A\mathbf{w}+B\mathbf{w}$ holds for each $\mathbf{w}$, hence $\|(A+B)\mathbf{w}\| \leq \|A\mathbf{w}\|+\|B\mathbf{w}\| \leq \|A\|\cdot\|\mathbf{w}\|+\|B\|\cdot\|\mathbf{w}\|$; hence, by (2.1.10), $\|A+B\| \leq \|A\|+\|B\|$. To show that $\|A\| \leq \|A\|_2$, observe that $\|A\|_2$ is a possible β in (2.1.10).

Ex. 2.1.3 From the proof of (2.1.4), $\langle \mathbf{w}, \mathbf{s}\rangle = \|\mathbf{w}\|\cdot\|\mathbf{s}\|$ if and only if the quadratic in (2.1.3) has two equal zeros, thus if and only if $\|\mathbf{w}+\alpha\mathbf{s}\| = \mathbf{0}$ for some α, thus if and only if $\mathbf{w}+\alpha\mathbf{s} = \mathbf{0}$.

Ex. 2.2.1 From differentiability, $\|\theta(\mathbf{w})\| < 1\|\mathbf{w}-\mathbf{c}\|$ when $\|\mathbf{w}-\mathbf{c}\| < \delta_1$, say. Then $\|\mathbf{f}(\mathbf{w})-\mathbf{f}(\mathbf{c})\| < \varepsilon$ when $\|\mathbf{w}-\mathbf{c}\| < \delta(\varepsilon) = \min\{1, (\|\mathbf{f}'(\mathbf{c})\|+1)^{-1}\varepsilon\}$.

Ex. 2.2.3 $h(\mathbf{x}) = [f(\mathbf{c})+f'(\mathbf{c})(\mathbf{x}-\mathbf{c})+\theta_1(\mathbf{x})][g(\mathbf{c})+g'(\mathbf{c})(\mathbf{x}-\mathbf{c})+\theta_2(\mathbf{x})$

$$= f(\mathbf{c})g(\mathbf{c})+[g(\mathbf{c})f'(\mathbf{c})+f(\mathbf{c})g'(\mathbf{c})](\mathbf{x}-\mathbf{c})+\theta(\mathbf{x})$$

where $\theta(\mathbf{x}) = g(\mathbf{x})\ \theta_1(\mathbf{x})+f(\mathbf{x})\ \theta_2(\mathbf{x})$. Using Ex. 2.2.1, $g(\mathbf{x})$ and $f(\mathbf{x})$ are bounded, when $\|\mathbf{x}-\mathbf{c}\|$ is small. Hence, for some constant k,

$$|\theta(\mathbf{x})| \leq k(|\theta_1(\mathbf{x})|+|\theta_2(\mathbf{x})|) \leq k(\varepsilon\|\mathbf{x}-\mathbf{c}\|+\varepsilon\|\mathbf{x}-\mathbf{c}\|)$$

whenever $\|\mathbf{x}-\mathbf{c}\|$ is sufficiently small.

Ex. 2.2.5 The stated expression for $f(\mathbf{c}+\mathbf{w})-f(\mathbf{c})$ follows on expansion, noting that $\mathbf{w}^{\mathrm{T}}A\mathbf{c} = \mathbf{c}^{\mathrm{T}}A^{\mathrm{T}}\mathbf{w} = \mathbf{c}^{\mathrm{T}}A\mathbf{w}$. Then $2\mathbf{c}^{\mathrm{T}}A\mathbf{w}$ is linear in $\mathbf{w}$; and $|\mathbf{w}^{\mathrm{T}}A\mathbf{w}| \leq$ const. $\|\mathbf{w}\|^2$, hence $f'(\mathbf{c}) = 2\mathbf{c}^{\mathrm{T}}A$ as stated.

Ex. 2.3.1 (i) $f'(x, y) = [yg(x)^{y-1}g'(x),\ g(x)^y \log g(x)]$; assume $g(x) > 0$.

(ii) Denoting $f'(u, v)$ by $[f_u, f_v]$, $F'(x, y) = [f_u(g(x)h(y), g(x)+h(y)),$ $f_v(g(x)h(y), g(x)+h(y))]\begin{bmatrix} h(y)g'(x) & g'(x) \\ g(x)h'(y) & h'(y)\end{bmatrix}$.

(iii) $\cos(x \sin y)[\sin y,\ x \cos y)]$.

(iv) $[g(x+y), g(x+y)]$.

Ex. 2.3.2 Denote the derivative of $f(u, v, w)$ by $[f_u, f_v, f_w]$. Then the derivatives of $f(x, g(x,y), h(x, y))$ is

$$[f_u, f_v, f_w]\begin{bmatrix} 1 & 0 \\ g_x & g_y \\ h_x & h_y \end{bmatrix} = [f_u+f_vg_x+f_wh_y,\ f_vg_y+f_wh_y].$$

The first component of the latter vector is the desired partial derivative with respect to x. The traditional notation for this is

$$\frac{\partial f}{\partial x}+\frac{\partial f}{\partial v}\frac{\partial g}{\partial x}+\frac{\partial f}{\partial w}\frac{\partial h}{\partial x}.$$

Ex. 2.3.3 Differentiating $f(\alpha x) = \alpha^k f(x)$ with respect to α, using the chain rule, gives $f'(\alpha x)x = k\alpha^{k-1}f(x)$. Substituting $\alpha = 1$ gives the result.
Ex. 2.3.4 From the mean-value theorem,

$$f(x^*, y)-f(x, y) = f_x(u, y)(x^*-x)$$

for some u in the the line segment joining (x, y) to (x^*, y), where $(u, y)\in E$ by the convexity. By hypothesis, $f_x(u, y) = 0$.
Ex. 2.3.5 $f\circ g = I$, where I denotes the identity map. By the chain rule, applicable since f and g are differentiable, $f'(g(y))g'(y) = I$.
Ex. 2.3.6 $y = f(x) \Leftrightarrow y = f(0)+Ax+\psi(x)$ where $\psi(x) = o(x) \Leftrightarrow A^{-1}y \equiv v = x+\theta(x)$ where $\theta(x) = A^{-1}\psi(x) = o(x)$. Thus $|\psi(x)| < \varepsilon'|x|$ whenever $|x| < \delta(\varepsilon')$, hence $|\theta(x) < \varepsilon|x|$ whenever $|x| < \Delta(\varepsilon) = \delta(|A|\varepsilon)$. Taking $\varepsilon = \frac{1}{2}$, for $0 < v < \frac{1}{2}\Delta(\frac{1}{2})$, $F(\frac{2}{3}v) \leq \frac{2}{3}v+\theta(\frac{2}{3}v)-v \leq \frac{2}{3}v+\frac{1}{2}(\frac{2}{3}v)-v = 0$; and $F(2v) = 2v+\theta(2v)-v \geq 2v-\frac{1}{2}(2v)-v = 0$. Since F is continuous, $F(\bar{x}) = 0$ at some $\bar{x}$ in $(\frac{2}{3}v, 2v)$.
Ex. 2.3.7 In Theorem 2.2, $\mathbf{s} = f(\mathbf{w}) = A\mathbf{w}+\boldsymbol{\theta}(\mathbf{w})$. Defining $A(\mathbf{w})$ by $\mathbf{s} = A(\mathbf{w})\mathbf{w}$, $[A(\mathbf{w})-A]\mathbf{w}/\|\mathbf{w}\| = \boldsymbol{\theta}(\mathbf{w})|\|\mathbf{w}\| \to 0$ as $\|\mathbf{w}\| \to 0$; thus $A(\mathbf{w}) \to A$ as stated. Similarly, obtain $\mathbf{g}(\mathbf{s}) = B(\mathbf{s})\mathbf{s}$ with $B(\mathbf{s}) \to B$ as $\|\mathbf{s}\| \to 0$. Then $(\mathbf{g}\circ\mathbf{f})(\mathbf{w}) = \mathbf{g}(\mathbf{s}) = B(\mathbf{s})A(\mathbf{w})\mathbf{w}$. As $\|\mathbf{w}\| \to 0$, $\|\mathbf{s}\| \to 0$ (since $\|\mathbf{s}\| \leq (\|A\|+1)\mathbf{w}$ when $\|\mathbf{w}\|$ is sufficiently small), so $B(\mathbf{s}) \to B$; also $A(\mathbf{w}) \to A$ as above. Hence $B(\mathbf{s})A(\mathbf{w}) \to BA$; thus $(\mathbf{g}\circ\mathbf{f})(\mathbf{w}) = BA\mathbf{w}+\boldsymbol{\psi}(\mathbf{w})$ where $\boldsymbol{\psi}(\mathbf{w})/\|\mathbf{w}\| \to 0$ as $\|\mathbf{w}\| \to 0$.
Ex. 2.4.1 $\|\varphi(\mathbf{u})-\varphi(\mathbf{v})\| = \|(\mathbf{s}-M\mathbf{u})-(\mathbf{s}-M\mathbf{v})\| = \|M(\mathbf{u}-\mathbf{v}\| \leq \|M\|\cdot\|\mathbf{u}-\mathbf{v}\|$. Since $\|M\| < 1$, φ is a contraction mapping. A solution of $(I+M)\mathbf{w} = \mathbf{s}$ is a fixed point of φ. Thus there is a unique solution $\mathbf{w}$ for each $\mathbf{s}$; note that this $\mathbf{w} = (I+M)^{-1}\mathbf{s}$.
Ex. 2.4.2 $|\varphi(w)-\varphi(x)| = |cw^2-cx^2| = |c(w+x)|\cdot|w-x|$. If $x, w \in (-\delta, \delta)$ where $2|c|\delta < 1$, then $|c(w+x)| \leq 2|c|\delta$, and φ (restricted to this domain) is a contraction mapping. The fixed point x of φ solves $y-cx^2 = x$. Using the contraction mapping leads to the approximation $x \approx y-c(y-cy^2)^2 = y-cy^2+$ higher-order terms. By comparison, solving the quadratic (choosing the root in $(-\delta, \delta)$) gives $x = (2c)^{-1}[-1+(1+4cy)^{1/2}] \approx (2c)^{-1}[-1+1+2cy-2(cy)^2] = y-cy^2$.

Ex. 2.4.3 $f'\left(\begin{bmatrix} x \\ y \end{bmatrix}\right) = \begin{bmatrix} 2x & 2y \\ 2y & 2x \end{bmatrix}$ is nonsingular except for (x, y) where its determinant, $4(x^2 - y^2)$, vanishes. Hence, except on the two lines $y = \pm x$, the solvability follows from the remark after Theorem 2.5. From the chain rule,

$$g'\left(\begin{bmatrix} u \\ v \end{bmatrix}\right) = f'\left(\begin{bmatrix} x \\ y \end{bmatrix}\right)^{-1} = [(4(x^2 - y^2))]^{-1} \begin{bmatrix} 2x & -2y \\ -2y & 2x \end{bmatrix}$$

$$\text{where } \begin{bmatrix} u \\ v \end{bmatrix} = f\left[\begin{pmatrix} x \\ y \end{pmatrix}\right].$$

Ex. 2.4.4

$$f'\left(\begin{bmatrix} x \\ y \end{bmatrix}\right) = \begin{bmatrix} -e^{-x}\cos y & -e^{-x}\sin y \\ -e^{-x}\sin y & e^{-x}\cos y \end{bmatrix}$$

has determinant $-e^{-x}$, which never vanishes. So f is locally one-to-one near all points (x, y). (f is not globally one-to-one since

$$f\left(\begin{bmatrix} x \\ y + 2\pi \end{bmatrix}\right) = f\left(\begin{bmatrix} x \\ y \end{bmatrix}\right).)$$

Ex. 2.5.1 Assume $g'(x) \neq 0$; then $g'(x)$ defines an invertible linear mapping from $\mathbb{R}$ to $\mathbb{R}$.

Ex. 2.5.2 The chain rule gives $-8x + 2yg'(x) = 0$; at $(x, y) = (0, -1)$, obtain $g'(0) = 0$. Or, directly, $g(x) = -(1 - 4x^2)^{1/2}$, choosing the $-$ sign to make $g(0) = -1$; then $g'(x) = 2x(1 - 4x^2)^{-1/2}$, so $g'(0) = 0$.

Ex. 2.5.3 $f(0, 0, 0) = (0, 0)$;

$$f'(x, y, z) = \begin{bmatrix} 1 & 1 & 1 \\ 1 - 2z & -1 & -2x \end{bmatrix};\ f'(0, 0, 0) = \begin{bmatrix} 1 & 1 & 1 \\ 1 & -1 & 0 \end{bmatrix}.$$

Since the submatrix $\begin{bmatrix} 1 & 1 \\ 1 & -1 \end{bmatrix}$ is nonsingular, there exists a local solution $(x, y) = \psi(z)$ near $(0, 0, 0)$. Applying the chain rule to $f(\psi(z), z) = 0$ gives

$$\psi'(z) = \begin{bmatrix} 1 & 1 \\ 1 & -1 \end{bmatrix}^{-1} \begin{bmatrix} 1 \\ 0 \end{bmatrix} = \tfrac{1}{2} \begin{bmatrix} -1 & -1 \\ -1 & 1 \end{bmatrix} \begin{bmatrix} 1 \\ 0 \end{bmatrix} = \begin{bmatrix} -\frac{1}{2} \\ -\frac{1}{2} \end{bmatrix}.$$

Ex. 2.5.4 The derivative is given by the matrix

$$\begin{bmatrix} 3 & 1 & -1 & 2u \\ 1 & -1 & 2 & 1 \\ 2 & 2 & -3 & 2 \end{bmatrix}.$$

At $(x, y, z, u) = (0, 0, 0, 0)$, replace u by 0 in this matrix. The system of equations can be solved if and only if the relevant determinant is nonsingular.

(i) $\begin{vmatrix} 3 & 1 & -1 \\ 1 & -1 & 2 \\ 2 & 2 & -3 \end{vmatrix} = 0$; not solvable.

(ii) $\begin{vmatrix} 3 & 1 & 0 \\ 1 & -1 & 1 \\ 2 & 2 & 2 \end{vmatrix} \neq 0$; solvable.

(iii) $\begin{vmatrix} 3 & -1 & 0 \\ 1 & 2 & 1 \\ 2 & -3 & 2 \end{vmatrix} \neq 0$; solvable.

Ex. 2.7.1

For $f\left(\begin{bmatrix} x \\ y \end{bmatrix}\right) = e^{x+y}$, $f'\left(\begin{bmatrix} x \\ y \end{bmatrix}\right) = [f_x, f_y] = [e^{x+y}, e^{x+y}]$, and

$$f''\left(\begin{bmatrix} x \\ y \end{bmatrix}\right) = \begin{bmatrix} f_{xx} & f_{xy} \\ f_{yx} & f_{yy} \end{bmatrix} = e^{x+y}\begin{bmatrix} 1 & 1 \\ 1 & 1 \end{bmatrix}.$$

Then

$$f\left(\begin{bmatrix} x \\ y \end{bmatrix}\right) = f\left(\begin{bmatrix} 0 \\ 0 \end{bmatrix}\right) + [1, 1]\begin{bmatrix} x \\ y \end{bmatrix} + \tfrac{1}{2}[x, y]\begin{bmatrix} 1 & 1 \\ 1 & 1 \end{bmatrix}\begin{bmatrix} x \\ y \end{bmatrix} + \cdots.$$

Ex. 2.7.2 $f_x(0, 0) = \lim_{x\to 0} x^{-1}[f(x, 0) - f(0, 0)] = 0$. For $(x, y) \neq (0, 0)$, $f_x(x, y) = y(x^4 + 4x^2y^2 - y^4)/(x^2+y^2)^2$. Hence $y^{-1}[f_x(x, y) - f_x(x, 0)] = (x^4 + 4x^2y^2 - y^4)/(x^2+y^2)^2 \to +1$ as $y \to 0$, for fixed $x \neq 0$. But $y^{-1}[f_x(0, y) - f_x(0, 0)] = y^{-1}(-y^5)/y^4 \to -1$ as $y \to 0$. Thus $f_{xy}(0, 0) = -1$. Since $f(x, y) = -f(y, x)$, $f_{yx}(0, 0) = +1$. The above calculations show that $f_{xy}(x, y)$ is not continuous at $(x, y) = (0, 0)$.

Ex. 2.7.3 From the remark following the proof of Theorem 2.7, $|\theta(x)| \leq b\|\mathbf{x}-\mathbf{a}\|^3$. Hence $\theta(\mathbf{x}) < \|\mathbf{x}-\mathbf{a}\|^2$ whenever $\|\mathbf{x}-\mathbf{a}\| < \varepsilon/b$. When M is positive definite, a theorem of linear algebra (see Appendix A) shows that $\mathbf{v}^{\mathrm{T}}M\mathbf{v}/\mathbf{v}^{\mathrm{T}}\mathbf{v} \geq c$, where c is the smallest eigenvalue of M, with $c > 0$ since M is positive definite. Then, for $\mathbf{x} \neq \mathbf{a}$, denoting $\mathbf{v} = \mathbf{x}-\mathbf{a}$, $f(\mathbf{x})-f(\mathbf{a}) \geq c\mathbf{v}^{\mathrm{T}}\mathbf{v}-\varepsilon\mathbf{v}^{\mathrm{T}}\mathbf{v} > 0$ provided $\varepsilon < c$ and $\|\mathbf{v}\| < \varepsilon/b$.

Ex. 2.7.4 Let $(x, y) \to (0, 0)$ along the radial line $y/x = t$; then $f(x, y) = t/(1+t^2) \to t/(1+t^2)$ as $x \to 0$. So f is not continuous in (x, y) at $(0, 0)$.

Ex. 2.7.5 From Equation (2.7.5), $f''(a)(u, v) = v^{\mathrm{T}}Mu = \sum_{i,j=1}^{n} M_{ij}u_j v_i$, which is a linear function of u for each fixed v, and a linear function of v for each fixed u. If f is $\mathbb{R}^2$-valued, each M_{ij} is replaced by a vector in $\mathbb{R}^2$.

Chapter 3

Ex. 3.1.1 Consider, for example, $U = \mathbb{R}$, $E = [1, 2]$, $f(u) = u^2$. The maximum on E occurs at $u = 2$, but $f'(2) = 4 \neq 0$. Note that the proof of Theorem 3.1 needs *all* directions from the maximum. The positive direction from 2 in not available in E, since E is not open.

Ex. 3.1.2 As r increases from 0, $f(r \cos\theta, r \sin\theta)$ increases for fixed $\theta \in (0, \pi)$, and decreases for fixed $\theta \in (\pi, 2\pi)$.

Ex. 3.1.3 (i) $f(x, y) = x^2+4xy+2y^2-2y$. A stationary point must satisfy both $f_x = 2x+4y = 0$ and $f_y = 4x+4y-2 = 0$, whence $(x, y) = (1, -\frac{1}{2})$. Then $f_{xx} = 2$, $f_{xy} = 4$, $f_{yy} = 4$, $f_{xx}f_{yy}-f_{xy}^2 = -8 < 0$, hence a saddlepoint.

(ii) $f(x, y) = x^4-4xy$. $f_x = 4x^3-4y = 0$, $f_y = -4x = 0$, so $(0, 0)$. $f_{xx} = f_{yy} = 0$, $f_{xx}f_{yy}-f_{xy}^2 < 0$, so $(0, 0)$ is a saddlepoint.

(iii) $f(x, y) = x^3+y^2$. $f_x = 3x^2 = 0$, $f_y = 2y = 0$, so $(0, 0)$. Here $f_{xx} = 0$, $f_{xy} = 0$, $f_{yy} = -2$, so $f_{xx}f_{yy}-f_{xy}^2 = 0$; so the eigenvalue test, in this instance, does not decide the kind of stationary point. However, when $y = 0$, f increases as x increases, and f decreases as x decreases, so $(0, 0)$ is a saddlepoint.

(iv) $f(x, y) = x^3-3xy^2$. $f_x = 3x^2-3y^2 = 0$, $f_y = -6xy = 0$, so $(x, y) = (0, 0)$. Here $f_{xx} = f_{xy} = f_{yy} = 0$ at $(0, 0)$. This is a saddlepoint, as in the previous case.

(v) $f(x, y) = ye^{-x^2}$. $f_x = -2xye^{-x^2}$, $f_y = e^{-x^2}$. Since e^{-x^2} does not vanish, there are no stationary points for this function.

(vi) $f(x, y) = (ax^2+by^2)e^{-x^2-y^2}$, where $0 < a < b$. Here $(f_x, f_y) = e^{-x^2-y^2}((ax^2+by^2)(-2x)+2ax, (ax^2+by^2)(-2y)+2by)$. A stationary point requires $x = 0$ or $ax^2+by^2 = a$, together with $y = 0$ or $ax^2+by^2 = b$, giving the solutions as tabulated below:

Stationary point	$A = f_{xx}$	$B = f_{yy}$	$H = f_{xy}$	
$(0, 0)$	$2a > 0$	$2b > 0$	> 0	Minimum
$(0, \pm 1)$	$e^{-1}(2a-2b) < 0$	$e^{-1}(-4b) < 0$	> 0	Maximum
$(\pm 1, 0)$	$e^{-1}(-4a) < 0$	$e^{-1}(2b-2a) > 0$	< 0	Saddlepoint

(vii) $f(x, y) = x^2y^2+8xy+x^2+y^2$. $f_x = 0$ and $f_y = 0$ give $x(y^2+1)+4y = 0$ and $y(x^2+1)+4x = 0$. Substituting $x = -4y/(y^2+1)$ into $y(x^2+1)+4x = 0$ gives $y = 0$ or y^4+2y^2-15, whence $y^2 = -5$ (no real solution) or $y^2 = 3$. This gives three stationary points, as follows:

Stationary point	$A = f_{xx}$	$B = f_{yy}$	$H = f_{xy}$	$AB-H^2$	
$(0, 0)$	2	8	8	-20	Saddlepoint
$(3^{1/2}, -3^{1/2})$	8	8	-4	80	Minimum
$(-3^{1/2}, 3^{1/2})$	8	8	-4	80	Minimum

Ex. 3.1.5 At $(0, 0)$, $f_x = 0$ and $f_y = 0$. Since

$$\frac{8(r\cos\theta)^4(r\sin\theta)^4}{((r\cos\theta)^4+(r\sin\theta)^2)^2} \leq \frac{8\,r^8\sin^4\theta}{r^4\sin^4\theta} = 8r^4,$$

f is differentiable at $(0, 0)$. Also (from the inequality cited)

$$|f(x, y)-f(0, 0)| \leq y^2+4y^2 \to 0 \text{ as } (x, y) \to (0, 0).$$

Ex. 3.1.8

$$\begin{aligned} f(\mathbf{a}+\mathbf{v})-f(\mathbf{a})-f'(\mathbf{a})\mathbf{v} &= (\mathbf{c}^{\mathrm{T}}(\mathbf{a}+\mathbf{v})+(\mathbf{a}+\mathbf{v})^{\mathrm{T}}A(\mathbf{a}+\mathbf{v}))-(\mathbf{c}^{\mathrm{T}}\mathbf{a}+\mathbf{a}^{\mathrm{T}}A\mathbf{a}) \\ &\quad -(\mathbf{c}^{\mathrm{T}}+2\mathbf{a}^{\mathrm{T}}A)\mathbf{v} \\ &= \mathbf{v}^{\mathrm{T}}A\mathbf{v} \geq 0 \end{aligned}$$

if A is positive definite (or semidefinite). By Theorem 3.3, f is convex. The definition (3.1.6) of a convex function may, alternatively, be verified directly for this function.

Ex. 3.2.1 The Lagrange multiplier equations (3.2.3) gives

$$1+\lambda(2x/4) = 0,\ 1+\lambda(2y/9) = 0,\ (x^2/4)+(y^2/9) = 1.$$

These solve to $(x, y) = (-4/(13)^{1/2}, -9/(13)^{1/2})$, and $\lambda = \frac{1}{2}(13)^{1/2}$. It is clear from a diagram (noting that this (x, y) is in the third quadrant) that this stationary point is a minimum.

Ex. 3.2.2 The Lagrange multiplier equations are

$$2xy^2z^2+\lambda(2x) = 0,\ 2x^2yz^2+\lambda(2y) = 0,$$
$$2x^2y^2z+\lambda(2z) = 0,\ x^2+y^2+z^2 = c^2.$$

These solve to $(x, y, z) = (\pm c/3^{1/2}, \pm c/3^{1/2}, \pm c/3^{1/2})$, all sign combinations being allowed. (Here $-\lambda = y^2z^2 = x^2z^2 = x^2y^2$ gives $\pm x = \pm y = \pm z$.) The maximum value function is $(c^2/3)^3$.

Ex. 3.2.3 The Lagrange multiplier equations are

$$2x+\rho(2x)+\sigma(2) = 0,\ 2y+\rho(2y)+\sigma(3) = 0,$$
$$2z+\rho(0)+\sigma(1) = 0,\ x^2+y^2 = 1,\ 2x+3y+z = 1.$$

The Lagrange multiplier $\lambda = [\rho, \sigma]$ here. Note that all the solutions of the system of equations must be sought. We have $2(1+\rho)x+2\sigma = 0$, $2(1+\rho)y+3\sigma = 0$, $2z = -\sigma$. If $1+\rho = 0$ then $\sigma = 0$, $z = 0$, $2x+3y = 1$; substituting $x = \frac{1}{2}(1-3y)$ into $x^2+y^2 = 1$ gives $13y^2-6y-3 = 0$, hence $y = (3\pm 2(12)^{1/2})/(13)$. If $1+\rho \neq 0$ then $y/x = (-3\sigma)/(-2\sigma) = 3/2$ (or $x/y = 2/3$). Substituting into $x^2+y^2 = 1$ gives $x^2 = 4/13$. This gives the stationary points (x, y, z) and the corresponding $f(x, y, z) = x^2+y^2+z^2$ as follows.

$$((2\pm 3(12)^{1/2})/13, (3\pm 2(12)^{1/2})/13, 0),\ f = 1 \text{ (minumim)};$$
$$(2/(13)^{1/2}, 3/(13)^{1/2}, 1-(13)^{1/2}),\ f = 15-2(13)^{1/2};$$
$$(-2/(13)^{1/2}, -3/(13)^{1/2}, 1+(13)^{1/2}),\ f = 15+2(13)^{1/2} \text{ (maximum)}.$$

Ex. 3.2.4 $8yz+\lambda(2x/a^2) = 0, 8zx+\lambda(2z/b^2) = 0, 8xy+\lambda(2z/c^2) = 0$, $(x/a)^2+(y/b)^2+(z/c)^2 = 1$. (The vertices of the box lie on the ellipsoid.) Then $x^2/a^2 = y^2/b^2 = z^2/c^2$, hence $\pm x/a = \pm y/b = \pm z/c = 3^{-1/2}$.

Ex. 3.2.5 $n^{-1}(x_1 \ldots x_n)^{1/n}\ x_j^{-1}+\lambda = 0\ (j = 1, 2, \ldots, n)$; $\sum_1^n x_j = nk$. Thus k is the arithmetic mean; denote by G the geometric mean $(x_1x_2\ldots x_n)^{1/n}$. At the maximum for the problem, $G = \lambda n x_j$ for each j, hence each $x_j = k$, so $G = k$. Thus the maximum value which G may take is k.

Ex. 3.2.6 For n large, approximate $\log n!$ by const. $-n+(n+\frac{1}{2})\log n$. The Lagrange multiplier equations are $1+\log(g_k+x_k)-\log x_k+\alpha e_k+\beta = 0$, where α and β are Lagrange multipliers. The stated result follows with $\alpha = 1/\theta$ and $-\beta = \mu/\theta$.

Ex. 3.3.3 $2y+\lambda(-x) = 0, 2x+2^{1/2}(3y^2)+\lambda(2y) = 0, -\frac{1}{2}x^2+y^2 = 1$. These have solution $(x, y) = (-2^{1/2}, -2^{1/2})$, $\lambda = 2$. The Lagrangian is $L = 2xy+2^{1/2}y^3+\lambda(-\frac{1}{2}x^2+y^2-1)$. At $(-2^{-1/2}, -2^{-1/2})$, the matrix $M = L'' =$

$$\begin{bmatrix} -2 & 2 \\ 2 & -8 \end{bmatrix}.$$

So the auxiliary problem (Equation (3.3.4)) requires stationary points of

$$[u_1 \quad u_2]\begin{bmatrix} -2 & 2 \\ 2 & -8 \end{bmatrix}\begin{bmatrix} u_1 \\ u_2 \end{bmatrix} \text{ subject to } [1, \ -2]\begin{bmatrix} u_1 \\ u_2 \end{bmatrix} = 0.$$

Thus $u_1 = 2u_2$, and the function reduces to $-2(2u_2)^2+4(2u_2)u_2 -8u_2^2 = -8u_2^2$. This stationary point is a maximum, so the given constrained problem has a maximum.

Ex. 3.4.1 The Kuhn–Tucker conditions for a minimum at $z = \bar{z}$ are:

$$\bar{z}^{\mathrm{T}}A+b^{\mathrm{T}}-\lambda^{\mathrm{T}}M = 0,\ \lambda \geq 0,\ \lambda^{\mathrm{T}}(M\bar{z}-q) = 0.$$

Here the Lagrange multiplier vector λ is taken as a column. A minimum is guaranteed if A is positive definite (but may also happen with less assumption). If M has rows M_i, let $J = \{i : M_i\bar{z} = q_i\}$ (active constraints). Assume then that $\{M_i : i \in J\}$ is a linearly independent set of vectors.

Ex. 3.4.2 The Lagrangian is $2y^2-x^2y+\lambda(\frac{1}{2}x^2+y^2-1)$. The Kuhn–Tucker conditions (necessary for a constrained minimum at (x, y)) are then:

$$-2xy+\lambda x = 0,\ 4y-x^2+2\lambda y = 0;\ \lambda(\tfrac{1}{2}x^2+y^2-1) = 0; \qquad (*)$$

together with $\lambda \geq 0$ necessary for a minimum. The solutions (x, y, λ) of (*) are tabulated as follows, together with $p = 1-(\frac{1}{2}x^2+y^2)$ and $f(x, y)$.

x	y	λ	p	$f(x, y)$	
$\pm 4/3$	$1/3$	$2/3$	0	$-10/27$	Minimum
0	-1	-2	0	$+2$	Maximum
0	0	0	1	0	Saddlepoint
0	1	-2	0	$+2$	Maximum

The identification of these critical points as maximum, minimum, or saddlepoint is proved later, in Exercise 3.5.1.

Ex. 3.4.3 The Kuhn–Tucker conditions are

$f_j'(c_j)-\lambda_j+\mu = 0, \lambda_j \geq 0\,(j = 1, 2, \ldots, n); c_1+\ldots+c_n = 1, c_j \geq 0.$

The gradients of the $n+1$ constraints are the basis vectors $e_1, \ldots, e_n$ for $\mathbb{R}^n$, together with $e = (1, 1, \ldots, 1)^T$. Since at most n of the $n+1$ constraints are active, the active gradients here are linearly independent. Then, if $c_j > 0$ then $\lambda_j = 0$ and $f_j'(c_j) = \theta \equiv -\mu$; if $c_j = 0$ then $f_j'(c_j) = \theta+\lambda_j \geq \theta$.

Ex. 3.4.4 A linear combination of convex functions, with non-negative coefficients, is also a convex function. For the sufficiency proof,

$$\begin{aligned} f(\mathbf{z})-f(\mathbf{c}) &= \mathbf{L}(\mathbf{z})-\mathbf{L}(\mathbf{c})-\lambda\mathbf{g}(\mathbf{z})+\lambda\mathbf{g}(\mathbf{c}) \leq \mathbf{L}(\mathbf{z})-\mathbf{L}(\mathbf{c}) \\ &\quad \text{since } -\lambda\mathbf{g}(\mathbf{z}) \geq 0 \text{ and } \mathbf{g}(\mathbf{c}) = 0 \\ &\geq \mathbf{L}'(\mathbf{c})(\mathbf{z}-\mathbf{c}) = 0 \text{ using Theorem 3.3.} \end{aligned}$$

Ex. 3.5.1 $L^*(x,\ y;\ \lambda;\ p) = 2y^2-x^2y+\frac{1}{2}\lambda x^2+\lambda y^2+\lambda p-\lambda$. Hence $L^*\left(\frac{4}{3}+\xi, \frac{1}{3}+\eta; \frac{2}{3}; p\right) = -\frac{10}{27}+\left\{\frac{8}{3}\eta^2-\frac{8}{3}\xi\eta\right\}-\eta\xi^2+\frac{2}{3}p$. Here, the cubic term may be neglected (when $|\xi|$ and $|\eta|$ are sufficiently small) in comparison with the quadratic form $\{\cdot\}$. The constraint $\frac{1}{2}\left(\frac{4}{3}+\xi\right)^2+\left(\frac{1}{3}+\eta\right)^2 = 1$ gives $\frac{4}{3}\xi+\frac{2}{3}\eta+p \approx 0$ on linearizing (thus neglecting higher-order terms); thus $\xi \approx -\frac{1}{2}\eta-\frac{3}{4}p$. Substituting this into L^* gives $L^* \approx -\frac{10}{27}+4\eta^2+p\left(\frac{2}{3}+2\eta\right)$. Thus $L^* -\left(-\frac{10}{27}\right) \geq 0$, so the critical point is a minimum. Similarly, $L^*(\xi, -1+\eta; -2; p) = 2-\eta\xi^2 -2p$; the constraint gives $\frac{1}{2}\xi^2-2\eta+\eta^2+p = 0$, so that $2\eta \geq 0$. So $L^*-2 \leq 0$, giving a maximum. Note that the higher-order terms are needed here. The unconstrained stationary point (0, 0) is clearly a saddlepoint. $L^*(\xi, 1+\eta; -2; p) = 2-2\xi^2-\xi^2\eta-2p \approx 2-2\xi^2-2p$. The constraint gives $2\eta+p \approx 0$. Substituting $\eta \approx -\frac{1}{2}p$ gives $L^*-2 \approx -2\xi^2-2p$, so a maximum.

Chapter 4

Ex. 4.1.2 $\arcsin \frac{1}{2}$.

Ex. 4.2.1 $h(y) = 1$ for $0 < y < e^{-1}$, $h(y) = \log(1/y)$ for $e^{-1} < y < 1$.

$\int_0^{h(y)} xy\, dx = \frac{1}{2}y$ for $0 < y < e^{-1}$, or $\frac{1}{2}y[\log(1/y)]^2$ for $e^{-1} < y < 1$.

Integration with respect to y then gives

$$\tfrac{1}{4}e^{-2}+\int_{e-1}^{1}\tfrac{1}{2}y[\log(1/y)]^2dy$$

$$= \tfrac{1}{4}e^{-2}+\int_0^1\tfrac{1}{2}e^{-t}t^2e^{-t}\,dt \text{ after substituting } y = e^{-t}$$

$$= \tfrac{1}{4}e^{-2}+[\tfrac{1}{16}e^{-2t}(-2-4t-4t^2)]_0^1$$
$$= \tfrac{1}{8}-\tfrac{3}{8}e^{-2}.$$

Ex. 4.2.3 The integral equals

$$\iint_G e^{-r^2}r\,dr\,d\theta = \int_0^{\pi/2}d\theta\int_0^c e^{-r^2}r\,dr = \tfrac{1}{4}(1-e^{-c^2}).$$

Ex. 4.2.4 One loop of the lemniscate is described by the equation in polar coordinates, $r^2 = \cos 2\theta$, for $-\pi/4 \le \theta \le \pi/4$. The integral equals

$$2\int_0^{\pi/4}d\theta\int_0^{(\cos 2\theta)^{1/2}}r(1+r^2)^{-2}\,dr = 2\int_0^{\pi/4}d\theta\Big[-\tfrac{1}{2}(1+r^2)\Big]_0^{(\cos 2\theta)^{1/2}}$$

$$= 2\int_0^{\pi/4}\frac{\sin\theta\cos\theta}{2-2\sin^2\theta}\,d\theta = \tfrac{1}{2}\log(3+2^{3/2}).$$

Ex. 4.2.5 The integral equals the repeated integral

$$8\int_0^a x\left\{\int_0^{b(1-(x/a)^2)^{1/2}}y\left[\int_0^{c(1-(x/a)^2-(y/b)^2)^{1/2}}z\,dz\right]dy\right\}dx$$

$$= 8\int_0^a x\left\{\int_0^{b(1-(x/a)^2)^{1/2}}\tfrac{1}{2}yc^2(1-(x/a)^2-(y/b)^2)\,dy\right\}dx$$

$$= 8\int_0^a\tfrac{1}{4}c^2b^2x(1-(x/a)^2)^2\,dx = \tfrac{1}{3}a^2b^2c^2.$$

Ex. 4.2.7 Volume equals $\pi\int_0^c(c^2-x^2)\,dx = \tfrac{2}{3}\pi c^3$.

When $f(x) = (c^2-x^2)^{1/2}$, $f'(x) = -x(c^2-x^2)^{-1/2}$ (which is not finite at the endpoint $x = c$). The area is obtained as the integral

$$2\pi\int_0^c(c^2-x^2)^{1/2}[1+x^2/(c^2-x^2)]^{1/2}\,dx = 2\pi c^2.$$

The triple integral for the volume of the hemisphere equals

$$4\int_0^c\left\{\int_0^{(c^2-x^2)^{1/2}}\left[\int_0^{(c^2-x^2-y^2)^{1/2}}dz\right]dy\right\}dx$$

$$= 4\int_0^c(\pi/4)(c^2-x^2)\,dx = \tfrac{2}{3}\pi c^3.$$

Ex. 4.2.8 Consider the region E defined by $x \ge 0$, $y \ge 0$, $x^2+y^2 \le 3$, $x^2-y^2 \le 1$. The required $\iint_G = 4\iint_E$. For (x, y) in E, the equations $p = x^2+y^2$, $q = x^2-y^2$ define a one-to-one transformation

$$\begin{bmatrix} x \\ y \end{bmatrix} = \varphi(\begin{bmatrix} p \\ q \end{bmatrix}) = 2^{-1/2}\begin{bmatrix} (p+q)^{1/2} \\ (p-q)^{1/2} \end{bmatrix}.$$

Then $\det \varphi'(\begin{bmatrix} p \\ q \end{bmatrix}) = -\frac{1}{4}(p^2-q^2)^{-1/2}$. The required integral then equals

$$I = 4\int\int \tfrac{1}{2}(p+q)\, \tfrac{1}{4}(p^2-q^2)^{-1/2}\, \mathrm{d}p\, \mathrm{d}q,$$

with a minus sign prefixed if an oriented integral is required, taken over the region defined by $p \geq 0$, $q \geq 0$, $q \leq p$, $q \leq 1$, $p \leq 3$. Integrating with respect to q gives $\frac{1}{2}p \arcsin(q/p) - \frac{1}{2}(p^2-q^2)^{1/2}$; when $0 < p < 1$, the range is $[0, p]$, giving $\frac{1}{2}(1+\frac{1}{2}\pi)p$; when $1 < p < 3$, the range is $[0, 1]$, giving $\frac{1}{2}(p \arcsin(1/p) - (p^2-1)^{1/2} + p)$. Integrating by parts, $\int p \arcsin(1/p)\, \mathrm{d}p = \int \arcsin(1/p)\, \mathrm{d}(\frac{1}{2}p^2) = [\frac{1}{2}p^2 \arcsin(1/p) + \frac{1}{2}(p^2-1)^{1/2}]$. Hence

$$I = \tfrac{1}{2}(1+\tfrac{1}{2}\pi)\int_0^1 p\, \mathrm{d}p + \tfrac{1}{2}\int_1^3 p \arcsin(1/p)\, \mathrm{d}p + \tfrac{1}{2}\int_1^3 (p-(p^2-1)^{1/2})\, \mathrm{d}p$$

$$= \frac{1}{4}\left(1+\frac{1}{2}\pi\right) + \frac{1}{2}\left\{\frac{9}{2} \arcsin\left(\frac{1}{3}\right) + \frac{1}{2}\sqrt{8} - \pi/4\right\}$$

$$+\left\{2 - \frac{1}{4}(-\log(3+2\sqrt{2}) + 6\sqrt{2})\right\}.$$

The boundary is smooth enough to be regular; we omit the verification.

Ex. 4.2.9 The volume equals

$$4\int_0^{ah^{1/2}} \left\{\int_0^{b(h-(x/a)^2)^{1/2}} (h-(x/a)^2-(y/b)^2)\, \mathrm{d}y\right\} \mathrm{d}x$$

$$= 4\int_0^{ah^{1/2}} \tfrac{2}{3}b(h-(x/a)^2)^{3/2}\, \mathrm{d}x$$

$$= \frac{8}{3}h^2 ab\int_0^1 (1-t^2)^{3/2}\, \mathrm{d}t \text{ on setting } x = ah^{1/2}t$$

$$= \tfrac{1}{2}h^2 ab\pi.$$

Ex. 4.3.5 Since

$$\varphi'\left(\begin{bmatrix} u \\ v \end{bmatrix}\right) = \begin{bmatrix} a\cos v & -au\sin v \\ b\sin v & bu\sin v \\ -c(1-u^2)^{-1/2} & 0 \end{bmatrix},$$

$$\det\left(\varphi'\begin{pmatrix} u \\ v \end{pmatrix}^{\mathrm{T}}\varphi'\begin{pmatrix} u \\ v \end{pmatrix}\right)$$

$$= \begin{vmatrix} a^2\cos^2 v + b^2\sin^2 v + c^2/(1-u^2) & (b^2-a^2)u\cos v\sin v \\ (b^2-a^2)u\cos v\sin v & a^2u^2\sin^2 v + b^2u^2\cos^2 v \end{vmatrix}.$$

Then $\hat{p}(q)$ equals the square root of this determinant.
In particular, consider $a = b = c$. Then this determinant reduces to $a^2u^2/(1-u^2)$, so that here $\hat{p}(q) = au/(1-u^2)^{1/2}$. Now, for a hemisphere $z = a(1-(x/a)^2-(y/a)^2)^{1/2} \equiv f(x, y)$, $(1+f_x{}^2+f_y{}^2)^{1/2} = (1-(x^2+y^2)/a^2)^{-1/2} = (1-u^2)^{-1/2}$. To calculate surface area, this function must be multiplied by the area element, $u\,\mathrm{d}u\,\mathrm{d}v$, for plane polar coordinates u, v; this leads to $u(1-u^2)^{-1/2}\,\mathrm{d}u\,\mathrm{d}v$, in agreement with the $\hat{p}(q)$ expression found above. (**Warning**: the expression $(1+f_x{}^2+f_y{}^2)^{1/2}$ belongs to cartesian coordinates.)
Ex. 4.4.2 For the first path, $\int(y^k\,\mathrm{d}x + x^k\,\mathrm{d}y)$ equals (when $k = 4$) $2b^kaI_5+0$, and (when $k = 5$) $2b^kaI_6 + 2ab^kI_6$, where

$$I_n = \int_0^{1/2} \sin^n\theta\,\mathrm{d}\theta;\ \text{thus } I_5 = \frac{4}{5}\cdot\frac{2}{3} \text{ and } I_6 = \frac{5}{6}\cdot\frac{3}{4}\cdot\frac{1}{2}\cdot\frac{\pi}{2}.$$

The integrals for the second path are the negatives of these values.
Ex. 4.4.3 $\int_\Gamma$ is zero, whether anticlockwise or clockwise. (Observe that $P_y = Q_x$ holds, and there is no singularity inside the path.)
Ex. 4.4.4 The line integral will equal zero for any path that does *not* loop around the origin. In this example, $P_y = Q_x$ holds for all (x, y) *except* $(0, 0)$, where the derivatives are infinite.
Ex. 4.4.7 Does the last path mentioned loop around the origin?
Ex. 4.4.9 The area equals

$$8\int_0^1 \mathrm{d}u \int_0^{\pi/2} \hat{p}(q)\,\mathrm{d}v,$$

where $q = (u, v)$, and $\hat{p}(q)$ is given by Exercise 4.3.5. This integral cannot be evaluated in closed terms (unless elliptic functions are used).
Ex. 4.5.1 $x(x^2+y^2+z^2)\,\mathrm{d}x \wedge \mathrm{d}y \wedge \mathrm{d}z$.
Ex. 4.5.2 $[A(x, y)D(x, y) - B(x, y)C(x, y)]\,\mathrm{d}x \wedge \mathrm{d}y$.
Ex. 4.5.3 (i) $(2xy-2xy)\,\mathrm{d}x \wedge \mathrm{d}y = 0$.

(ii) $dx \wedge dy \wedge dz - dy \wedge dz \wedge dx = 2\, dx \wedge dy \wedge dz$.
(iii) $2y \cos(x^2+y^2)\, dy \wedge dx \wedge dz$.

Ex. 4.5.6 Let φ have components φ_1 and φ_2. From definition of φ^*,

$$\varphi^*\lambda = (f \circ \varphi)(z)\Bigl(\sum_i \frac{\partial \varphi_1(z)}{\partial z_i}\, dz_i\Bigr) \wedge \Bigl(\sum_j \frac{\partial \varphi_2(z)}{\partial z_j}\, dz_j\Bigr),$$

where (from Ex. 4.5.2.) $f(x, y) = A(x, y)\, D(x, y) - B(x, y)\, C(x, y)$, and $\begin{bmatrix} x \\ y \end{bmatrix} = \varphi\left(\begin{bmatrix} z_1 \\ z_2 \end{bmatrix}\right)$.

If φ is given by the matrix M, having components M_{ij}, then

$$\varphi^*\lambda = f(Mz) \sum_{i,\, j\, =\, 1}^{2} M_{1i}M_{2j}\, dz_i \wedge dz_j = f(Mz)(\det M)\, dz_1 \wedge dz_2.$$

(See also the remark following Theorem 4.7.)

Index

Some special symbols